Teaching *Macbeth*

Teaching *Macbeth*

A Differentiated Approach

Lyn Fairchild Hawks

NCTE

National Council of Teachers of English
340 N. Neil St., Suite #104, Champaign, Illinois 61820
www.ncte.org

Internal graphics are Adobe Stock images by Natallia Filonchyk; croisy; Azuzl; val_iva; YuliaRafael Nazaryan; Alexey Pavluts; Alexander Potapov; istry; and berdsigns.

Staff Editor: Bonny Graham

Interior Design: Doug Burnett

Cover Design: Jody Boles

Cover Image: iStock.com/tomertu

NCTE Stock Number: 51204; eStock Number: 51228
ISBN 978-0-8141-5120-4; eISBN 978-0-8141-5122-8

It is the policy of NCTE in its journals and other publications to provide a forum for the open discussion of ideas concerning the content and the teaching of English and the language arts. Publicity accorded to any particular point of view does not imply endorsement by the Executive Committee, the Board of Directors, or the membership at large, except in announcements of policy, where such endorsement is clearly specified.

NCTE provides equal employment opportunity to all staff members and applicants for employment without regard to race, color, religion, sex, national origin, age, physical, mental or perceived handicap/disability, sexual orientation including gender identity or expression, ancestry, genetic information, marital status, military status, unfavorable discharge from military service, pregnancy, citizenship status, personal appearance, matriculation or political affiliation, or any other protected status under applicable federal, state, and local laws.

Every effort has been made to provide current URLs and email addresses, but, because of the rapidly changing nature of the web, some sites and addresses may no longer be accessible.

Library of Congress Cataloging-in-Publication Data

Names: Hawks, Lyn Fairchild, 1968- author.
Title: Teaching Macbeth : a differentiated approach / Lyn Fairchild Hawks.
Description: Champaign, Illinois : National Council of Teachers of English, [2022] | Includes bibliographical references and index. | Summary: "Offers ways to teach Macbeth to engage all students with different readiness levels and interests, providing lessons that highlight key scenes, film analysis activities, close reading assignments, and preassessments and summative assessments"—Provided by publisher.
Identifiers: LCCN 2021049837 (print) | LCCN 2021049838 (ebook) | ISBN 9780814151204 (trade paperback) | ISBN 9780814151228 (adobe pdf)
Subjects: LCSH: Shakespeare, William, 1564-1616. Macbeth—Study and teaching.
Classification: LCC PR2823 .H39 2022 (print) | LCC PR2823 (ebook) | DDC 822.3/3—dc23/eng/20211029
LC record available at https://lccn.loc.gov/2021049837
LC ebook record available at https://lccn.loc.gov/2021049838

Contents

Acknowledgments

The first time I ever read Macbeth's desperate words, that trilogy of "Tomorrows," chills raced across my skin. The magic of that speech left me speechless. Full of ennui and angst, stoicism and poetry, Macbeth's moment of depression made so much sense to me at sixteen.

When vaulting ambition says there can be only one winner, *Macbeth* is more than relevant. When equivocation comes from fair yet false faces, when cruelty gets covered up, and when power and privilege strive that some be "heard no more," *Macbeth* speaks to us still. I have deep love for Shakespeare, an artist who asks big questions of us, and who wonders if we might find courage and compassion in the ashes after the fall.

Thank you, Angela Connor, for wrangling us crazy teens so we might meet the Bard, and laugh and yell, "What, you egg!" You led me to teaching.

Thank you, all my teaching mentors. Roma Hammel, you showed me how to make a safe, creative, and rigorous space in the classroom. Sarah Mayper, you taught me how to get kids on their feet to make a joyful noise. Dan Mindich, you brought delight and dilemma together in simulations, that life-changing curriculum. We miss you so much.

Gordon Jack, thank you for your insights as I paired books with *Macbeth*. To my Vermont College of Fine Arts colleagues who recommend great kidlit till the crack of doom: thank you! Dr. Jack Barnwell, your endless love of the Bard inspires me; keep those quotes coming! Elizabeth Simmons, web goddess: I couldn't make all these materials available without you. Thank you for cheering me on!

Kurt Austin and Bonny Graham, thank you for making the next book in this series happen!

Behind me as I write these words is a poster from the American Shakespeare Company titled "Which Shakespeare Play Should You See?" It's a tongue-in-cheek, choose-your-own-adventure flowchart, and a gift from my parents. Stephen and Katherine Fairchild were the ones who taught me to love books. They support every dream and venture I've chased. I love you!

Thank you, Antonia Fairchild, for your brilliant producer, director, and actor advice for how to approach this play. Thank you for talking me through these scenes and films. I love you.

My dearest Greg Hawks, my love who is a gifted teacher and writer: thanks for understanding why I shout the Bard's lines at the cable news ticker. You bring me Bob Dylan songs and PBS documentaries that end up in the books. You are my heart!

Introduction

What You Will Find in This Section

- Access to the companion website and additional resources
- Tips for getting started
- Beliefs and philosophy
- A rationale for teaching *Macbeth*
- A preview of challenging subjects
- A glossary for differentiated instruction
- Tips for reading the play while preparing your unit

Companion Website and Additional Resources

Let's face it: there's never enough stuff for differentiation. I've designed more than fifty handouts to help you teach a group of students with multiple levels of readiness as well as myriad interests and intelligences. Using the principles and strategies in this book, you can use the digital handouts as is, or, adapt them to your particular context and students. Visit my companion website to find these additional materials where noted throughout this book.

Go to lynhawks.com/extramacbeth and log in for exclusive content using this password: wyrdsisters.

Making This Guide Work for You

This book offers many ideas, activities, handouts, and lessons because both you and your students deserve choices. Much of this book can be sampled, remixed, and shaken however you like. Since you know your students best, every chapter has been developed with an eye to what I'll call DYO: design your own. In several chapters, I peel back to the strategic bones to mention underlying pedagogy and strategy so you can design your best versions. You also have my digital handouts that you can redesign in a direction that suits your classroom context.

Here's the thing: to differentiate well, you must be a designer-juggler. You analyze your students' readiness levels, interests, and learning preferences to create a range of experiences: tiered readiness, mixed readiness, and whole-class activities.

Were I to give you every permutation of differentiated possibility, I'm afraid you'd shout like Macbeth: "What, will the line stretch out to the crack of doom?" (act 4, scene 1, 116). So I hope my sampling of models will help you go forth and make what's right for your students.

If you are a novice teacher, if you have never taught Shakespeare, or you are new to differentiated instruction:

- Start with the glossary on page 209 (also reprinted on the inside front cover).
- Pay close attention to Notes on Differentiation at the end of activities.

If you have intermediate or advanced experience with the play and differentiation:

- Skim the glossary to learn this guide's acronyms, and then adapt lessons as needed.
- Follow DYO tips to start creating activities best suited to your classroom.

What Do You Believe?

The following beliefs and understandings drive this guide's approach to teaching Shakespeare's works. In my studies with educators and researchers such as Tracy F. Inman, Jay McTighe, Julia L. Roberts, Joyce Van Tassel-Baska, Carol Ann Tomlinson, and Grant Wiggins, I have developed a manifesto of what I believe differentiation is, inspired by their work and that of others. What are *your* beliefs?

- Differentiation empowers, gives space to, and amplifies voices of all students, no matter their readiness levels, interests, or learning preferences.
- Differentiation strategies and antiracist education can partner to ensure all students make daily progress while also feeling safe, seen, heard, and included.

- Student interests should be an integral part of English language arts exploration.
- All students can be creators and makers. They should all investigate Essential Questions, build new understandings, and create their own products and performances, driven by interest and engagement preference.
- Differentiated instruction means teachers evolve their practice with each group of students and redesign materials as needed.
- Teachers who differentiate are observers and guides using a range of strategies to ensure all students make progress during a unit. All students should make progress during a Shakespeare unit in the core skills of reading, writing, speaking, and listening.
- All students should have access to classic works in the canon such as Shakespeare's plays and poems, and they should interpret and own this particular play.
- Plays should be viewed and performed.
- Students do not have to read every word of a script meant to be performed.
- All texts should be disrupted. Shakespeare should be challenged with modern eyes.
- What's considered canon should be questioned. Contemporary texts should be taught alongside or instead of Shakespeare.
- Every text is an opportunity for social-emotional learning.
- All students can be artists. They should have opportunities to practice skills such as creative writing, drawing, and acting.
- All students should have some fun.

What do you believe about differentiation? About teaching Shakespeare? Start your Teacher Manifesto where space is provided, below.

Why Teach *Macbeth*?

Whether you're all in and all hail with *Macbeth,* or whether you bite your thumb at this Bard forced upon thee, just about anyone reading a work more than four hundred years old can feel removed, if not unmoved. But William Shakespeare gets us way more than we might think.

He survived political, social, and religious strife. He dealt with bloody discord in the streets. He felt pressure from the powers-that-be. He survived regime change and, yes, plagues. He lost a child. Not only can he relate to us, but he even has something to say to teens who know about conflict and change, deep and dark desires, loss and grief, and reaping what you sow.

He's got some great insults, too.

> Go, prick thy face and over-red thy fear,
> Thou lily-livered boy
> —act 5, scene 3, 14–15
>
> *What, you egg!*
> —act 4, scene 2, 81

And witches. Who doesn't like witches?

Macbeth stays with us because it explores timeless concepts and questions about good and evil. It deals with fear and courage, order and chaos, and guilt and remorselessness. It makes us interrogate leadership and the transfer of power. It makes us examine what we crave and why we crave it. It makes us ask whether we will do that thing we know we shouldn't. It makes us explore the tortured mind in decline, one that has succumbed to the worst kind of temptations.

Macbeth stays current because it has the antihero breaking bad, suspense and stakes and a riddle in its last plot twist, and even slapstick humor about what booze does to a body. Macbeth and Lady Macbeth are a psychiatrist's dream—or nightmare—and worth a deep dive into the whys and wherefores of human behavior. Or maybe they're just a cautionary tale about getting a good night's sleep. Whether it's high or low, surface or deep, Shakespeare is there.

There's another side to this, however: *Macbeth* also hangs around because schools, budgets, and traditions don't offer other voices. It's no slight to Shakespeare to admit that *Macbeth* has traction because of ingrained habits. So while the play is timeless, it's also old and crusty unless it is taught well. And meanwhile, many other voices still never get the mic. So what do we do?

The good news is this: *Macbeth* is a compelling match for contemporary texts that wrestle hard with similar themes. It is a powerful match for newer texts that show us the same or new paradigms for leadership, conscience, and character. Chapter 10, "Independent Reading," is something to consider first before you crack open *Macbeth* with students.

Why am I teaching *Macbeth*?

Because ______________________________

____

Because ______________________________

____

Because ______________________________

____

What creative strategies do I already use that might work with a text like *Macbeth*?

____

____

____

____

Challenging and Sensitive Subjects

Address the Tough Stuff

Murder most foul, and a beheading. Suicide. Witches. Madness and delusion. Racist and sexist language. Evil. Nihilism. Tyranny. Yep; it's a lot. I address a range of difficult issues throughout this book and how to best approach them.

These awful human deeds and frightening cosmic questions can be handled well in the safe space of the literature classroom, where we can go far deeper into the issues than unsupervised students do alone. It's one way of turning what could be poison into tonic. Literature is not only an opportunity for us to slow down and sniff the roses (and the offal) of the human condition; it's also a chance to analyze said condition.

A lot of people die in *Macbeth*, but why and how they die is worth interrogating. What happens to the violent perpetrators leads to good conversation and analysis.

- Why should a "dead butcher and his fiend-like queen" (act 5, scene 9, 36) elicit our pity and concern?
- Why do some who seemed "normal" before commit murder most foul?
- What desires drive evil people and evil regimes?
- What are triggers for suicide? How do we prevent them?
- Why are some people unmoved by death or violence?
- Are there evil supernatural forces? How do we know? What do we do?
- What is nihilism and its consequences?

Preview Upcoming Events and Support Students as Needed

Let students know the plot events before you give them the play. See Handout 26. *Macbeth* Key Events at a Glance (found at the website lynhawks.com/extramacbeth) and Chapter 6, "Key Scenes to Teach," for more information.

As with all sensitive topics, be sure to preview discussion material with students the day before, or in whatever way your school community recommends you introduce material. Be ready to explain the importance of the topic to your literary and historical studies around the play.

Be aware of students who might be facing personal struggles related to any of these issues. For example, if you know a student has recently suffered a death in the family, you might preview the fact you will be discussing Macbeth's stoic if not dismissive reaction to Lady Macbeth's death. Suggest that a conversation can be illuminating and cathartic, until it's not; at which point, if a student feels overcome by emotion, they can use a code set up between you to request a break. Certain students undergoing serious trauma may need to opt out of class and do an alternate assignment elsewhere. You know to seek family, school, and community resources as needed if a student shares distress in response to lesson content.

Acknowledge Different Cultural and Personal Experiences

Sample lessons note different cultural associations and sensitivities around certain topics. Connotations of *witch*, for example, differ among cultural and religious groups, as do *manhood* and *womanhood*. See Chapter 3, "Big Ideas: Essential Questions, Discussions, and Journals," and Chapter 6, "Key Scenes to Teach," for suggestions on how to introduce such topics. If we're unsure of what students know or believe, it helps to introduce such topics with historical context, while also telling students we are open to learning more about what other cultures believe, historically or currently. We don't need to be the experts; we can demonstrate the curiosity we want our students to have.

> This guide uses the Oxford School Shakespeare *Macbeth* because of its excellent text references, easy-to-read design, and strong prefatory and endnotes. If your school has a budget for Dover editions that students can annotate and keep, those are also an economical choice.
>
> If you love curriculum design and want a range of resources, I recommend getting another of my books in the Differentiated Approach series—*Teaching* Romeo and Juliet or *Teaching* Julius Caesar. Many activities, handouts, and strategies transfer well to *Macbeth*. I also recommend Mary Ellen Dakin's *Reading Shakespeare with Young Adults*.

Glossary for Differentiated Instruction

This text uses a number of terms and their acronyms frequently throughout the lessons, so I've provided a glossary of terms, found both at the end of the book and on the inside front cover.

Core Competencies

Identifying at least one core reading skill and writing skill, and what I call the micro skills therein, is a crucial first step to planning any English language arts unit. Once you know your skill focus, then you can determine the tiers to identify what students need to master when. See Chapter 1, "Decisions to Make and Core Competencies," for more guidance.

Common Core State Standards

The Common Core State Standards (CCSS) are helpful, succinct statements of learning goals. Because *Macbeth* is often taught to high school students, I use tenth- and eleventh-grade CCSS standards as the on-target skill goals to model competency choice and tiering. See Chapters 1, 4, 5, and 6 to find standards listed.

Modes of Discourse: Writing

I chose persuasive writing and argument as well as expository writing as two modes students could practice during this unit. Since there are as many skill priorities as there are schools and students, you are the best judge of what to use and how to adapt what I provide.

Getting Ready to Teach: Reading the Play

Preparing to teach the psychological depth, plot, and poetry of *Macbeth* means it's worth taking time to sit with this most beauteous script. I recommend not only that you read it carefully with your favorite beverage in hand, annotating it slowly, but that you also watch a number of film interpretations. See Chapter 6 for some recommendations.

Here are some other activities that might help you walk in the shoes of your students:

- Try the Pre-Play Poll before and after reading, found in Chapter 5, "Hook Activities."
- Pick your favorite Big Ideas and create Essential Questions. See Chapter 3.
- Track your favorite motifs. See the motifs list provided in Chapter 3.
- Read passages aloud to hear the poetry and feel chills across your skin.
- Watch two different *Macbeth* films with someone and discuss which is better, and why.
- Read different literary criticism of Shakespeare's plays, from the beginnings of criticism to postcolonial, feminist, queer, critical race theory, and / or Marxist.
- Try a Close Reader (CR) from Chapter 9, "Close Readers, Translation, and Annotation" and see what you discover.
- Look at the project and essay prompts found at Handout 44. Projects, Project Prompts, Rubric, and Compacting and Handout 40. Essay Prompts (found at lynhawks.com / extramacbeth). Decide which ones you would pick now and which you might have picked as a student.

1 Decisions to Make and Core Competencies

What You Will Find in This Chapter

- A list of questions to consider when planning your unit
- A model of how to set readiness ranges for reading and writing skills
- Recommendations for these decisions

Decision Questions

"I love teaching," a colleague once told me, "but I don't like planning lessons." There are so many design decisions to be made that lesson planning really can overwhelm us. I once read that teachers make as many, if not more, decisions per hour as air traffic controllers. We have to combine intense situational awareness with a high level of domain-specific knowledge, never mind empathy. This is not a job for the faint of heart or casual practitioner.

Good differentiation takes careful design. To start, I do what I tell students to do, using Anne Lamott's brilliant words: just go "bird by bird" (19). If these decisions are new for you, start with just a few questions in this chapter. Pick your first, most important bird, and go from there. Your students, school, and standards will lead you to the one requiring most attention. For example, if your school prioritizes performance on a certain type of writing test, begin with differentiation of writing skills and how you can merge *Macbeth* with those goals.

Here are some decisions to make while designing your differentiated *Macbeth* unit. I provide suggested answers throughout this guide.

- What core reading and writing skills will my students practice?
- What will be the readiness ranges?
- How will I preassess readiness?
- Where and when will students read the play?
- How much of the play will we read?
- What else might we read?

- What will students write, and when?
- How will students pursue their interests?
- What problem-based learning might we do?
- What project-based learning might we do?
- What cooperative or collaborative learning will we do?

What Core Reading and Writing Skills Will My Students Practice during the Unit?

Table 1.1 indicates key skill sets students can develop during this guide's activities. If your students need to practice other skills, follow DYO tips to address other skills.

Table 1.1. Core Competencies: Micro and Macro Skills

READING	WRITING	SPEAKING & PERFORMANCE
■ translation ■ annotation ■ text analysis for denotation, connotation, key words, figurative language, sound devices, and meter ■ evidence identification ■ character, plot, setting, theme, tone, and style analysis	■ identifying purpose ■ writing for an audience ■ writing in various modes of discourse such as narrative and persuasion ■ following a process from ideation to editing ■ creating and finding substantive evidence ■ creating a claim ■ providing context, commentary ■ organizing ideas and creating structure ■ employing rhetorical devices ■ revising ■ editing	■ identifying purpose ■ speaking to an audience ■ volume ■ emphasis and pacing; cadence ■ poise and body language
RESEARCH	**COLLABORATION & COOPERATION**	**CREATION/MAKING**
■ question development ■ identifying authoritative sources ■ taking meaningful notes ■ citing sources ■ organizing information ■ developing a thesis	■ listening ■ reflecting ■ ideating ■ planning ■ note-taking ■ facilitating ■ compromising ■ consensus-building ■ sharing	■ identifying purpose ■ identifying audience ■ planning ■ revising ■ evaluating ■ fluency, flexibility, and elaboration

I recommend picking one core reading skill, one core writing skill, and maybe one other as the focus for the unit. Each skill is a macro skill with micro skills. For example, you can't develop a claim in your argument without logic, reasoning, and summary micro skills. Each skill also has a few ranges of performance. Think about the skill steps and knowledge required for each step as you tier assignments. Before making your final decisions, you may want to consult chapters such as Chapter 4, "Preassessment and Formative Assessment," Chapter 9, "Close Readers, Translation, and Annotation," and Chapter 10, "Independent Reading." Obviously, you will be teaching other skills besides two, but I don't recommend a long list because of the layers within each skill.

You will also see how the core skills of finding substantive evidence and making claims thread through numerous activities I design: a skill necessary to most professions.

This guide offers several activities that include both macro and micro skills.

What Will Be the Readiness Ranges?

How do you distinguish between ELL, NOV, OT, and ADV levels of skill?

1. Begin from a baseline set of standards (grade-level expectations in your state or district) and name these "OT." Consider using the CCSS.
2. Then move two to four grade levels below these standards to select your ELL and NOV levels, while moving two to four grade levels above to select your ADV levels. Two to four is a suggested range; if you have several students needing ranges closer or farther apart, pitch your readiness range to their needs. I usually establish three ranges.
3. Do you have learning specialists and classroom assistants? If you work with ELL and special education support personnel, consult and collaborate to refine these skill tiers.
4. See Chapter 4 for how you might scale readiness levels. These levels can apply to any tiered activity or task you design, such as CRs to writing prompts.

Sample of Readiness Ranges

In Table 1.2, you can see how I took one reading skill from the CCSS (grades 7, 9, and 12) and spelled out micro skills for each macro skill.

There are enough micro skills within one macro skill to keep everybody busy. This is why focusing on one key skill or standard can "go for miles" in a unit. The challenge is in choosing and distinguishing what a range of performances looks like. I study the language of the CCSS carefully and then analyze every noun, verb, and adjective till I feel sure I've imagined what it takes for a student to master the entire skill. See how I've analyzed various CCSS standards here and found where different readiness levels share micro skills, as well as where they differ. For your own planning, head to lynhawks.com/extramacbeth for a blank handout, Handout 45. Identifying Macro and Micro Skills.

Table 1.2. Micro and Macro Skills for Reading and Textual Analysis

Skill: Reading, Text Analysis		
Level	**Macro Skill**	**Micro Skills: Students must**
ELL & NOV Standard	CCSS.ELA-LITERACY.RL.7.1: *Cite several pieces of textual evidence to support analysis of what the text says explicitly as well as inferences drawn from the text.*	■ Know and apply the definition of textual evidence. ■ Translate text (find denotations). ■ Infer meaning from text (find connotations). ■ Find several instances of evidence. ■ Look at a body of evidence and paraphrase, summarize, and state a claim about what the text says.
OT Standard	CCSS.ELA-LITERACY.RL.9-10.1: *Cite strong and thorough textual evidence to support analysis of what the text says explicitly as well as inferences drawn from the text.*	■ Know and apply the definition of textual evidence. ■ Translate text (find denotations). ■ Infer meaning from text (find connotations). ■ Find several instances of evidence that are thorough, meaning the student has surveyed the text as a whole. ■ Look at a body of evidence and then paraphrase, summarize, and state a claim about what the text says, taking into account the whole text and balancing a range of ideas.
ADV Standard	CCSS.ELA-LITERACY.RL.11-12.1: *Cite strong and thorough textual evidence to support analysis of what the text says explicitly as well as inferences drawn from the text, including determining where the text leaves matters uncertain.*	■ Know and apply the definition of textual evidence. ■ Translate text (find denotations). ■ Infer meaning from text (find connotations). ■ Find several instances of evidence that are thorough, meaning the student has surveyed the text as a whole. ■ Look at a body of evidence and then paraphrase, summarize, and state a claim about what the text says, taking into account the whole text and balancing a range of ideas. ■ Find the gray or open-ended nature of a text's meaning and consider alternate meanings; articulate the nuance and questions therein.

Where and When Will We Read the Play?

How much will you read in class? Will you assign Shakespeare reading for homework?

I recommend reading a few key scenes with students in class, while performing and viewing the rest. For more on my rationale, see Chapter 6, "Key Scenes to Teach," and Chapter 10. Listed here are decisions to make and my suggested answers:

- *Which scenes best exemplify the play?* In Chapter 6, I offer several suggestions for core scenes. These will be your foundational scenes for lesson design and classwork, and/or for homework assignments. See Figure 1.1, a reading decisions graphic organizer, for some guiding questions to ask yourself as you make decisions about student reading assignments.
- *When and how will we read these scenes?* Use class time to read and analyze one to two times a week. Some or all reading of the play can be done at home if you have students who enjoy detective work, if you make those assignments detective work that mirror roles of professions, and if you set interest-based goals students meet while creating a unique product or performance. After-school reading should be motivational because students have an interest in decoding or discovering something. I offer homework suggestions and strategies in Chapters 6 and 10.
- *How will I assess knowledge of other scenes?* Don't quiz on other scenes, or worry about whether they are read.
- *If homework time is freed up for independent reading, what independent reading options might I offer?* See Chapter 10 and handouts on my website. After reading this section, you might want to consult those to decide how to include other texts.
- *How will students know the plot of the play?* Point students to a plot outline, such as the ones provided in most texts, or the one I provide in Chapter 6.
- *How will my students truly understand the scenes we read?* See Chapter 9. Students' work of translation, analysis, and exploration of Big Ideas can happen with you and their classmates. Close Reader handouts, discussion questions, and other activities demonstrate how this might be done. See Chapters 3, 6, and 9.

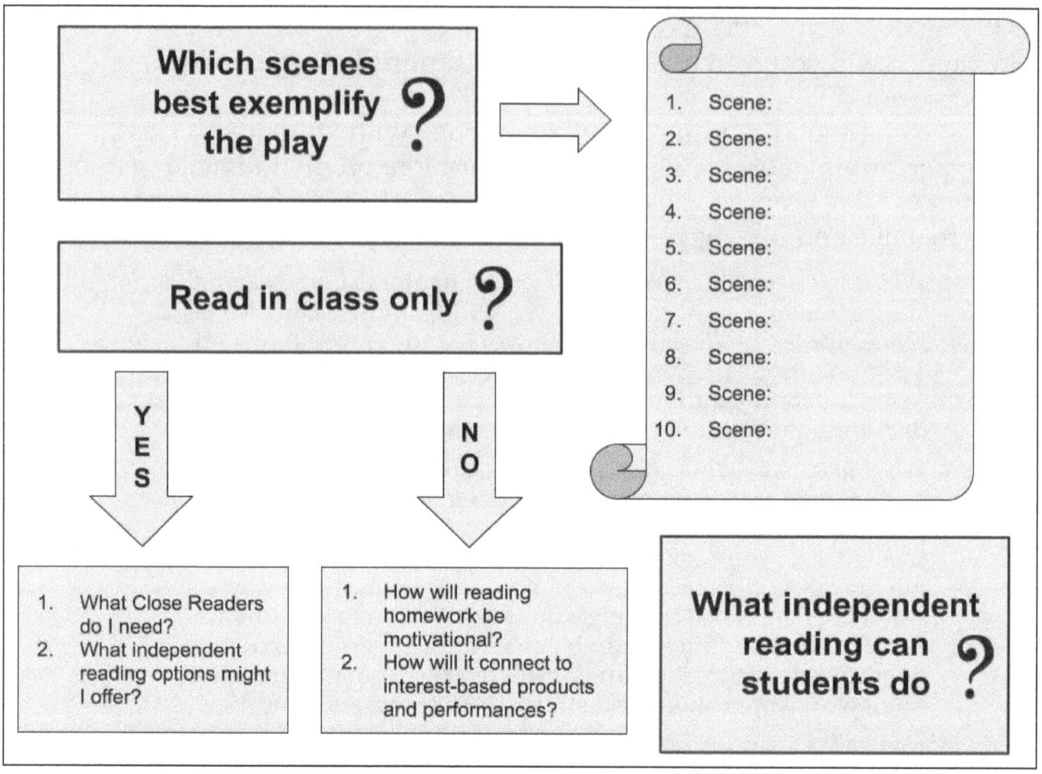

Figure 1.1. Reading decisions graphic organizer.

What Will Students Write, and When?

Chapter 11, "Summative Assessments," offers several answers, as do suggested writing activities in Chapters 5, 6, and 9. I recommend students begin with creative, exploratory writing in class and at home (stories, poems, raps, songs) as well as journals. I also recommend assigning brief text analyses, followed by more robust, in-class timed assignments.

As you plan other tasks, whether cooperative or collaborative learning, problem-based or project-based learning, and performance activities, consult Chapter 7, "Film and Graphic Novel Activities," and Chapter 8, "Performance Activities," as well as my website handouts for ideas, strategies, and samples.

2 Unit Calendar

What You Will Find in This Chapter

- A rationale for a calendar
- A sample calendar

"I can't spend more than three weeks on *Macbeth*," you say.

Understood. In certain schools, it's not recommended that you "teach the same book" for a long time. But what if the learning objectives change weekly because you're practicing micro skills crucial to the macro skill? What if students are reading other texts along with *Macbeth*?

What if they are practicing more than one form of writing?

Then you're doing far more than "teaching the same book."

Ask those in charge if you might use *Macbeth* as a thematic frame and unifying text for the range of skills you can teach during an extended unit. Feel free to use this text as a rationale.

While I teach* Macbeth, *my students will:

- practice reading skills applicable to all types of literature study, including in-depth translation, annotation, and analysis;
- complete other readings, such as independent, interest-based texts;
- generate writing in different modes of discourse and practice core writing skills (using evidence and strong claims); and
- pursue inquiry-driven projects, discussions, performances, and other tasks, allowing the practice of maker and researcher skills.

There is no perfect unit length. This calendar suggests one way of pacing the unit, assuming a traditional five-day, fifty-minute-period schedule. This pacing reflects decisions to allow students ample time to pursue interests and practice core reading and writing skills you have identified. See Chapter 1 to help you select key skills and design a series of learning experiences that help your students master literacies they need.

Six to eight weeks is my ideal time for a unit driven by reading and writing skill mastery, Big Idea exploration, and project- and problem-based learning, all while juggling an older text.

Suggested Activities for Weeks 1–3

- Preassess writing and reading skills. See Chapter 4, "Preassessment and Formative Assessments."
- Hook students with activities using Essential Questions relevant to their lives. Introduce key characters and the plot as a whole. Hook students so they care about the people and the situations and can make personal connections. See Chapter 5, "Hook Activities."
- Ask ADV students to begin their compacting work. For extensive details about logistics of setting up compacting, see Handout 44. Projects, Rubric, and Compacting at lynhawks.com/extramacbeth.
- Teach close reading and viewing skills using a few key scenes. Lead a few low-stakes performance and viewing activities. See Chapter 6, "Key Scenes to Teach," Chapter 8, "Performance Activities," and Chapter 9, "Close Readers, Translation, and Annotation."
- Teach skill and content knowledge mini-lessons as needed.
- Invite all students to choose an inquiry lens (Big Idea and question) and project focus. See Chapter 3, "Big Ideas, Essential Questions, Discussions, and Journals," and also projects suggested in Handout 44 at lynhawks.com/extramacbeth.
- For homework, ask students to pursue thematically connected, interest-based independent readings and writing assignments and/or projects.

Alternate Plan, Weeks 1–3

Do you have a group of students who are mostly ELL and NOV? Here's a recommendation for this student grouping:

- Create CR activities for cinematic viewing of two versions of the play—I suggest the Goold, Coen, Polanski, and Kurzel film versions—and alternate these two types of lessons for the first two weeks:
    - Film Analysis Days: Devote thirty minutes to film viewing, followed by CR annotation of scenes, using a professional role approach (see Chapter 9). Spend twenty minutes in pair or triad work discussing Big Ideas. Try to view major scenes in one film version by the end of the two weeks.

- Hooks, Key Scene, and CR Days: Use hook activities (Chapter 5) and key scene activities (Chapter 6) and/or CR activities (Chapter 9) at least once a week.
- Perform scene excerpts as often as you can. Play with language and rejoice in the weirdness of Shakespeare's words.

- By week 3, begin moving into more key scene and CR work.

Suggested Activities for Weeks 4–5

- Invite students to pursue a thematically connected problem of interest and work cooperatively with peers while close reading and viewing analysis continues. If your students are fairly independent, give them a lot more choice and time, and require that core reading and writing skills be an element of the final product or performance. For homework, ask students to begin independent project planning.
- Teach skill and concept mini-lessons as needed per local, state, or national standards in class.
- Lead performance and viewing activities in class.

Alternate Plan, Weeks 4–5

For a class of mostly ELL and NOV students:

- Introduce picture, chapter, and middle grade works that are thematically connected to *Macbeth* and do project-based, cooperative activities around reading and critical inquiry. See Chapter 10, "Independent Reading," for these titles.
- Finish the play in class using CRs, performance, and cinematic viewing activities.
- Give a limited range of project forms (200–800 words of writing and tapping into other intelligences) while allowing students to pick Big Ideas, interests, and intelligence focus.

Suggested Activities for Weeks 6–8

- Ask students to begin collaborative or independent project work in an area of interest.
- Lead culminating discussions.
- Wrap up study of the play with timed readings and writings in class that demonstrate core skills ranging from annotation to essay writing.
- Ask students to present projects that demonstrate core skills.

Alternate Plan, Weeks 6–8

For a class of mostly ELL and NOV students:

- Give extra days for timed readings and writings, as well as opportunities to revise in class.
- Consider using alternate texts (student-selected ones) for timed writings.
- Ask students to present projects.

Sample Calendar

MONDAY	TUESDAY	WEDNESDAY	THURSDAY	FRIDAY
Weeks 1–3 Hook activity Homework: Independent reading and creative writing	Hook activity Homework: Independent reading and creative writing	CR analysis and performance activities; film analysis Homework: Independent reading and creative writing	CR analysis and performance activities; film analysis Homework: Independent reading and creative writing	CR analysis and performance activities; film analysis Homework: Independent reading and creative writing
Weeks 4–5 PBL cooperative task or CR and film analysis Homework: Independent project work	PBL cooperative task or CR and film analysis Homework: Independent project work	PBL cooperative task or CR and film analysis Homework: Independent project work	PBL cooperative task or CR and film analysis Homework: Independent project work	PBL cooperative task or CR and film analysis Homework: Independent project work
Weeks 6–8 Projects and timed writing and readings Homework: Independent project work	Projects and timed writing and readings Homework: Independent project work	Projects and timed writing and readings Homework: Independent project work	Projects and timed writing and readings Homework: Independent project work	Projects and timed writing and readings Homework: Independent project work

3 Big Ideas, Essential Questions, Discussions, and Journals

What You Will Find in This Chapter

- A rationale for finding Big Ideas and Essential Questions
- A process for selecting Big Ideas and EQs to drive your unit
- A list of Big Ideas
- A discussion of motifs
- Considerations for challenging and sensitive topics
- Discussion and journal questions
- Tips for assigning and assessing journals
- Tips for leading Socratic discussion

Students Care about Big Ideas

One of my favorite moments of teaching was during a *Romeo and Juliet* unit when ninth grader Sam held forth with wisdom. Sam, who never did homework but could act Shakespeare with gusto, was an accomplished wrestler who could turn a somersault from a standing position. He was the one who got his head stuck between the slats of a wooden chair during a class skit, playing the lion to a fellow classmate's lion tamer. Sam also fought the label of troublemaker; I thought he was a gifted comedian. Sure, he often was the center of something slightly chaotic, but he loved learning and wanted class to mean something. I just needed to work harder to make it worth his while—and keep certain chairs at bay. So on the day we discussed this Essential Question—were Romeo and Juliet prisoners of fate or following their free will?—Sam announced to the class, "Fate is just a religious word for coincidence."

It turned the discussion in a whole new direction, and it stopped me in my tracks. I still think of his fascinating insight, aka Essential

Understanding as © Sam. Big Ideas are a chance for all students to test out theories, form new hypotheses, and wrestle with possibilities. Big Ideas activate empathy as students encounter a variety of perspectives. Big Ideas hold tension, nuance, dilemma, and discovery. Big Ideas and Essential Questions should drive whole-class activities. I now always ask, How do my lessons make room for the Sams to explore Big Ideas?

How do my lessons make room for us as educators to explore Big Ideas too? During the writing of this book, I saw headlines with the words *tyranny* and *equivocation*. Shakespeare's timeless stories always seem to make the news. *Macbeth* was a match for the social, political, and systemic issues and conflicts, while *Macbeth*'s characters resonated with those I saw in contemporary films, reality shows, and young adult novels. I even saw characters in people I know. All of these connections made me want to discuss and interrogate the play.

> Big Ideas and Essential Questions are for everyone. Integrate them in all activities, and invite all to pose questions and find answers. What will students discover, explore, create, design, and solve using Big Ideas from *Macbeth*?

If we want all our students to access Big Ideas, think critically, and create meaningful products and performances, then all activities must be question driven. Essential Questions—deep questions—should drive not only discussions and essays but also the smallest daily activity: journal entries, pair work, close reading, mini-projects.

Of all the Big Ideas and open-ended questions you could discuss, what will be best for your class? Students can help us choose. Matching *Macbeth* to your students' interests, dilemmas, and challenges will always be a win. Using students' needs as the lens provides a valuable opportunity for students to become more self-aware, reflective, and proactive.

> Why do good people turn bad?
> How do you handle a bully—or remove a tyrant?
> What is real and what is imagination?
> How do I describe this sadness I'm feeling?

Partner with your students to identify key ideas that will serve as the lens and focus for the unit. Educator and researcher Joyce Van Tassel-Baska calls these *concepts*:

> The concepts fundamental to the human condition are also fundamental to human learning. . . . Concepts are, by definition, abstractions, and they require higher levels of thought to absorb, understand, and extend. Concept learning is fundamental to knowledge acquisition in every discipline and in everyday living, and our comprehension of abstract ideas affects our behavior from kindergarten to the corporation, in the classroom and in the community. We cannot function effectively in society without understanding concepts such as justice, authority, responsibility, and honor. (Van Tassel-Baska and Little 125)

Our students carry into classes their Love and Fear, Good and Evil, Systems and Order, and so much more. These abstract, neutral nouns require clarification and conversation. Concepts are spurs to Essential Questions and become the root words of the Essential Understandings students should develop by the end of a lesson or unit.

In their *Understanding by Design* curriculum and planning strategies, Wiggins and McTighe call these generalizations derived from such concepts Essential Understandings. Inviting students into this process creates buy-in from the start. If Change or Justice or Womanhood is a conceptual foundation of a lesson, why not see what kids already know about that concept and what else they want to know? Why not see how these inquiries translate into interesting thesis statements and essays and into unique projects?

- *Why do good people turn bad?* In act 1, Macbeth is a guy on the rise with everything going for him. He's a loyal, trustworthy soldier, admired by his king. By the end of the play, he's the "hell-hound" (act 5, scene 8, 3) and "dead butcher" (act 5, scene 9, 36), and a head dangling from Macduff's hand. What happened? Have you seen the rise and fall of people you know? Yourself?
- *How do you handle a bully—or remove a tyrant?* Macbeth assassinates his king, Duncan, to get to the throne, a decidedly evil act. But when Macduff kills Macbeth, why is that assassination considered legitimate? How do you handle those who want to be the end-all and be-all?
- *What is real and what is imagination?* Macbeth hears a few prophecies and his mind is off and running. He starts seeing possibilities, whereas Banquo sees danger and temptation instead. Meanwhile, Lady Macbeth sees only the "golden round" (act 1, scene 5, 27), a vision maybe fed by demons. How has your perception clouded memory or the moment? Deep desires? Why do you have a different point of view from that of others?

- *How do I describe this sadness I feel? Is life worth living?* Macbeth sees pettiness, foolishness, and dust in his nihilist last moments. How do we articulate our pain and ennui to others? Why is life worth living?

These questions are not just play-relevant; they're us-relevant. Almost every student has been betrayed or been a betrayer (Loyalty and Betrayal). Many of us question authority and wish to be the one in charge (Power). Almost everyone wonders if we can trust our own perceptions (Delusion). Almost everyone feels scared and rudderless sometimes (Fear). Questions like these can get students to a fever pitch of thinking, discussion, and writing.

Identifying Big Ideas with the help of your students can also be a preassessment. For a wider perspective on the whys and wherefores of preassessment, go to Chapter 4, "Preassessment and Formative Assessments." See the Big Ideas I suggest in Handout 1. Pick Your Favorite Big Ideas as well as Handout 4. Big Ideas in *Macbeth*, both found at lynhawks.com/extramacbeth.

> **DYO Takeaway Tip:**
> Create an Essential Question for each task you design. How will this open-ended query lead to interesting products and performances? Visit lynhawks.com/extramacbeth for Handout 4. Big Ideas in *Macbeth* for models of questions.

How to Find Big Ideas to Match with Your Students

So how do you involve students in the selection of Big Ideas?

1. Before the unit begins, ask your students to choose their favorite Big Ideas. You can assign Handout 1. Pick Your Favorite Big Ideas (lynhawks.com/extramacbeth). Use your preferred polling tool to let students rank order ideas, asking, *Which of these Big Ideas are most significant to your life right now?* Allow students to look up word meanings and discuss the meanings together while they work.
2. Select the top three ideas the majority of students want to discuss. As you design lessons, use them for everything from hook activities to essay prompts to project prompts. See Chapter 5, "Hook Activities," and Chapter 11, "Summative Assessments," and the Projects materials available at lynhawks.com/extramacbeth for tasks guided by Big Ideas.

3. Allow students to choose their Big Idea(s) for essays, projects, and even smaller tasks such as journal entries or Close Readers.
4. Don't forget to select your favorite Big Ideas too. When you're enthused about certain concepts, students will often follow.
5. Use Handout 2. Pre- and Post-Play Poll: Where Do You Stand? in Chapter 5 to see where students stand with Big Ideas in *Macbeth*. Close the unit with the same poll to see if students' perspectives have evolved. Consider editing and adapting these statements as needed.
6. Teach students how to generate good Essential Questions about Big Ideas. To help guide the development of strong questions, see Handout 3. Let's Clarify: Asking Good Questions (available at lynhawks.com / extramacbeth).
7. Use Big Ideas as your lens for prepping character analysis, CRs, and film activities.
8. Choose two to three Essential Questions to drive Socratic discussions. See guidance later in this chapter for designing these discussions.

For a model of how one educator designed lessons for his student population, I recommend checking out "Reader Idea: Reading 'Macbeth' through the Lens of Ferguson." This lesson provided by The Learning Network via *The New York Times* takes a Big Idea important to one group of sophomores in Illinois—Trust—and creates a meaningful *Macbeth* unit around difficult current events at the time, which was Michael Brown's death in Ferguson, Missouri. The Essential Question is *Why do we trust?*

Naming Big Ideas

Like Hamlet said to Horatio, there are more Big Ideas in heaven and earth than are dreamt of in our philosophy—or something like that! In other words, if you or your students have a better synonym or a more effective word for a Big Idea, by all means, use that. What's the difference between Fortune and Luck? Leadership and Authority? Tyranny and Bullying? When it comes to the last pair, Macbeth is guilty of both, whether grabbing the crown and sending out his hired assassins or insulting his servants daily. These two words relate but differ. Students can build word families to find the right synonyms. Let them do the deep dive of differentiating between definitions, connotations, and nuances among words.

Keep in mind that all of us respond to certain words differently, thanks to our language acquisition status, prior experience with certain words, worldview, and readiness level. My Big Ideas are suggestions inspired by the text, using either Shakespeare's own words, ideas that critics have identified, or ones that I see. Shakespeare contains multitudes, so you may know and find different synonyms and discover new Big Ideas not mentioned here.

Tips for Choosing Big Ideas

1. *Pick abstract, general concepts.* It's up to our students to bring specific evidence to prove this idea exists and that the playwright has something to say about it.
2. *Use nouns only.*
3. *Use these words as the key words in Essential Questions and Essential Understandings.*
4. *Use Big Ideas that matter to your students.*

Challenging Topics and Opportunities for Growth

Power. Privilege. Manhood. Womanhood. There are challenging topics in *Macbeth* worth considering with sensitivity and thoughtfulness.

Power and Privilege

The Essential Questions that I recommend ask students to look at power, privilege, systems, and hierarchies in their own lives as well as those of the characters in *Macbeth*. See Handout 2. Pre- and Post-Play Poll: Where Do You Stand? (in Chapter 5) and Handout 4. Big Ideas in *Macbeth* (lynhawks.com/extramacbeth) for these specific questions.

Because we can't talk about power and privilege in America without also discussing race and race relations, we should prepare for these conversations thoughtfully. You know best how ready your students are to discuss these concepts as a group and how ready you are to facilitate such discussions. For this task, I recommend Matthew R. Kay's *Not Light, but Fire: How to Lead Meaningful Race Conversations in the Classroom*, a robust, thorough guide to having conversations about race, power, and privilege. For more suggestions for working through discomfort, check out the recommendations from educator Dena Simmons in her article "How to Be an Antiracist Educator."

The very act of teaching Shakespeare relates to power. Do we ascribe too much power to Shakespeare himself? Do we consider his works "perfect" and protect him from critique? These are questions asked by #DisruptTexts, a movement self-described as "a crowdsourced, grass roots effort *by* teachers *for* teachers to challenge the traditional canon in order to create a more inclusive, representative, and equitable language arts curriculum that our students deserve" (Disrupttexts.org). Educators such as Tricia Ebarvia and Kimberly Parker who are working to expand the canon invite us to challenge our own biases, center BIPOC (Black, Indigenous, People of Color) voices, and think critically as we work in community (Ebarvia). Some practical ways this book disrupts the power and privilege of the canon is by excerpting rather than whole-book teaching, and pairing this play with independent/student-choice reading and other contemporary works. We also disrupt the canon when we connect the Big Ideas to us, our priorities, and our students in our community.

How do we interrogate a time-honored text? One way, besides using Big Ideas as our Socratic lens, is by welcoming other archetypes, plots, and settings as excellent models of storytelling while teaching *Macbeth*. In *Craft in the Real World*, Matthew Salesses recommends that we expand the definition of *literary* to include other cultures' story traditions. He notes, "We still talk about plot the way Aristotle wrote about it over two thousand years ago, when he argued that plot should be driven by character" (xv).

> We have come to teach plot as a string of causation in which the protagonist's desires move the action forward. The craft of fiction has come to adopt the terms of Fretyag's triangle, which were meant to apply to drama, and of Aristotle's poetics, which were meant to apply to Greek tragedy. (27)

This excellent guide helps educators see that there's more than one way to teach craft, which is inseparable from cultural expectations and ideology (4). Using models from Japanese, Chinese, and African fiction, Salesses broadens our canonical lens with powerful questions that can make for excellent Socratic discussion in our classrooms. I strongly recommend reading the chapter "What Is Craft? 25 Thoughts" and developing exercises that consider and/or rewrite *Macbeth* through the lens of the Japanese four-act structure *kishotenketsu* (27), or asking students to attempt that structure in their own creative writing. In other words, we can help students understand that there are more ways in heaven and earth to craft a plot than are dreamt of in the Bard's philosophy.

What do Lorraine Hansberry, William Shakespeare, and Sophocles have in common? Not have in common? What makes great works? We can teach texts in conversation and in historical context. If we don't relegate a very few authors and texts to the timeless category but instead find a chain of links among many from a variety of points of view, we are also teaching a more expansive, truthful history of literature. We are also helping students see similarities across thinkers and creators. The Bard is as timeless as the Greeks and Romans who sparked his imagination, and as timeless as Hansberry, who makes *A Raisin in the Sun* both a Greek tragedy and yet entirely her own drama. Walter Younger's quest for power in 1950s America has overlaps with as well as differences from Macbeth's, just as his intoxication scene has humorous parallels with the Porter's scene; Beneatha Younger's definition of womanhood and power stands in fascinating contrast to not only Mama's but also Lady Macbeth's; and the tyranny of white supremacy does its ugly work in the same way as the witches' evil in *Macbeth*.

Manhood and Womanhood

There are plenty of declarations about these two gender identities in *Macbeth*, including how each gender should express and conduct itself. When I define *manly* and *womanly* for the sake of Big Ideas, I am firmly grounding these terms in the play's worldview. Meanwhile, the average dictionary I consulted doubled down on very traditional definitions not far from those understood by British people in 1606. Whereas *manly* had associations of heroism and strength, *womanly* was associated with roles (mother, matron) and age (girl, maiden, woman).

We all know there's a lot more to men and women than machismo or girlishness. Language is power. So consider trying the activity Man Up! It's a Woman's Job in the Chapter 5. It helps students prepare for a four-hundred-year-old view of gender with its own complexities, while also finding more empowering words for students' names for *personhood*.

Your students may identify across a spectrum of sexual orientations, gender identities, and gender expressions. Your LGBTQIA+ students, including those who identify as nonbinary and transgender, will appreciate that classroom language, questions, and topics stay open to a range of gender definitions while discussing Shakespeare's text.

Distinguishing Big Ideas and Motifs

As I note in the Let's Make a Motif Motto mini-lesson in *Teaching* Julius Caesar: *A Differentiated Approach*, a motif

> is a repeated symbol in a literary work that is often a sensory, physical, concrete image. Motifs carry Big Ideas on their backs. Let's take the American flag: what big ideas does the flag represent? What about the rose you give someone on Valentine's Day? If these images appear frequently in a work of literature, they can act as motifs, carrying the concepts of freedom and patriotism or love and romance. (133)

Table 3.1 provides a list of motifs for students to track. There are many connotation, denotation, and figurative language activities and mini-lessons you might do in conjunction with these images. Note that I have listed words that may seem redundant (*darkness, night, black*). The reason for this is to provide enough motifs to find as well as ways to see word families. While *fog, air,* and *smoke* are different, they tend to be present when mysterious and/or evil things occur, so I linked these. You can group words as you choose before sending students out to scavenge the text.

Table 3.1. Motifs for Students to Track in *Macbeth*

Motifs				
banquet	birds	black	blood	children or babies
clothing	daggers	darkness	death	devil
doors	doubling	dreams	eyes	fog or air or smoke
food	ghosts	hands	heath or hedge	hell
horses	light	masks	milk	multiplication
night	red	robes	serpents	sleep
stairs	stars	time	water	white

Motif Lesson Ideas

- A quick way for students to search for motifs is to use MIT's full text of *Macbeth* (http://shakespeare.mit.edu/macbeth/full.html) and ask them to use the Command-F or Control-F search functions to find every reference. Students can record all quotes in a document and then work in pairs or triads to identify denotations and connotations of various synonyms and to track patterns and trends of where these words tend to appear. Ask students to answer this question: What is significant about the appearance of this motif in this particular scene and with this particular set of characters?
- Use a digital tool such as ThingLink or Canva to let students create mottos, PSAs, or other messaging around motifs. The focus prompt is "What is Shakespeare saying when this motif appears?" Students' digital products might include a base image with captions linked to a Big Idea. You can ask students to fill in a blank such as "When you see _____, watch out for _____." For example: "When things get foggy, beware of EQUIVOCATION."

- Since students may not know bird species, you can provide these types of birds to look for: *choughs, crows, falcons, maggot-pies, martlets, owls, ravens, rooks, wrens*—and all the associations made with such birds. What behaviors are these birds known for?
- *Macbeth* mentions many other creatures that live in ocean or land ecosystems, so you might assign some students to track any other references related to living creatures and plumb their associations. Some creatures like serpents and sharks have an image problem with humans, so that could be an interesting discussion of associations with evil and demonic power.
- Students can also track allusions to Greek and Roman mythology and other characters.

> It is remarkable that almost all the scenes which at once recur to memory take place either at night or in some dark spot. The vision of the dagger, the murder of Duncan, the murder of Banquo, the sleep-walking of Lady Macbeth, all come in night-scenes. . . . The moon is down and no stars shine when Banquo, dreading the dreams of the coming night, goes unwillingly to bed, and leaves Macbeth to wait for the summons of the little bell. When the next day should dawn, its light is "strangled," and "darkness does the face of earth entomb."
>
> —A. C. Bradley (qtd. in Lerner 173)

Big Ideas for Character Analysis

Another way to make Big Ideas relevant is for students to use Shakespeare's words to self-describe while also making connections with characters in *Macbeth*. We want them to understand there's a difference between being mischievous and tricky; between being strategic and manipulative; between being guilty and culpable. To get students understanding nuances, they must build word banks and dive deep into connotations.

In the chapter "Generating Character Vocabulary" of *Reading Shakespeare with Young Adults*, Mary Ellen Dakin suggests offering vocabulary lists to help students develop banks of powerful, nuanced words. She also recommends character bio poems. In the following list, I suggest using her strategies and then riff off her ideas, adding my idea for student bio poems.

Vocabulary Lesson Ideas

- Give students a bank of adjectives to describe characters, including Big Idea words, their synonyms, and words that are descriptive of characters or antonyms for characters (Dakin). See Handout 5. If the Shoe Fits . . . Our Bank of Adjectives on page 23. Assign two to five words per pair or triad, asking students to find definitions and illustrate them using art supplies or digital tools. For a WCA, on-your-feet activity, ask students to create a quick live commercial or video for their word. Students can take notes on each other's definitions and use these words in CRs, discussion, and task prompts for the rest of the unit. Prompt: *Prepare a commercial teaching these words. The commercial should share the correct definitions using a meaningful situation that will interest your audience; share the nuances among synonyms; and be visual and dynamic so we don't hit "Skip ad."*
- Create a class vocabulary gallery using digital tools. This can be a study guide for students to use before a quiz. It can also be a timed writing resource during vocabulary quizzes. I ask students to write a coherent personal story using five to ten new words. This gallery might contain a mood board (Canva or Pinterest) using a word and its synonyms or interactive images (ThingLink) where the key image for a word is also captioned and linked to definitions and explanatory videos. Or students might use word clouds, mind maps, or other visual brainstorming tools such as Google Drawings to let students visually represent Big Ideas, their synonyms, and antonyms. Prompt: *Prepare a visual for your words and their synonyms. Create a unique image, using an interactive image tool, a design template, a mood board, or some other drawing tool.* Students can also use Handout 56. *Macbeth* Wordle to play an in-class game with word banks of five-letter words from *Macbeth*.
- Invite students to write a Just Because bio poem using one adjective. The adjective can come from the word bank on Handout 5. If the Shoe Fits . . . Our Bank of Adjectives or elsewhere. It can be a positive, neutral, or negative word. This poetic template, in use in classrooms for decades, allows students to prove and disprove the way a word describes them. It allows a student to explore myriad connotations and better define themselves. You can Google tons of student examples or use the sample poems I have created, loosely based off of and inspired by ones my students wrote over the years. See Handout 6. Write a Just Because Poem at lynhawks.com / extramacbeth.
- Would You Rather Be. . . ? discussion. This activity, adapted from Dakin's book, begins a fun deep dive into word connotation. Take the words representing the most undesirable character traits and ask students to claim any word and argue how it's

better (more positive or desirable) than another. When wrapping study of the play, you might revisit this discussion, asking students to make claims using these words about various characters and to provide evidence.

- Would you rather be *anxious* or *paranoid*?
- Which is worse—to be *disloyal* or *treacherous*?
- Is it better to be *suspicious* or *trusting*?
- Would you rather be a victim of *bad luck* or *fate*?

Handout 5. If the Shoe Fits . . . Our Bank of Adjectives

This word bank offers adjectives describing some characters in *Macbeth,* synonyms, and also Big Idea words we might explore. Note the bold words in particular. Words are grouped in word families, where connotations have connections.

Acquisitive **Ambitious** Aspiring Driven Enterprising Opportunistic Strategic	Altruistic Benevolent **Compassionate** Considerate Empathetic Selfless Self-sacrificing	Cunning Deceitful Dishonest Disloyal Dodging **Equivocating** Evading Hedging **Manipulative** Prevaricating Lying
Conscientious Honest **Loyal** Trusting **Trustworthy**	**Fated** **Fortunate** Lucky **Magical**	Hierarchical **Orderly** Systematic Systemic
Assertive **Authoritative** Commanding Masterful Self-Assured	Adaptable **Changeable** Conformable Flexible Malleable Mutable Variable	Aggrieved Angry Galled Incensed Irate Piqued Vexed **Wrathful**
Anxious Mistrusting Nervous Paranoid Skeptical **Suspicious**	Callous Cynical **Nihilistic** Stoic	**Chaotic** Confused Disorderly Tumultuous
Bold Brave **Courageous** Daring Fearless Heroic Valiant Valorous	**Cowardly** Craven Fearful Spineless Timid Timorous	Bullying **Cruel** Ferocious Harsh Merciless Pitiless Ruthless Threatening Vicious Wicked

continued on next page

Bad Base Corrupt Dishonorable **Evil** Foul Ignoble Immoral Sinful Ungodly Unholy Wrongful	Bleak Cynical Depressed Despondent Discouraged Glum **Fatalistic** Sad	Endangered Exposed Feeble Frail Incapacitated Infirm Unprotected **Vulnerable** Weakened
Accountable Blameworthy Culpable **Guilty** Liable Responsible	Confused Creative **Delusional** Deranged Imaginative Inspired Inventive Paranoid Pretentious Visionary	Abandoned Foolhardy Hasty Impetuous **Impulsive** Passionate Rash Spontaneous Uninhibited
Macho Male **Manly** Masculine Strong Tough Virile	Good **Honorable** Moral Noble Principled Right-minded Upstanding Virtuous	Compelling Convincing Eloquent Influential **Persuasive** Potent
Mighty **Powerful** Robust Strong	Arrogant Haughty Lofty Lordly **Prideful** Superior	Advantaged Affluent Elite Favored Fortunate Lucky **Privileged**
Insightful Intuitive Oracular Predictive Prescient Prognostic **Prophetic** Revelatory Sibylline Spiritual Vatic	**Magical** Mystical Occult Otherworldly Paranormal Preternatural Spectral Supernatural	Admiring Courteous Deferential Dutiful Humble **Respectful** Reverent Subservient

continued on next page

Conquering Successful Triumphant Undefeated Vanquishing **Victorious** Winning	Absolute Arbitrary Autocratic Despotic Dictatorial Fascistic Oppressive Repressive Terrorizing Totalitarian **Tyrannical** Undemocratic	Acrimonious Avenging Maleficent Resentful Unforgiving **Vengeful** Vindictive
Barbaric Bloodthirsty Brutal Cutthroat Homicidal Hotheaded Intemperate Murderous Rampaging Savage Terrorizing Thuggish **Violent** Wild	Female Feminine Girlish Ladylike Maidenly Maternal Motherly **Womanly**	Antithetical Conflicting Contradictory Irreconcilable Oppositional Paradoxical

DYO Socratic Questions

So how do we create meaningful Essential Questions? Knowing how to develop open-ended questions that interrogate Big Ideas is key, whether you plan to design essay, journal, or creative writing questions; facilitate face-to-face or asynchronous discussion; create Close Readers; or coach students finding project questions. These why, how, what, and what-if queries ensure meaningful critical thinking opportunities.

To develop truly Socratic, open-ended questions driven by Big Ideas, we must be clear on the skill sets and scaffolding involved. In my work training teachers, I've found that where some people get stuck is understanding the difference between and overlap across the upper levels of Bloom's Taxonomy. Analysis, evaluation, and creation questions sometimes seem to blur. I've created a list below of question types to help understand the distinctions.

Types of Questions

Analysis Questions: Questions that ask us to dissect, compare and contrast, label by category or definition, find patterns and trends, and/or link cause and effect.

Evaluation Questions: Questions that ask us to interpret and value by a standard, tradition, rule, and/or taste or preference. Evaluation does require analysis, but there must be a rubric—a set of standards—to use for evaluation, which requires more depth than definition or categorization.

Creation Questions: Questions that ask us to analyze and evaluate in order to create a new interpretation, synthesis, design, template, or understanding.

Some last thoughts on DYO:

- Star the model questions I provide in the next section that you think will generate the most conversation with your students. Ask yourself what makes these questions so interesting.
- Develop EQs for other Big Ideas.

Play-Related and Relevance Questions

- Play-related questions are what I call "local" queries led by Big Ideas, interrogating character, plot, and other elements of the text. Like a magnifying glass, these questions look closely at the story itself. Play-related questions work well with Close

Readers and essay prompts, asking students to find evidence directly in the text.

- Relevance questions are "global" queries exploring Big Ideas; they are Essential Questions that relate to students' lives. They invite students to explore their current beliefs, knowledge and definitions, attitudes, preferences, and experiences related to these Big Ideas. Just like play-related questions, relevance questions demand evidence: appropriate personal anecdotes with real-life examples, any statistics or facts students know, historical and current events, and evidence students locate through research. Relevance questions are also life skill questions: the social-emotional, character-driven questions that might make us better people if we spend some serious time reflecting.
- Relevance questions are also the "So what?" purpose of essay topics. I ask students to find a related relevance question to explore as part of the essay topic. Example: *What is the author telling us about loyalty? Evil? Courage? Why should we care?*
- Relevance questions are great hooks for any class activity.

In Chapters 5 and 6, note how I weave both types of questions through activities and tasks. In Chapters 10 and 11, these questions drive assignments.

Essential Questions

Not all of the following questions are given equal weight and time, but that is not an indication of my priorities as much as it is an indication of which Big Ideas fascinate me most. Again, student interests and your interests should drive the generation of Essential Questions. See Chapter 5 for tips on how to teach students to design their own. See lynhawks .com/extramacbeth for more Big Ideas, their relevance, and play-related questions at Handout 4. Big Ideas in *Macbeth.*

Ambition

Relevance Questions

- [Analysis] What are signs that a person has a lot of ambition?
- [Analysis] What systems and obstacles prevent ambitious people from succeeding? Why?
- [Analysis] How can ambition sometimes surmount such obstacles?
- [Evaluation] When is ambition healthy? When is it toxic?

- [Evaluation] What ambitions should our government leaders have?
- [Evaluation] What type of success is worth pursuing ambitiously?
- [Evaluation] When should people "stay in their lane" and restrain their ambition?
- [Evaluation] When should people restrain others' ambition?
- [Evaluation] Do highly ambitious people deserve more success? Why or why not?
- [Creation] What type of system would allow all people to pursue their ambitions?

Play-Related Questions

- [Analysis] What are the differences between Macbeth's and Lady Macbeth's ambition?
- [Analysis] What are the differences between Macbeth's and Macduff's ambition?
- [Analysis] What effects does Macbeth's ambition have on others?
- [Analysis] How does the era of *Macbeth* influence characters' ambitions?
- [Evaluation] How might Macbeth have better used his ambition?
- [Evaluation] How might Lady Macbeth have better used her ambition?
- [Evaluation] What type of ambition does this play seem to applaud? Is there anyone who handles ambition well?
- [Creation] What is Shakespeare saying about Macbeth's ambition?

Compassion

Relevance Questions

- [Analysis] How can one be compassionate when others aren't?
- [Evaluation] Who is the most compassionate person you know, and why?
- [Evaluation] What types of work in our society are known as compassionate?
- [Creation] What if compassion appeared in a typically not-so-compassionate field or industry? What would that look like?

Play-Related Questions

- [Analysis] Where does compassion appear in a play full of betrayal and cruelty? Why does it appear in certain places in the story?

- [Evaluation] How do Duncan's and Macbeth's reigns differ when it comes to compassion? What makes one more compassionate than the other?
- [Creation] What is Shakespeare saying about "th' milk of human kindness" (act 1, scene 5, 16) in a chaotic world gone mad with violence?

Conscience

Relevance Questions

- [Analysis] How does conscience affect our choices?
- [Analysis] What values form your conscience? What is right and what is wrong?
- [Evaluation] If your conscience still bothers you about a past action, why is that?
- [Evaluation] Who is a leader you respect whom you believe leads from conscience?
- [Creation] How would you redesign a group structure, system, institution, or other type of social structure to include more conscience-led decisions?

Play-Related Questions

- [Analysis] Where is Macbeth's conscience most evident?
- [Analysis] What values form his conscience?
- [Analysis] Why does Macbeth lose his conscience?
- [Analysis] What is his life like without a conscience?
- [Evaluation] Who should bear the guiltiest conscience and most culpability for all the evil that occurs in this play?

Courage

Relevance Questions

- [Analysis] What actions and choices define courage?
- [Analysis] What similar and different types of courage are required for war versus political leadership?
- [Evaluation] Who in your life is most courageous?
- [Evaluation] Whom in public life or leadership do you admire most for their courage?

Play-Related Questions

- [Analysis] Who is bravest, Lady Macbeth or Macbeth? Macbeth or Macduff? Macbeth or Banquo?
- [Analysis] Where in *Macbeth* do people "screw [their] courage to the sticking-place" (act 1, scene 7, 60)?

- [Evaluation] Who is the bravest person in *Macbeth*?
- [Evaluation] When is Macbeth most courageous? Least?
- [Evaluation] Who is least courageous in *Macbeth*?
- [Creation] What is Shakespeare saying about heroic acts of courage? What is Shakespeare saying about the type of courage it takes to lead a nation?

Deception

Relevance Questions

- [Analysis] What strategies do devious people use?
- [Analysis] How does one extricate oneself from a web of deception?
- [Evaluation] What is the most devious thing I have done?
- [Creation] What could I design to expose deviousness?
- [Creation] What could I create that would be honest and transparent?
- [Creation] If we could read minds, what would our world look like without deception?

Play-Related Questions

- [Analysis] How do the witches deceive Macbeth?
- [Analysis] What are the most devious strategies the Macbeths employ to grab power?
- [Analysis] What in the play makes people vulnerable to the Macbeths' deceptions?
- [Analysis] How does Macbeth deceive himself? How does Lady Macbeth deceive herself?
- [Evaluation] Who is most devious, Lady Macbeth or Macbeth?

Delusion

Relevance Questions

- [Analysis] What are the signs of delusion?
- [Analysis] What causes delusion?
- [Analysis] How do delusions of grandeur impact families, organizations, and societies?
- [Analysis] How do we remedy the lack of information and understanding that leads to delusion?
- [Evaluation] When does delusion cross the line from limited awareness to mental illness?
- [Creation] How do we prevent our leaders from falling prey to delusion? How do we do the same for ordinary citizens?

Play-Related Questions

- [Analysis] What are the signs of delusion in Macbeth and Lady Macbeth?
- [Analysis] What causes Macbeth's delusions? Lady Macbeth's?
- [Analysis] What are signs that the witches are real and not a delusion—and vice versa?
- [Evaluation] How and when do Macbeth's beliefs and perceptions cross into pathology (disease, whether physical or mental)?
- [Evaluation] How and when do Lady Macbeth's beliefs and perceptions cross into pathology (disease, whether physical or mental)?

Evil

Relevance Questions

- [Analysis & Evaluation] How can we know what is evil?
- [Analysis] Why do people commit evil acts?
- [Analysis] When is evil hard to identify? Why?
- [Analysis] How can we combat evil?
- [Evaluation] Is it evil to suggest or predict something? Why or why not?
- [Evaluation] What is the most evil thing I have done?
- [Creation] How do we design social and political structures to protect citizens from evil?

Play-Related Questions

- [Analysis] Why do Macbeth and Lady Macbeth commit evil acts? What causes, reasons, and motivations can you identify?
- [Analysis] Is evil inside or outside the characters in *Macbeth*?
- [Analysis] How is evil beneficial to some in the play?
- [Evaluation] In the witches' scenes, what in their ways and works are evidence of evil?
- [Evaluation] In the Christian faith, people say, "Hate the sin, not the sinner." Is this motto true in *Macbeth*? Are the sinners so sinful they cannot be loved?
- [Creation] What is Shakespeare saying about the nature of evil? How does it work? Who is responsible for it?

Equivocation

Relevance Questions

- [Analysis] How do you know when someone is equivocating?

- [Analysis] What's the difference between equivocation and lies?
- [Evaluation] Is any level of equivocation a lie?
- [Analysis] Why do people equivocate?
- [Creation] How do we prevent people in power from equivocating?
- [Evaluation] Would you rather deal with a truth-teller or an equivocator? Is there such a thing as too much honesty?

Play-Related Questions

- [Analysis] How are the witches' prophecies equivocation or doublespeak?
- [Analysis] How are Lady Macbeth's and Macbeth's words equivocation or doublespeak?
- [Creation] What does Shakespeare say about equivocators?

> FEAR.
> **Alas poor country, almost afraid to know itself.**
> —*Macbeth*, Act IV, scene 3
>
> In 1605 there was a plague. Theatres were closed. In 1606 Shakespeare wrote **Macbeth**.
>
> In 2020 there was a plague. Theatres were closed. In 2020 we read **Macbeth**.
>
> There is not one mention of the plague in **Macbeth**, but fear is mentioned over 48 times.
>
> The acting company of our "startlingly good" (*The Times*) 2018 production including Michelle Terry and Paul Ready, reunite for a semi-staged reading of this ominous play about power, fear, the bloody murder of the most powerful figure in the country, and the tenacious ambition of a despotic leader who will seemingly do anything in the pursuit and maintenance of power.
>
> #ShakesFear
>
> —"*Macbeth*: A Conjuring."

Imagination

Relevance Questions

- [Evaluation] What is wonderful about the human imagination?

- [Evaluation] What is horrible about the human imagination?
- [Analysis] What are the benefits and challenges of having the gift of fantasy?
- [Analysis] Can we control our imaginations?
- [Evaluation] What should be the moral limits of imagination (fantasy)?
- [Creation] Oscar Wilde once said art should be for art's sake. What should be the standards for artistic imagination?

Play-Related Questions

- [Analysis] How is Macbeth's imagination sometimes a terrorist?
- [Analysis] Does Macbeth control his imagination or does it control him?
- [Analysis] How much does Macbeth's imagination alter what the witches and others tell him? Where does his imagination alter reality?
- [Analysis] Where does Macbeth have an opportunity to limit his imagination? Why doesn't he take that opportunity?
- [Analysis] How is Shakespeare's poetry able to make Macbeth's "horrible imaginings" beautiful?

Leadership

Relevance Questions

- [Analysis] What is the difference between leadership and tyranny?
- [Analysis] What elements of society encourage and create tyranny?
- [Analysis] How does my culture or community define leadership? Who should lead, and why? How should they lead, and why?

Play-Related Questions

- [Analysis] How would you describe Macbeth's leadership style and methods?
- [Analysis] What is the leadership structure in *Macbeth*'s Scotland? What are its strengths and flaws?
- [Evaluation] Is Duncan a good leader?
- [Evaluation] Does Malcolm look like he will be a good leader?

Loyalty

Relevance Questions

- [Analysis] How do we show loyalty to family or friends?
- [Analysis] How do we show loyalty to our leaders or our country?
- [Evaluation] What is the ultimate test of loyalty?
- [Evaluation] When is loyalty honorable, and when is it toxic? When do demands of loyalty cross a line?

Play-Related Questions

- [Analysis] What kind of loyalty does Macbeth show? To whom or to what?
- [Analysis] Why and how do Macbeth's loyalties change?
- [Evaluation] What is the worst type of betrayal shown in this play?
- [Evaluation] Who seems to be the most loyal person in this play?

Magic

Relevance Questions

- [Analysis] What is magic?
- [Analysis] Why should someone attempt magic? Why shouldn't someone?
- [Analysis] What do witches represent in my culture or community?
- [Evaluation] What moral standards should be involved in magic?

Play-Related Questions

- [Analysis] What is the method and means of the witches' magic?
- [Analysis] Does the witches' magic make Macbeth do anything?
- [Evaluation] Is the witches' magic evil or immoral?
- [Creation] What is Shakespeare saying about witches and witchcraft?

Manhood

Relevance Questions

- [Analysis] What is manhood? What roles do men play in my culture? What are their responsibilities? How should men look? How should men behave?

- [Analysis] What are the benefits and challenges of identifying as a man?
- [Analysis] What types of power do men hold in my culture? In our society?
- [Analysis] What are positive and negative terms describing male gender identity? What are different ranges on the spectrum of male gender identity?
- [Evaluation & Creation] To what standards should men be held?

Play-Related Questions

- [Analysis] What does it mean to "take it like a man" in *Macbeth*?
- [Evaluation] Who is a true "man" in *Macbeth*?
- [Creation] What is Shakespeare's view of manhood?

Paradox

Relevance Questions

- [Analysis] In what ways are opposites true in your life? How is what's foul sometimes fair and vice versa?
- [Evaluation] How do you feel about opposites in your life?

Play-Related Questions

- [Analysis] What in each of the characters is both "foul" and "fair"?
- [Analysis] What in the society of *Macbeth*'s Scotland is both "foul" and "fair"?
- [Analysis] How are loss and victory intertwined in this play?
- [Analysis] How are appearances full of contradictions in this play?
- [Creation] What is Shakespeare saying about the nature of reality if it's so full of paradoxes?

Power

Relevance Questions

- [Analysis] Who has power in your life? In our society? How do you know?
- [Analysis] How does your identity provide or prevent access to necessary resources (Simons), resources that give you power?
- [Analysis] How does your power take up space or silence others? (Simons)

- [Analysis] How does others' power through their identities provide or prevent access to necessary resources (adapted from Simons)?
- [Analysis] Have you ever gotten a taste of power and then found yourself unable to handle the responsibility?
- [Analysis] Have you seen others get a taste of power and abuse it?
- [Analysis] Why is power so addictive?
- [Creation & Evaluation] How should people in power conduct themselves? What should be the standards?

Play-Related Questions

- [Analysis] Do the witches possess power? If yes, in what ways? What seems to be the source(s) of the witches' power? If no, why not?
- [Analysis] Who possesses more power—Macbeth or Lady Macbeth—in their relationship? Who has most power in leading the plot?
- [Analysis] Who is without power in this play? Why? What happens to them?
- [Evaluation] Who uses power most wisely in the play?
- [Creation] What view of government power, political power, and leadership does Shakespeare present? Is there an ideal?

Womanhood

Relevance Questions

- [Analysis] What is womanhood? What roles do women play in my culture? How should women look? How should women behave? What are their responsibilities? Why?
- [Analysis] What are the benefits and challenges of identifying as a woman?
- [Analysis] What types of power do women hold in my culture? In our society?
- [Analysis] What are positive and negative terms describing female gender identity? What are different ranges on the spectrum of female gender identity?
- [Evaluation & Creation] To what standards should women be held?

Play-Related Questions

- [Analysis] What do lines in *Macbeth* communicate about women, such as "a woman's story at a winter's fire / Authorized by her grandam" (act 3, scene 4, 65) or "womanly defense" (act 4, scene 2, 73)?

- [Evaluation] Who is a true woman in *Macbeth*?
- [Creation] What is Shakespeare's view of womanhood?

DYO EQs

At Handout 4 found at lynhawks.com/extramacbeth you can review several other Big Ideas that might better suit your students. You might create at least one relevance and one play-related query for each Big Idea and have these available to offer students for essays, projects, journals, and other tasks.

Build a list of quotes that might make great discussion fodder for these concepts. These can be quotes from thinkers across the ages, quotes from current events and contemporaries, and even quotes from your family, friends, students, and others. The goal is to get a bank of generalizations and assumptions rooted in this Big Idea, in the same way that the Pre-Play Poll and Post-Play Poll offer some. In The Learning Network lesson about *Macbeth* and its connections to Michael Brown's death in Ferguson, instructional coach Michael Roethler offers such a bank with quotes to students such as "I don't trust words, I trust actions" or "Trust is like paper: once it's crumpled, it can't be perfect again" (The Learning Network).

Head to lynhawks.com/extramacbeth for Handout 54. Big Idea Planning.

Assigning Journal Entries

Journals are a safe, reflective, and creative space for students to explore personally relevant Big Ideas. Relevance questions make great journal prompts.

I've always liked giving students a long list of options related to the week's discussions. I invite students to write one hundred to five hundred words per question. They can fold over pages they don't need me to read. I expect to read one out of three entries each time. I want to create a space where students can explore ideas, tell stories, rehearse theories, and happen upon epiphanies. These are great warm-ups for class discussion. Feedback comes in the form of straight credit and my questions, asking them to think more deeply or specifically. I don't expect revisions. These are formative thinking "rehearsals."

Sometimes students reveal traumatic stories, so when I introduce this assignment, I always let students know that if I learn of anything that might endanger them, it's my duty to share it with those who can support them. I always seek advice from guidance staff.

Leading Socratic Discussions

The Goal of Socratic Discussion

Socratic seminars challenge students to explore important issues; to communicate clearly, substantively, and respectfully; and to deepen their understanding of texts. As Mortimer Adler notes in *The Paideia Program*, the goal is "enlarged understanding of ideas and values by means of maieutic or Socratic questioning and active participation" (8).

Discussions are for everyone and should be a WCA grouping as often as possible. Bringing students together weekly for discussion tells them not only that their views matter but also that they are text investigators and idea wranglers, able to engage in intellectual inquiry.

Meaningful discussion requires clear ground rules and rigorous questions. In a successful Socratic seminar, students own the conversation, and ideally they choose the questions to discuss. The teacher's role is to keep questioning alive, to encourage use of the text for evidence, to encourage thoughtful commentary on evidence, to provide feedback on discussion progress, to nurture positive behaviors, and to delegate discussion facilitation as soon as students are ready, eventually playing observer rather than catalyst.

Steps for Planning Discussions

- Designing effective lead questions takes time. They need revision and testing with students until they can "go for miles." I always bring three to five Essential Questions and then a bank of clarifying questions. Clarifying questions might be any on the guide offered on Handout 3. Let's Clarify: Asking Good Questions at lynhawks.com/extramacbeth.
- Before the first discussion, establish and review ground rules using Handout 7. Socratic Seminar Evaluation Rubric (lynhawks.com/extramacbeth). If students lack prior experience, assume initial discussions may be shorter and less expansive until students understand routines and build confidence and skill.
- Before a discussion, ask students to prepare notes using Handout 8. Socratic Seminar Notes (at lynhawks.com/extramacbeth). In class, have students sit in a circle or U shape, and place any observers in an outer ring. If conducting an online discussion, assign students to comment as observers in an online document, bulletin board, or discussion thread while you facilitate the group discussion. Students should come prepared with both notes and texts.
- You can assign roles such as question leader (the person who ensures ample time for discussion of each question, poses new

questions, and invites new questions) and evidence checker (the person who asks students to defend their claims with quotations, paraphrases, or reasons).

- Depending on personality types and learning styles, some students prefer speaking in generalizations, while others prefer speaking in specifics. Whatever their preference, all must learn to quote or paraphrase the text to defend an argument, and all must eventually extrapolate topical subgroups and generalizations (the Big Ideas and Essential Understandings) from the specifics. Good speakers and writers can move fluidly between the concrete and the abstract, a fundamental skill you're coaching during discussions, along with listening well and building on others' ideas.
- Personal anecdotes can enrich a discussion. Such stories are a great place to begin as students build a discussion community with you. A strong personal anecdote is relevant to the topic and helps a reader or listener connect more deeply with the text. For example, "I don't trust Lady Macbeth because she says that she and Macbeth should look like a flower but really be a snake. I used to have a friend in fifth grade who was exactly like that; said one thing to my face, another behind my back. Anyone who is strategically fake should not be trusted." Some students will need gentle guidance away from stories that get too personal or off topic.
- Encourage students to take notes. Especially when preparing for summative assessments, students will be glad they noted great ideas shared in discussion, ones they can use in their essays, with credit to their peers. Handout 8. Socratic Seminar Notes (lynhawks.com/extramacbeth) offers one method of note-taking during discussions.

Giving Feedback

- I keep brief notes on all students. You might build a spreadsheet using categories in Handout 7. Socratic Seminar Evaluation Rubric (lynhawks.com/extramacbeth), making a tab for each student. Whenever students excel or need guidance, you can mark a Y or N and jot notes as needed. Every few discussions, make a positive, highly specific observation, ask one question, and/or leave constructive criticism. You can read some of the compliments aloud at the end of a discussion or before the next one as a reminder of which skills to practice. You can share these areas for growth with students as areas for everyone's growth. In my gradebook, everyone received straight credit for being part of the discussion, with bonus points to those who go above and beyond.

- Pick a few skills to assess in the beginning and then begin to add more levels of skill as you move forward with discussions. Determine which are foundational, core skills that most if not all students should demonstrate by the end of the unit, and which are advanced ones that you might nudge some more gifted students toward.
- Treat the first weeks of discussion as formative, and plan on a summative discussion in the final week of the unit.

Possible Seminar Formats and Permutations

- *WCA*: Have all students experience a seminar together as a unit opener and a unit closing. The most heterogeneous mix allows the richest variety of perspectives, where students with practical wisdom might educate those with more sheltered perspectives, and verbal-linguistic students can model a love of close reading, debate, and language for less avid readers.
    - If you have a large class and a greater range of readiness levels, allow plenty of time for skill development. Consider beginning Socratic seminars with a more accessible text and twenty-five-minute experiences until students grow more comfortable with the guidelines. Another way to warm up to literary text discussion is to introduce the rules and then use a film clip as the first text. For example, you might pose a question before viewing act 1: "Macbeth is a guy who wants a promotion. He wants the crown. Should he go for it?" and then ask students to watch act 1, scene 3, looking for any evidence in the film clip to support either answer. Follow-up questions you might ask could include:
        - What words from various characters seemed to signal Macbeth should go after the crown?
        - Where did you see images, actions, or sounds in this film clip that encourage Macbeth to go after the crown?
        - Where did you see anything else seemingly auspicious for Macbeth's ambition?
        - Is Macbeth wrong to want the crown?
        - Is Macbeth wrong or right to heed the witches? What do we mean by "wrong" or "right"?
        - Is evil present here? How do you know?
    - Model for students how you listen, reflect back, and clarify various students' claims, assumptions, and understandings, trying to dig for greater clarity and evidence. Provide positive feedback for students who live up to the rubric.

- Rely heavily on relevance questions for initial WCA discussions to hook most students while emphasizing two core skills: listening well and offering evidence.
- I use fishbowls and peer review, with all students getting a chance to be in and out of the circle, when I first introduce the expectations of Socratic seminar.

- *Tiered-readiness (TR) differentiation*: NOV, OT, and ADV groups can discuss different questions separately in TR groups of seven to ten students, or TR groups can be matched up to observe and evaluate each other (fishbowl style) and then switch. Assign different questions to each group to create the richest discussion later when the class regroups. Note that relevance questions can be more ELL-NOVI friendly for the first discussions. Regroup as a WCA to hear insights from each group.
- *Mixed-readiness (MR) differentiation*: Make two discussion groups of ten to fifteen each: one, an ELL-NOV-OT mix and the other, an OT-ADV mix. Have each group discuss different questions while the other group watches fishbowl style and assesses discussion participants' skill using the rubric. Regroup as a WCA so that each group of fishbowl observers can celebrate their peers' strong insights or demonstrations of Socratic seminar skill.

You can teach a discussions skills mini-lesson to an ELL-NOV group needing further practice and help with translation while also giving more time and attention to students whose ideas, knowledge, and experience might be fairly complex but not as easily expressed. Meanwhile, other TR groups of OT-ADV students will run recorded discussions in groups of ten or fewer. The next day, switch and offer mini-lessons in needed skills to OT-ADV while the ELL-NOV group records its discussion.

4 Preassessment and Formative Assessment

What You Will Find in This Chapter

- A rationale for preassessment
- A process for preassessment
- Sample formative assessments: preassessments, in-process assessments, and postassessments for skill competencies and interests
- Tips for designing your own

Why Preassess?

"Diagnostic assessment (preassessment) is as important to teaching as a physical exam is to prescribing appropriate medical regimens" (qtd. in Roberts and Inman 47). This statement by Carol Ann Tomlinson and Jay McTighe, two leaders in differentiated instruction, says it all. We should ask, *What do our students already know? What can they already do? What do they need to know and learn how to do?* Unlike Macbeth, who'd rather "throw physic to the dogs" (act 1, scene 5, 48), we are curricular physicians looking for signs of health and symptoms of disease.

Consider the lessons you provide—whether WCA, MR, or TR activities—a "wellness path" for students to explore their interests, strengthen their skill competencies, and seek remedy for skill gaps. Preassessment is one step in a continuous process of assessment and responding to students' various needs, as Julia L. Roberts and Tracy F. Inman note in *Strategies for Differentiating Instruction: Best Practices for the Classroom* (49). If medicine is too heavy a metaphor, try photography instead: preassessment provides a snapshot of a moment in time for the writing portfolio or scrapbook so we can later see development and growth.

Research also proves the added benefits of pretesting before a unit, since error generation and the correction of misunderstandings lead to increased retention (Pan).

Preassessment is also a chance to discover new information about students and have a little fun. When students know we care about their interests and passions, and that we are willing to find a way to integrate them into Shakespeare study, we get a whole new level of buy-in.

Sample preassessments, in-process assessments, and postassessments follow in this chapter, as well as tips for your own design. If your school, district, and/or state has different skill competencies and expectations, check out the DYO section of this chapter (see p. 82) and edit digital handouts as needed. For cumulative, summative assessments, see Chapter 11, "Summative Assessments."

How Do I Assess Readiness?

Three questions can help you design assessment when planning your unit:

- Which core skill competencies should all students master by the end of this unit?
- What are the macro and micro levels of these competencies? (See Chapter 1 for a model.)
- What will be the check-ins for formative assessments: preassessment, in-process, and postassessment?

> Pre-assessment, in-process assessment, and post assessment should give learners consistent opportunity to demonstrate their knowledge, understanding, and skills related to topics of study. Assessments related to student readiness, interests, perspectives, and learning preferences provide educators with a consistently emerging understanding of each learner's needs in the classroom.
>
> —National Middle School Association and the National Association for Gifted Children, qtd. in Roberts and Inman 49

Establishing a Safe Space

My tenth graders' eyes were as big as if they'd seen Banquo's ghost. "I don't get any of it!" some said as they contemplated the *Macbeth* passage with fear and loathing. It was the week prior to my *Macbeth* unit, and I'd given them about fifteen lines from the play to annotate. But I'd sprung the pretest on them, and they didn't understand what I was up to, not at all.

"Come on, you know *some* words," I reassured them. "Make sense of it as best you can. Don't worry. If you try—show some kind of effort—you'll get full credit!"

Still, during the whole period they seemed frustrated, despite reassurances that I meant what I said. I hadn't thought about their prior experiences with Shakespeare, or how they heard the term *timed response* as synonymous with "high-stakes test." I realized I needed to better introduce why we preassess and how I planned to differentiate instruction based on this assessment.

Roberts and Inman recommend that you let students know your rationale for preassessment (50). Here is some suggested language.

> I preassess to learn more about your prior skills and knowledge.
>
> As your curriculum designer and instructional coach, I need to get data in order to practice the best teaching methods.
>
> These tasks carry no grade penalty. You get credit for writing something.
>
> Please do your best. Do your best so that I can design the best lessons, activities, and assignments for you.

Roberts and Inman also suggest many preassessment strategies and formats. The types I offer here are interest inventories, a matching quiz, and writing tasks.

Emily Pendergrass notes that some key components are essential for the successful differentiated classroom that uses preassessment effectively:

- Is your learning community based on respect?
- Do students trust you? Do they know you want them to succeed?
- Do you use preassessment data rather than feelings to make choices about TR and MR groups? (Pendergrass)

Another key set of inquiries for vetting lesson activities are these:

- Do the tasks we provide all students in TR and MR groups indicate a respect for not only their interests but also their ability to grow as critical thinkers?
- Are the tasks we design for all creative and fun?

We should ask ourselves these questions whenever we flexibly group students so that we communicate excitement and hope for what students can do now and in the future.

Designing for Core Competencies and Sample Assessments

Let's say a teacher named Alicia is designing her ninth-grade *Macbeth* unit and wants to ensure her students master two core skills: persuasive writing and argument, as well as figurative language knowledge, interpretation, and creation. She makes the following plans for formative and summative assessments throughout the unit, giving her preassessments the week prior to the unit.

Alicia uses writing portfolios with her students. For more on writing portfolios, see Chapter 11. Her plan is detailed in Tables 4.1 and 4.2. All assessments mentioned in these tables are featured as samples in this chapter or in Chapter 11.

Table 4.1. Argument Assessment Plan

Skill	**Preassessment (Formative) (Before Week 1)**	**In-Process Assessment (Formative) (Weeks 2–6)**	**Postassessment (Summative) (Week 8)**
Students will: ■ Write arguments to support claims in an analysis of substantive topics or texts, using valid reasoning and relevant and sufficient evidence. (CCSS.ELA-LITERACY.W.9-10.1) ■ Introduce precise claim(s), distinguish the claim(s) from alternate or opposing claims, and create an organization that establishes clear relationships among claim(s), counterclaims, reasons, and evidence. (CCSS.ELA-LITERACY.W.9-10.1.A)	Handout 9. Preassessment: Write a Persuasive Message	■ Twice-weekly entrance and exit tickets—write a persuasive claim—after key scene lessons ■ A Fair Brand, A Foul Proposition, and Tiniest Superpower creative writing assignments	Essay, Podcast, Poster, or Performance (see Chapter 11)

Table 4.2. Figurative Language Assessment Plan

Skill	Preassessment (Formative) (Before Week 1)	In-Process Assessment (Formative) (Weeks 2–6)	Postassessment (Summative) (Week 8)
Students will: Demonstrate understanding of figurative language, word relationships, and nuances in word meanings. CCSS.ELA-LITERACY.L.9-10.5.A: ▪ Interpret figures of speech (e.g., euphemism, oxymoron) in context and analyze their role in the text. CCSS.ELA-LITERACY.L.9-10.5.B: ▪ Analyze nuances in the meaning of words with similar denotations.	Handouts 10–13 Figurative Language and Sound Devices: label the image and sound devices, and interpret one.	▪ Creative writing exercise #1: I Am Literally and Figuratively . . . ▪ Creative writing exercise #2: Soundscapes ▪ Peer review literary analysis	▪ Timed analysis: Macbeth's Tomorrow and Tomorrow and Tomorrow speech ▪ Timed creative writing: My Ennui Special Effects ▪ Or experimental poetry gallery and peer review (will decide after midpoint of unit) ▪ (see Chapter 11)

Use Handout 46. Preassessments, In-Process, and Postassessment Planning Chart available at lynhawks.com/extramacbeth to determine skills you hope to preassess, to assess during the unit, and to assess at the end of the unit. Don't forget macro and micro skills. For more tips and models, see Chapter 1.

Sample Preassessments, In-Process Assessments, and Postassessments

This guide offers preassessments to determine student interests, translation skills, figurative language skills, expository writing skills, and persuasive writing skills.

Preassessing for Interests

Preassessing for interests will help you design flexible MR groupings for CRs, projects, and problem-based learning activities. It's also helpful knowledge to have when advising a student on which essay and project topics to pick.

Find out what students love to do and what inspires their passion. Use Handout 14. The Bardometer: Your Interest Inventory (lynhawks .com/extramacbeth), or create a poll of your own. Note that I have listed professions on my interest inventory because they relate to character professions in *Macbeth*. Be ready for students to ask, "What's the difference between a psychologist and a psychiatrist?" or "What's a chief of staff?"

Lesson for Interest Preassessment

One fun way to preassess is to offer learning centers where students can experiment for the day and demonstrate their interests and abilities. Create different stations where students choose their top two or three and spend part of the class at each, working either independently or in groups to make a statement about a Big Idea. You can let students know that you are curious to see what ideas they have about a completely open-ended idea, and that you have no "right answer" in mind for these products. You might be surprised by the creative artistry, imagination, and play that ensues. Here are some sample centers you might create.

Sample Centers	Sample Tasks	Learning Center Materials
Writer's Studio	Poetry Explorations: Write a descriptive poem based on the scents you discover here, related to one of these Big Ideas: ■ Imagination ■ Delusion ■ Nature ■ Manhood ■ Womanhood ■ Magic ■ Ambition ■ Tyranny	■ Lavender-soaked cloth ■ Eucalyptus-soaked cloth ■ Sliced lemon ■ Sage ■ Cinnamon ■ Rosemary ■ Thyme ■ Cumin ■ Turmeric ■ Ginger ■ Any other strong-smelling natural spice [Note: Be sure to check that students aren't allergic to any of these. Do not let students touch essential oils directly.]
Actor's Studio	Freeze-Frame: Create and photograph a living statuary pose expressing a story related to the Big Ideas listed above.	■ Oversized T-shirts ■ Blankets ■ Sunglasses ■ Hats, scarves, gloves, and other accessories ■ Kitchen utensils (long spoon, spatula, tin foil, etc.)
Visual Artist's Studio	Images, collages, sketches, and paintings: Design a symbolic image, mixed-media piece, tattoo, or other design related to the Big Ideas listed above.	■ Paper (plain and colored) ■ Colored pencils ■ Paints ■ Crayons ■ Fabric swatches ■ Markers ■ Scissors

Music Studio	Lyrics, melody, and beats: Write and/or record a few lines of music, beats, or other musical expression related to the Big Ideas listed above.	■ Computer ■ Keyboard ■ Percussion instruments (shaker, drum, etc.)

In-Process Assessments for Interests

Allow students to choose their journal entry topics, creative writing topics, CR roles, project- and problem-based learning prompts, and academic writing prompts. If students select these based on interest, they will be more creative and committed to these tasks and products, and you will enjoy assessment more.

One method of informal assessment is to circulate while students are engaged in TR and MR tasks chosen by interest. You might ask students:

- What do you like about this role/topic/question/task? Why?
- How are you extending your knowledge in this area?
- What skill are you practicing?
- What skills would you like to develop?
- What's a new thought or realization you had today about this topic?
- Does this make you think about potential careers, as in, "I'd love to do this professionally" or "I'd never do this"?
- How has this exploration shown you something about your reading and writing skills?

Nurturing this metacognitive awareness in your students will not only relay to you key information about their skill development and interests, but it will also show your students you care about their interests. Meanwhile, keep observational notes of strengths or struggles students have to help you plan for future units. You can also share and celebrate student discoveries and interests in final comments, narrative evaluations, and conferences.

Postassessments for Interests

Ask students to complete a freewrite or an exit ticket answering these questions:

- One interest, talent, or skill that I was able to pursue during this *Macbeth* unit was . . .
- During this unit, I believe I developed or enhanced an interest, talent, or skill in . . .

- I know I got better at this interest, talent, or skill because . . .
- One question I'm interested in exploring now is . . .
- [optional] I will always remember when I . . .
- [optional] In the future, I hope to explore more of . . .
- [optional] Today a career or profession that might interest me is . . .
- [optional] A question I have about our next unit of study is . . .

Preassessing and Postassessing for Understandings

How do we know that students *understand* something? What does that vague word truly mean? Two questions I ask are:

- Can my students bring meaningful evidence from the text to develop a claim about this topic? In other words, do they know some facts, whether textual or otherwise?
- Can they use reason and analysis of diction to further explain their thinking? Is the logic solid and is the analysis accurate?

If their writing and speaking during all our tasks are getting better in these two areas, this is my proof they are developing more robust and well-defended thinking, and that they are grappling more deeply with Big Ideas and Essential Questions. Students have moved from surface understanding of Big Ideas and Essential Questions to in-depth understanding.

See Chapter 5, "Hook Activities," for the Tell Me Where You Stand preassessment asking students to choose their perspectives when the play opens. Also see Chapter 3 to find tips and activities that are useful when preassessing and postassessing student understandings.

In-process assessments for understanding can include journal entries, creative writing tasks, and other formative assessments such as Punnett squares, T-W-H or K-W-L charts, and Venn diagrams. I recommend that these be given full credit if you are grading, once students meet standards such as these:

- The student raises at least one interesting question.
- The student shares an opinion.
- The student gives an example to support an opinion.

Preassessing for Core Skill Competencies

Simple and brief preassessments to obtain evidence of student knowledge and skill are key. Sample preassessments for these areas follow: figurative language, persuasive writing, expository writing, evidence identification and claim creation, and text translation follow, as well as tips for assessment.

Figurative Language Knowledge and Skill: Formative Preasssessments

A preassessment for figurative language knowledge can test for basic knowledge, comprehension, and application skills: Can students match terms and definitions and create some examples?

I recommend giving the identification piece of any tier, whether Word Nerds or Word Sleuths (aka Part 1) as an individual, timed task and collecting that information right away. Then you might give the creative writing piece (Part 2)—the tic-tac-toe board—as an independent task followed by a pairs/triads peer review activity.

Another way to approach this process is to begin with a figurative language and sound devices mini-lesson as a WCA, and then follow with one of these two formative TR preassessments for figurative language to see what students retain:

- Word Nerd: The first TR preassessment could be used for a class with many ELL and NOV as well as OT students. It does not use Shakespeare's text.
- Word Sleuth: The second TR preassessment could be used for a class of students who are more OT and ADV. It uses Shakespeare's text.
- If you are offering the *Macbeth* unit at a time when you already know your students' readiness levels well, and the class spans a very heterogeneous group of levels, consider giving two different preassessments: the Word Nerd to ELL and NOV students and the Word Sleuth version to OT and ADV students.
- If you like both, you might use the Word Nerd version first as a preassessment and the Word Sleuth as a formative assessment later, offering these successively, perhaps two weeks apart, to see where students are at and how they are developing in this skill area.

Note that the in-process and postassessments are specifically devoted to creation: tasks in which students demonstrate the ability to harness figurative language and sound devices in their own writing. The first creative writing prompt focuses solely on metaphor as a model for how you can create a deep-dive activity to let students explore one form of figurative language.

Go to lynhawks.com/extramacbeth for digital versions of the following preassessments. Answer keys and assessment guidance are provided here in this guide.

For ELL and NOV students:

Handout 10. Figurative Language & Sound Devices Preassessment, Word Nerds, Part 1

Directions: What do you already know about figurative language and sound devices? Match as many terms to their definitions as you can. Don't worry if you can't match them all.

Do your best. You will get full credit for attempting this assessment.

Term	**My Answer** (number)	**Definition**
Synesthesia		1. a chiming (rhyme) of the vowel sounds
Cacophony		2. a succession of light, harmonious syllables
Double Rhyme		3. a figure of speech in which a part represents the whole object or idea
Synecdoche		4. also known as masculine rhyme; rhyme in the last syllable of the line
Assonance		5. a pattern of identical sounds created by consonants, especially in the final syllables of words
Paradox		6. a succession of harsh, slow-moving syllables
Consonance		7. also known as feminine rhyme; rhyme in the last two syllables of the line
Euphony		8. verse with five beats, or metrical feet, each beat containing one short (unstressed) syllable followed by one long (unstressed) syllable
Single Rhyme		9. a statement or concept which appears self-contradictory, but underlines a basis of truth
Metaphor		10. a figure of speech where inanimate or lifeless things are described as having human qualities
Euphemism		11. the frequent repetition of the same initial letter or sound
Antithesis		12. verse with four beats, or metrical feet, each beat containing one long (stressed) syllable followed by one short (unstressed) syllable
Hyperbole		13. a figure of speech where two contradictions are paired in one image, description, or expression

continued on next page

Personification		14. a figure of speech where contrasting words or sentences are placed next to each other in direct opposition
Simile		15. a figure of speech where an offensive idea is stated inoffensively with vagueness or more inoffensive terms
Oxymoron		16. A figure of speech created by substitution where one thing is said to be another
Alliteration		17. A comparison of two things, often using *like* or *as*
Onomatopoeia		18. A figure of speech that is an exaggeration where something is portrayed as being either greater or less than what it really is
Iambic pentameter		19. a figure of speech in which the description of one kind of sense impression is created by words that normally describe another, such as when sound is described in terms of things seen and felt
Trochaic tetrameter		20. a word formed by the sound related to what is named (e.g. *hiss* or *pop*)

Answer Key for Handout 10. Figurative Language & Sound Devices Preassessment, Word Nerds, Part 1

Term	Answer	Definition
Synesthesia	19	1. a chiming (rhyme) of the vowel sounds
Cacophony	6	2. a succession of light, harmonious syllables
Double Rhyme	7	3. a figure of speech in which a part represents the whole object or idea
Synecdoche	3	4. also known as masculine rhyme; rhyme in the last syllable of the line
Assonance	1	5. a pattern of identical sounds created by consonants, especially in the final syllables of words
Paradox	9	6. a succession of harsh, slow-moving syllables
Consonance	5	7. also known as feminine rhyme; rhyme in the last two syllables of the line
Euphony	2	8. verse with five beats, or metrical feet, each beat containing one short (unstressed) syllable followed by one long (unstressed) syllable
Single Rhyme	4	9. a statement or concept that appears self-contradictory but underlines a basis of truth
Metaphor	16	10. a figure of speech in which inanimate or lifeless things are described as having human qualities
Euphemism	15	11. the frequent repetition of the same initial letter or sound
Antithesis	14	12. verse with four beats, or metrical feet, each beat containing one long (stressed) syllable followed by one short (unstressed) syllable
Hyperbole	18	13. a figure of speech in which two contradictions are paired in one image, description, or expression
Personification	10	14. a figure of speech in which contrasting words or sentences are placed next to each other in direct opposition
Simile	17	15. a figure of speech in which an offensive idea is stated inoffensively with vagueness or more inoffensive terms
Oxymoron	13	16. a figure of speech created by substitution, where one thing is said to be another
Alliteration	11	17. a comparison of two things, often using *like* or *as*
Onomatopoeia	20	18. a figure of speech that is an exaggeration in which something is portrayed as being either greater or less than it really is
Iambic pentameter	8	19. a figure of speech in which the description of one kind of sense impression is created by words that normally describe another, such as when sound is described in terms of things seen and felt
Trochaic tetrameter	12	20. a word formed by the sound related to what is named (e.g., *hiss* or *pop*)

For ELL and NOV students:

Handout 11. Figurative Language & Sound Devices Preassessment, Word Nerds, Part 2

Directions: What do you already know about figurative language and sound devices? Choose three devices from the Tic-tac-toe board and design your own figurative language or sound devices based on the creative writing prompts.

- You can use the prompts below, or you can come up with your own ideas of what to describe.
- If you want to use other figurative language or sound devices, choose from the Word Bank.
- Be prepared to share your creations with a classmate.

Do your best. You will get full credit for attempting this assessment.

Tic-tac-toe

METAPHOR for you or a friend when mad	**SIMILE** for you or a friend when sad	**PERSONIFICATION** for a favorite object or thing
METAPHOR for someone who is deceitful	**SIMILE** for someone who is heroic	**PERSONIFICATION** of something that is tempting
HYPERBOLE for how bad or good something is	**ANTITHESIS,** where you express two coexisting, opposite feelings or situations	**EUPHEMISM** for something offensive in your life that you don't want to say straight up
ALLITERATION using a favorite consonant of yours in the first letters	**ONOMATOPOEIA** of how a car or bus or train sounds	**ASSONANCE** using a favorite vowel of yours
CONSONANCE of a favorite consonant of yours in the last syllables of words	**CACOPHONY** describing something that is cacophonous	**IAMBIC PENTAMETER** in one line describing something you love

Figurative Language and Sound Device Word Bank

Figurative Language Devices	Antithesis, Euphemism, Hyperbole, Metaphor, Oxymoron, Paradox, Personification, Simile, Synecdoche, Synesthesia
Sound Devices	Alliteration, Assonance, Cacophony, Consonance, Double Rhyme, Euphony, Iambic Pentameter, Trochaic Tetrameter, Onomatopoeia, Single Rhyme

My Examples

#1	
#2	
#3	

Assessment Approaches for Handout 10. Figurative Language & Sound Devices Preassessment, Word Sleuths, Part 1

Divide student work into three piles and scale within the pile.

1. OT A: Misses several matches; knows about 25 percent.
2. OT B: Misses some or half of the answers.
3. ADV: Misses few answers.

Now determine whether a small group or the whole class needs a minilesson.

Assessment Approaches for Handout 11. Figurative Language & Sound Devices Preassessment, Word Nerds, Part 2

When assessing Part 2, keep in mind that students have spent independent time creating their answers and then worked with a peer or in a triad, so they may have added some of their peers' ideas. I recommend having students give feedback to each other in real time, first reading aloud peers' work in pairs or triads and then nominating in the follow-up WCA activity those figures of speech they deem "most creative."

The shaded rows of tic-tac-toe board are the most complex levels of figures of speech and sound devices, simply because they are not as commonly known by high school students and/or require a deeper level of analysis and creation. You can add Part 2 to student portfolios and wait to assess at the end of the unit. See Chapter 11 for more information on this process.

"Most creative" can be defined as:

- *Unique and Experimental.* The student thinks "outside the box" with original pairings of images to ideas. Instead of "mad as a hornet," the student picks a surprising creature or description: *I'm ferocious as a feral cat / left out too long in the rain.*
- *Elaborative.* The student goes above and beyond to create an example, such as using a range of details or sound repetitions.
- *Complexity of Thought.* The student attempts the shaded squares.

For OT and ADV students:

Handout 12. Figurative Language & Sound Devices Preassessment, Word Sleuths, Part 1

Directions: What do you already know about figurative language and sound devices? Match Shakespeare's text to the type of literary device.

Do your best. You will get full credit for attempting this assessment.

Figurative Language and Sound Device Word Bank

Figurative Language Devices	Antithesis, Euphemism, Hyperbole, Metaphor, Metonymy, Oxymoron, Paradox, Personification, Simile, Synecdoche, Synesthesia
Sound Devices	Alliteration, Assonance, Cacophony, Consonance, Double Rhyme, Euphony, Iambic Pentameter, Internal Rhyme, Onomatopoeia, Single Rhyme

Figurative Language: Devices That Create Images

Literary Device, Figurative Language	Text	Translation Notes
	"Approach thou* like the rugged Russian bear, / The arm'd* rhinoceros, or th'*Hyrcan tiger" —Macbeth (act 3, scene 4, 100–101)	*Approach me *armed *the *from Hyrcania (name for region where now is modern-day Iran and Turkmenistan)
	"I drink to the general joy o'* the whole table." —Macbeth (act 3, scene 4, 89)	*of
	"He that's coming Must be provided for,* and you shall put This night's great business into my dispatch*" —Lady Macbeth (act 1, scene 5, 65–67)	*prepared for *control, *management
	"O,* full of scorpions is my mind, dear wife!" —Macbeth (act 3, scene 2, 37)	*Oh
	"Fair is foul and foul is fair" —the Witches (act 1, scene 1, 12)	
	"'Tis* safer to be that which we destroy Than by destruction dwell in doubtful joy." —Lady Macbeth (act 3, scene 2, 6–7)	*It is
	"I have almost forgot* the taste of fears. . . ." —Macbeth (act 5, scene 5, 9)	*forgotten

continued on next page

	"This supernatural soliciting* Cannot be ill, cannot be good" —Macbeth (act 1, scene 3, 129–30)	*persuasion
	"Our castle's strength Will laugh a siege to scorn.*" —Macbeth (act 5, scene 5, 2–3)	*target of mock- ery
	"Take thy face hence*" —Macbeth (act 5, scene 3, 19)	*away from here
	"Thy crown does sear mine* eye-balls" —Macbeth (act 4, scene 1, 112)	*my

Sound Devices: Devices That Create Mood, Rhythm, and Tone

Sound Devices	Text	Translation Notes
	"After life's fitful fever he sleeps well." —Macbeth (act 3, scene 2, 23)	
	"When shall we three meet again?" —the Witches (act 1, scene 1, 1)	
	"Out, damned spot! Out, I say!—One, two. Why, then, 'tis time to do 't. Hell is murky." —Lady Macbeth (act 5, scene 1, 31–32)	
	"Shipwrecking storms and direful* thunders break" Sergeant (act 1, scene 2, 26)	*dreadful, terrible, frightful
	Double, double toil* and trouble; Fire burn, and cauldron bubble. —the Witches (act 4, scene 1, 10)	*exhaust
	"This castle hath* a pleasant seat;* the air / Nimbly* and sweetly recommends itself / Unto our gentle senses." —Duncan (act 1, scene 6, 1–3)	*has *setting *freshly
	"Thrice the brindled* cat hath mew'd" —First Witch (act 4, scene 1, 1)	*streaked, striped, tabby
	"But get thee back; my soul is too much charged*" —Macbeth (act 5, scene 8, 5)	*burdened, laden, oppressed
	"Double, double toil and trouble" —the Witches (act 4, scene 1, 1)	
	God's benison* go with you; and with those / That would make good of bad, and friends of foes! —Old Man (act 2, scene 4, 40–41)	*blessing
	Round about the cauldron go; In the poison'd entrails* throw. —the Witches (act 4, scene 1, 4–5)	*insides, intestines

Answer Key for Handout 12. Figurative Language & Sound Devices Preassessment, Word Sleuths, Part 1

Figurative Language: Devices That Create Images

Literary Device, Figurative Language	Text	Translation Notes
Simile	"Approach thou* like the rugged Russian bear, / The arm'd* rhinoceros, or th'* Hyrcan tiger" —Macbeth (act 3, scene 4, 100–101)	*Approach me *armed *the *from Hyrcania (name for region where now is modern-day Iran and Turkmeni-stan)
Metonymy	"I drink to the general joy o'* the whole table." —Macbeth (act 3, scene 4, 89)	*of
Euphemism	"He that's coming Must be provided for,* and you shall put This night's great business into my dis-patch*" —Lady Macbeth (act 1, scene 5, 65–67)	*prepared for *control, *man-agement
Metaphor	"O,* full of scorpions is my mind, dear wife!" —Macbeth (act 3, scene 2, 37)	*Oh
Antithesis	"Fair is foul and foul is fair" the Witches (act 1, scene 1, 12)	
Oxymoron	"'Tis* safer to be that which we destroy Than by destruction dwell in doubtful joy." —Lady Macbeth (act 3, scene 2, 6–7)	*It is
Synesthesia	"I have almost forgot* the taste of fears. . . ." —Macbeth (act 5, scene 5, 9)	*forgotten
Paradox	"This supernatural soliciting* Cannot be ill, cannot be good" —Macbeth (act 1, scene 3, 129–30)	*persuasion
Personification	"Our castle's strength Will laugh a siege to scorn.*" — Macbeth (act 5, scene 5, 2–3)	*target of mockery
Synecdoche	"Take thy face hence" —Macbeth (act 5, scene 3, 19)	
Hyperbole	"Thy crown does sear mine* eye-balls" —Macbeth (act 4, scene 1, 112)	*my

continued on next page

Sound Devices: Devices That Create Mood, Rhythm, and Tone

Sound Devices	Text	Translation Notes
Alliteration	"After life's fitful fever he sleeps well." —Macbeth (act 3, scene 2, 23)	
Assonance	"When shall we three meet again?" —the Witches (act 1, scene 1, 1)	
Cacophony	"Out, damned spot! Out, I say!—One, two. Why, then, 'tis time to do 't. Hell is murky." —Lady Macbeth (act 5, scene 1, 31–32)	
Consonance	"Shipwrecking storms and direful* thunders break" Sergeant (act 1, scene 2, 26)	*dreadful, terrible, frightful
Double Rhyme	"Double, double toil* and trouble; Fire burn, and cauldron bubble." —the Witches (act 4, scene 1, 10)	*exhaust
Euphony	"This castle hath* a pleasant seat;* the air / Nimbly* and sweetly recommends itself / Unto our gentle senses." —Duncan (act 1, scene 6, 1–3)	*has *setting *freshly
Onomatopoeia	"Thrice the brindled* cat hath mew'd" —First Witch (act 4, scene 1, 1)	*streaked, striped, tabby
Iambic Pentameter	"But get thee back; my soul is too much charged*" —Macbeth (act 5, scene 8, 5)	*burdened, laden, oppressed
Internal Rhyme	"Double, double toil and trouble" —the Witches (act 4, scene 1, 1)	
Single Rhyme	God's benison* go with you; and with those / That would make good of bad, and friends of foes! —Old Man (act 2, scene 4, 40–41)	*blessing
Trochaic Tetrameter	"Round about the cauldron go; In the poison'd entrails* throw." —the Witches (act 4, scene 1, 4–5)	*insides, intestines

Handout 13. Figurative Language & Sound Devices Preassessment, Word Sleuths, Part 2

Directions: What do you already know about figurative language and sound devices? Choose three devices from the tic-tac-toe board and design your own figurative language or sound devices based on the creative writing prompts.

- You can use the prompts below, or you can come up with your own ideas of what to describe.
- If you want to use other figurative language or sound devices, choose from the Word Bank.
- Be prepared to share your creations with a classmate.

Do your best. You will get full credit for attempting this assessment.

Tic-tac-toe

HYPERBOLE for how bad or good something is when it comes to politics	**ANTITHESIS,** where you express two coexisting, contrasting elements in war	**EUPHEMISM** for something offensive in your life that you don't want to say straight up
METONYMY for a person in a certain position of authority	**PARADOX** for a truth built from two seeming contradictions, seeming absurd, yet true, when it comes to leading people	**SYNECDOCHE** for something that is a part of a whole and can represent it (such as what something is made of or contains) when it comes to institutions
ALLITERATION using a favorite consonant of yours in the first letters	**ONOMATOPOEIA** of how a car or bus or train sounds	**ASSONANCE** using a favorite vowel of yours
CONSONANCE of a favorite consonant of yours in the last syllables of words	**CACOPHONY** describing something that is cacophonous	**IAMBIC PENTAMETER** in one line describing something you love
EUPHONY to describe a serene, happy place	**DOUBLE RHYME** in a text message between two people in love	**TROCHAIC TETRAMETER** in a sports chant or cheerleader yell

Figurative Language and Sound Device Word Bank

Figurative Language Devices	Antithesis, Euphemism, Hyperbole, Metaphor, Oxymoron, Paradox, Personification, Simile, Synecdoche, Synesthesia
Sound Devices	Alliteration, Assonance, Cacophony, Consonance, Double Rhyme, Euphony, Iambic Pentameter, Trochaic Tetrameter, Onomatopoeia, Single Rhyme

continued on next page

My Examples

#1	
#2	
#3	

Assessment Approaches for Handout 13. Figurative Language & Sound Devices Preassessment, Word Sleuths, Part 2

When assessing Part 2, keep in mind that students have spent independent time creating and then worked with a peer or in a triad, so they may have added some of their peers' ideas. The shaded rows of the tic-tac-toe board are the most complex levels of figures of speech and sound devices, simply because they are less commonly known by high school students and/or require a deeper level of analysis and creation.

There are also more complex Big Ideas offered related to *Macbeth*. You can add Part 2 to student portfolios, but wait to assess until the end of the unit. See Chapter 11 for more information on this process. I recommend having students give feedback in real time in class by reading aloud peers' work, ones they deem "most creative."

Most creative can be defined as:

- *Unique and Experimental.* The student thinks outside the box with original pairings of images to ideas. Instead of the hyperbole *It's a million miles away,* the student might have chosen *The distance makes me think I could make it to Mars and back sooner.*
- *Elaborative.* The student goes above and beyond to create an example, such as using a range of detail or sound repetition. The student might even combine literary elements in one expression (note the alliteration above in "make it to Mars").
- *Complexity of Thought.* The student attempts the shaded squares, does so accurately, and makes interesting commentary about the subjects given.

Mini-Lessons on Figurative Language

Preassessments will show you what students already know and can do. When remediating gaps or extending skill and knowledge, consider brief mini-lessons of ten to thirty minutes: modeling and skill practice. Besides the range of figurative language mini-lessons available out there, check out "Shakespeare's Metaphors: A Deep Dive with Tenor, Vehicle, and *Macbeth*" (Fairchild and Fairchild).

Figurative Language In-Process Assessment (Formative)

In-process assessments are creative writing activities to be added to students' writing portfolios, ones that students may cite as signs of creative growth when effectively applying figurative language and sound devices. Students are also working at showing mastery of CCSS.ELA-LITERACY.W.9-10.3.D: "Use precise words and phrases, telling details, and sensory language to convey a vivid picture of the experiences, events, setting, and/or characters"—only in this case, the formative practice is in building a vivid picture of the self. Begin with a subject of greatest interest to our students—themselves and their lived experience—before moving to characters, setting, events, and experiences in literature. See Chapter 11 for a final Character Analysis Summative: Metaphor Poster MR activity, followed by a TR timed writing.

To accomplish these tasks, students will need either a mini-lesson on figurative language and sound devices and/or the answer key for Handout 10. Figurative Language & Sound Devices Preassessment, Word Nerds, Part 1 (see p. 53) in order to have a reference list of definitions.

I recommend reading aloud a few lines from *Macbeth* and then following with an inspirational modern poem exploring a related Big Idea. You might find poems at Poetry Foundation that are thematically connected, related to power, empowerment, terror, heroism, and protest. Ask students to listen for figures of speech.

- "Tonight, in Oakland" by Danez Smith (2015)
- "Boy Breaking Glass" by Gwendolyn Brooks (1987)
- "In the Middle of This Century" by Yehuda Amichai (2015)
- "Watts Bleeds" by Luis J. Rodriguez (1991)
- "(Riot Police)" by Sun Yung Shin (2012)

Go to lynhawks.com/extramacbeth for two sample creative writing in-process assessments. Consider assigning Handout 23. Creative Writing: I Am Literally and Figuratively . . . Extend That Metaphor or Handout 15. Creative Writing: Soundscapes.

Persuasive Writing

Preassessment

Why persuasive writing? Not only do students need this skill for everything from college essays to various careers, but they also need it for self-advocacy in myriad life challenges. The Macbeths are also trapped by their own powers of persuasion as well as those of the Witches, while Malcolm and Macduff argue with one another. Even the drunk Porter takes time to make an argument! The art of argumentation is both theme and medium throughout the play.

You can integrate formative practice in the art of persuasion by integrating macro and micro skills such as the ones suggested below from the CCSS. As mentioned in Chapter 1, you will be choosing your OT standard, but if we were to begin with ninth- and tenth-grade standards, you might make any of the following skills your persuasion macro skill:

- CCSS.ELA-LITERACY.W.9-10.1: Write arguments to support claims in an analysis of substantive topics or texts, using valid reasoning and relevant and sufficient evidence.
- CCSS.ELA-LITERACY.W.9-10.1.A: Introduce precise claim(s), distinguish the claim(s) from alternate or opposing claims, and create an organization that establishes clear relationships among claim(s), counterclaims, reasons, and evidence.
- CCSS.ELA-LITERACY.W.9-10.1.B: Develop claim(s) and counterclaims fairly, supplying evidence for each while pointing out the strengths and limitations of both in a manner that anticipates the audience's knowledge level and concerns.
- CCSS.ELA-LITERACY.W.9-10.1.C: Use words, phrases, and clauses to link the major sections of the text, create cohesion, and clarify the relationships between claim(s) and reasons, between reasons and evidence, and between claim(s) and counterclaims.
- CCSS.ELA-LITERACY.W.9-10.1.D: Establish and maintain a formal style and objective tone while attending to the norms and conventions of the discipline in which they are writing.
- CCSS.ELA-LITERACY.W.9-10.1.E: Provide a concluding statement or section that follows from and supports the argument presented.

Handout 9. Preassessment: Write a Persuasive Message on page 66 uses CCSS standards while also inviting students to find an interest (or propose a topic of greater interest) as they demonstrate the skill. I chose the Big Ideas of Temptation and Individuality to drive these writing assessments, whereas you may wish to redesign prompts to get at other Big Ideas that are relevant and exciting to your students.

You might want to expand or condense the standards for this assessment, or privately label what's on the following rubric as NOV, OT, and ADV skills. I suggest giving students a class period for this task and perhaps having them brainstorm the night before. You might also ask students to get in pairs or triads to brainstorm particular topics the class period before and then go home to think further before writing the next day on their own.

Handout 9. Preassessment: Write a Persuasive Message

Directions

Write a persuasive message in which you convince a friend, relative, or other person who is important to you (real or imaginary) that what they are about to do is wrong. This could be in the form of a physical letter or card, a very long email or text message, or any other format you would use to communicate—such as a speech you would practice and then deliver in person.

Please use the time given to complete this task.

Tips

- Think of a situation in which someone is tempted to do the wrong thing that might forever change their life. You can use any topic or situation that matters to you. You can invent a story or use a real-life experience as inspiration.
- Try to empathize with your audience. Try to understand their perspective, needs, and challenges. Write to this person and their situation specifically.
- Use your moral, spiritual, or personal codes to convince this person not to do what they want to do. Give specific reasons not to do the thing that tempts them. Be prepared to answer their counterclaims about why they think they should do this thing.

Rubric

- The message gives one or more meaningful reasons to appeal to the audience.
- The writer offers substantive examples to defend these reasons. These might be examples of potential issues, obstacles, consequences, or concerns.
- The writer uses logic and effective rhetorical strategies and avoids argument fallacies.
- The writer explains the reasoning with elaboration, explanation, and commentary.
- The writer responds preemptively to potential counterclaims.

Assessment

- If this is your first time teaching persuasive writing and/or your students are fairly new to it, you might identify one skill as OT and most essential for your *Macbeth* unit. Let's say that for this unit you really want to tackle reasoning or maybe evidence. Make a choice that you can thoughtfully, carefully track for all your students' skill development. Call that your baseline skill and identify the micro skills.
- Or if you and your students have prior experience, you can identify three macro skills and tier those as ELL-NOV, OT, and ADV.

Use some or all of the following rubric to quickly read and mark each piece, and then place each student writing in one of three piles: NOV, OT, or ADV. Adjust any aspect of the rubric depending on the expectations of your school, students, and/or grade levels.

Criteria	**NOV**	**OT**	**ADV**
Reasoning	The writing isn't yet clear or convincing to a particular audience. There may be some initial attempts at reasoning or insightful thinking that could be expanded. Argument fallacies may appear.	With some audience awareness, the writing offers at least one substantive reason and makes a case with some insight. There may be thinking outside the box to get audience attention. Argument fallacies may appear.	Keeping audience in mind throughout, the writing offers two or more convincing, clear reasons and creatively attacks the challenges unique to the writing situation. Argument fallacies do not appear.
Evidence	With one or a partial example, the evidence is missing or not yet fully convincing. There may be one interesting example that impresses.	With one or more examples, the evidence is interesting and working toward a solid case. Evidence may include raising potential issues, obstacles, consequences, or concerns.	With two or more examples, the evidence is powerful, compelling, and hard to refute. Evidence may include raising potential issues, obstacles, consequences, or concerns.
Elaboration	There is some or minimal elaboration to clarify the examples or convince the audience. There may be a moment of strong insight or social-emotional awareness. Audience awareness may be minimal.	Elaboration is present and sometimes provides thoughtful or clarifying means of convincing the audience on one or more examples. Audience awareness could be expanded.	Elaboration on each example is insightful, clarifying, and/or drives the argument home to the specific audience, communicating a concern for that audience.

Note that this element of language use is separated.

Criteria	ELL	NOV	OT	ADV
Use of language	Language shows a strong need for vocabulary expansion and grammar and syntax support. Voice, humor, and/or other unique stylistic choices may be present.	Language and syntax are simple and unvaried but clear enough. Voice, humor, and/or other unique stylistic choices may be present.	Language and syntax show some variety and complexity as well as clarity. Voice is present, and the author can use some humor and/or other unique stylistic choices.	Language and syntax are complex and varied. Expression is clear. Strong voice, humor, and/or other unique stylistic choices drive the writing.

Persuasive Writing In-Process Assessments

Entrance and Exit Tickets. Entrance and exit tickets are an efficient, meaningful way to do MR and TR formative activities, especially with literary analysis. You can grab a snapshot of student understanding without having to assess an entire essay, and you can quickly gain knowledge of where students are at with arguments, claims, reasoning, and evidence.

Give students limited time at the beginning or end of class, such as ten to fifteen minutes to outline an argument for you based on the day's activities. The first time, try MR pairs or triads, especially if you have several ELL and NOV students in class. After cinematic viewing, performance, or other activities, you might ask students to make a case for character behavior or choice. Examples might include:

- Should Macbeth listen to the Witches? Write him a message with two reasons for or against and two specific examples to prove.
- Should Macbeth listen to Lady Macbeth? Write him a message with two reasons for or against and two specific examples to prove.

In this MR group task, students will take on one of the three arguments below in pairs or triads and prove it using the text. Students must work under time pressure using both the text and any rhetorical tips for argumentation you like to teach. The product could be a persuasive paragraph, or it could be a visual argument with full sentence claims and bulleted examples. Students might use an infographic tool such as Venngage or an interactive image tool such as ThingLink. Time pressure can vary depending on your goals; sometimes, let an exit ticket be twenty to thirty minutes. Making this a competition across groups can be fun, with prizes for winners in Best Reasoning or Best Evidence.

- The Witches are delusion, all in Macbeth's head.
- The Witches are real women.
- The Witches are supernatural, more powerful than mortals.

For later weeks, move to TR group entrance and exit tickets, and then finally to independent ones that a student might answer on their own:

- Should Macbeth keep fighting?
- Would you keep fighting?
- Is Macbeth a hero or a fool, or something else? Persuade us of an apt term for him.

Creative and Persuasive Writing. Consider creative writing activities where students use both "fair" and "foul" persuasive techniques to advertise, market, and sell products or services, including argument fallacies. Here are some sample prompts, which can be in-class timed writings and homework assignments. Whether it's a traditional writing exercise or a visual exercise using digital tools such as ThingLink, Venngage, and Canva (interactive images, infographics, or posters/social media posts), succinct writing is the order of the day. Give these products and performances class time and gallery space for students to leave comments and give positive and constructive feedback.

- **Persuasive Brand.** You are a social media influencer sharing a favorite product that fits your brand. Develop a social media ad campaign with three posts using our "fair" persuasive techniques, a campaign that is designed to get the most clicks.
- **A Fair Brand.** Develop a product that will help our world somehow and with a brand that encourages one of these virtues from the play: Compassion, Courage, Heroism, Imagination, etc., using our "fair" persuasive techniques.
- **A Foul Proposition.** You are from Murd'ring Ministers, Inc., the agents of Evil that Lady Macbeth knows. Use quotes from the play to create a persuasive social media post with argument fallacies to get someone to engage in Betrayal or something Tyrannical. Use the persuasively "foul" techniques for your propaganda.
- **Tiny Superpower.** What is your tiniest superpower? What do you do well or know a lot about? In our Career Fair, you will pitch yourself persuasively for one minute by noting a unique skill. It might be making thank-you cards; it might be singing in the shower; it might be baking bread; it might be saying hello to strangers in the halls. But it must be (a) a tiny, random, natural act you do, and (b) not something you would put on a résumé.

Perform this live, record a short video, or use an avatar tool such as Voki.

- Imagine a world where Macbeth is running for a second term as president, aka king, on the merits of his past actions. Create a political ad campaign using persuasive techniques and the text of the play to sell his merits as a leader to the people.

For variety and fun, you can make this last activity MR or TR, with the most complex ad campaign being Macbeth trying to sell himself to the people in acts 4 and 5. Example: "You are the publicist for Macbeth and things aren't going quite so well for him in Acts 4 and 5. He needs a new image." Or, "The people need convincing that tyranny is a good thing."

After these activities, provide live or asynchronous peer review opportunities so that students can comment on the effective use of persuasive techniques, the use of powerful language in making claims, and the use of powerful evidence in proving such claims.

With the "foul" persuasive techniques, remind students early and often how we are all susceptible to such thinking and techniques. Note to students that it's wise to develop skills in identifying foul persuasive techniques so we don't fall prey to them. You can help them build skills for vetting propaganda, for example, by inviting students to seek argument fallacies in various statements, whether in current media or within character statements.

Persuasive Writing Postassessment

See Chapter 11 for a timed writing sample.

Expository Writing

Key skill sets of expository writing include identifying a main idea, stating it clearly, and proving it succinctly. Across the Differentiated Approach series, I recommend the expository writing assignment of the Satisfying Sandwich paragraph, a summary paragraph containing all these elements: a topic sentence, evidence, context, and commentary. See *Teaching* Julius Caesar: *A Differentiated Approach* for lessons and approaches, and see the website for Handout 47. The Satisfying Sandwich Paragraph, a template for writing a standard paragraph. Short writing with a high degree of rigor allows you to do deep-dive assessment followed by mini-lessons and skill practice as needed. You can assign this task multiple times for nonfiction writing, literary analysis, descriptive writing, and more, discussing with students how to modify the various elements for purpose and audience.

I suggest beginning with a topic of interest, such as the classic show-and-tell speech, what I call *narrative-persuasive writing*. This mode of discourse is essential to a successful college essay or job application cover letter. In my work with students on college essays, I help students brainstorm unique elements of their identity that distinguish them from the crowd as "uncommon" (Sawyer) and persuade a school that they are a good fit for the institution. One effective strategy is to have students look at their personal possessions, contents of a purse or bag or backpack, a desk or shelf or room, and/or social media posts to determine objects of importance (Sawyer). From that activity come several fascinating ideas and topics for Common App essay prompts, where we find ways for them to express their passions, interests, values, and, as one 2023 prompt says, those interests that "make you lose track of all time."

You can find models of successful college essays at Ethan Sawyer's College Essay Guy website or in his book *College Essay Essentials* that were sparked by identifying an object of importance. Also see Further Resources for a link to Tadeo Messenger's wonderful essay on his truck Big Betsy, printed in the 2020 *New York Times*, as well as other students' unique and creative nonfiction that gained them entrance to competitive schools. Consider providing students with a few models of these before doing the preassessment so that students understand the value and real-world relevance of this task. See my college essay consultant website for blog posts, a Great Essay Rubric, and models of student writing (www.success-story.lynhawks.com).

This task can also be a speech activity for any grade level in which students bring in a representative object and share how it is meaningful to them, after having prepared this writing. I've had students demonstrate freestyle bicycle tricks, share their favorite cookie recipe, and sing and strum guitar. I find students are never too old for show-and-tell, especially when I kick it off with things like sharing my Crazy Cat Lady action figure or my talismans from my writer's shrine. Show them your unique weirdnesses and they tend to be less reluctant to share theirs.

In Handouts 16–18 listed below, I offer three levels of challenge: ELL and NOV, OT, and ADV, available at lynhawks.com/extramacbeth. You can use these as preassessments and/or as formative assessments. Having three assessments gives you different degrees and expectations to support for each readiness level in your class.

- If you have a large range of readiness levels, use all three and adapt the prompts to different topics as you deliver them as formative, in-process assessments during the unit. In this way, you can see students grow in their respective readiness spheres.

- Whereas ELL-NOV students (Word Nerds) are given a highly structured format to follow, almost a recipe for how text should flow within the "satisfying sandwich" paragraph, OT and ADV students (Word Sleuths and Wordsmiths, respectively) are challenged to find their own structure.
- ADV students are given a prompt to hook readers at hello while also really exploring their unique writing voice and style.
- To be clear: you may be teaching ELL-NOV students with a greater understanding of writing voice and personality than their ADV peers, but the skill gap ELL-NOV students might have regarding structure and evidence must be addressed first without the distraction of exploring voice and hooks. Voice and hooks can be the focus of a creative writing assignment that same week and celebrated then.
- Meanwhile, ADV students with a more rigid understanding of topic sentences and examples need to be challenged to loosen up, hook their readers, and find personality in their details.

Find the following handouts at lynhawks.com/extramacbeth:

- Handout 16. My Object of Importance, Word Nerds
- Handout 17. My Object of Importance, Word Sleuths
- Handout 18. My Object of Importance, Wordsmiths
- Handout 19. Expository Writing Rubric.

Assessment

If this is your first time teaching expository writing and/or your students are fairly new to it, you might identify one skill as OT and most essential for your *Macbeth* unit. Let's say for this unit, you really want to tackle substantive examples that are highly specific. Or maybe you want to help students understand how elaborative commentary around an example circles back to the topic sentence or thesis. Again, as noted earlier, make a macro skill choice that you can thoughtfully and carefully track for all of your students' skill development, and then find the micro skills within.

The rubric on page 67 is my catch-all rubric for all types of literary analysis writing: the character analysis (dissection); the plot analysis (cause and effect); the tone or style analysis (dissection); and any comparison/contrast essay, etc. You can add or remove specific micro skill sets to this template.

Consider introducing this rubric to students when you are ready to home in on one particular skill. Consider breaking this rubric into scaffolded versions, increasing in amount of skills each time it reappears. Adjust the rubric based on expectations for your school, students, and/or grade levels.

If you use some or all of this rubric for preasssessment, quickly read and mark each piece and place student writing in one of three piles: NOV, OT, or ADV.

In-Process Expository Satisfying Sandwich Prompts

These prompts work well for short, timed writing assessments throughout a unit:

- What is an object of importance in this play so far? Why?
- Which character is the "one to watch"? Why?
- Who is the most admirable or least admirable character thus far? Why?
- How does this character compare to that character in terms of ___ [insert Big Idea]?
- What event in the play has so far "changed everything"? Why?
- What is a key element of setting in this play so far—an element of world building that you think will come back later to "haunt" someone? Why?

Expository Writing Postassessment

See Chapter 11 for a range of options.

Evidence Identification and Claim Creation

Preassessment for Evidence Identification

The following preassessment asks students to find evidence and details in two types of writing: fiction and nonfiction. If you feel students aren't ready for this type of assessment, you might revise it to be a mini-lesson on finding evidence. Evidence finding is a key emphasis because of the legal, forensic, and persuasive roles students can play during this unit.

Handout 20. Preassessment: Finding Evidence in Literature

Directions:

1. Read the passage and number each piece of evidence that answers the questions.
2. Then extract two pieces of evidence that you think support the most interesting or important element of each passage.

Passage #1: Banquo describes the Witches.

Story Action: General Banquo is walking on the battlefield with fellow general Macbeth after a battle is over. They run across three women (the Witches) and Banquo tries to figure out who they are.

1. What evidence do you see of Banquo's description of the Witches? Circle and number each piece of evidence you see.
2. What evidence tells you something about Banquo's beliefs about the Witches?
   - Quote a piece of evidence, using quotation marks.
   - Then elaborate in at least one full sentence using one adjective that captures his description.

Passage

What are these,*	**these women*	
So wither'd* and so wild in their attire,*	*wrinkled, old	*clothing
That look not like th'inhabitants* o'th'earth,*	*the residents *of the earth	
And yet are on't*?—Live you, or are you aught*	*on it	*nothing
That man may question? You seem to understand me,		
By each at once her choppy* finger laying	*chapped	
Upon her skinny lips; you should be women,		
And yet your beards forbid* me to interpret	*prevent	
That you are so.		

Answer to Question #2:

Answer Key for Handout 20. Preassessment: Finding Evidence in Literature

1. What evidence do you see of Banquo's description of the Witches? Number each piece of evidence you see.
    a. "Withered"
    b. "Wild"
    c. Do not look like "inhabitants of the earth"
    d. "aught / That man may question"
    e. "Choppy finger"
    f. "Skinny lips"
    g. "You should be women / And yet your beards forbid me to interpret / That you are so"

    ADV students should get most of these; OT, at least half; ELL-NOV one or a few.
2. What evidence tells you something about Banquo's beliefs about the Witches? Quote a piece of evidence, using quotation marks, and then elaborate in at least one full sentence using one adjective that captures his description.
    a. ELL-NOV-OT: *The Witches are old because . . .*
    b. ELL-NOV-OT: *The Witches are ugly because . . .*
    c. OT-ADV: *The Witches are otherworldly/supernatural/strange because . . .*
    d. OT-ADV: *The Witches are nonbinary because . . .*
    e. OT-ADV: another unique, provable insight or a combination of any two or more insights

Observe:

- Do students know how to quote?
- Paraphrase?
- Cite?
- Advanced skill includes paraphrasing, citing per MLA or APA style, and summing up the details in a multitopic topic sentence.

Make a list of skill strengths and skill gaps you see, ones you will address through either TR mini-lessons or activities.

Preassessing for Evidence Identification and Claim Creation

The following preassessment asks students to differentiate between evidence (details) and summary (topic sentences/thesis statements). See these Common Core State Standards for more details of what's being assessed:

- **NOV Standard,** 7th: CCSS.ELA-LITERACY.RL.7.1. *Cite several pieces of textual evidence to support analysis of what the text says explicitly as well as inferences drawn from the text.*
- **OT Standard:** CCSS.ELA-LITERACY.RL.9-10.1. *Cite strong and thorough textual evidence to support analysis of what the text says explicitly as well as inferences drawn from the text.*
- **ADV Standard,** 12th: CCSS.ELA-LITERACY.RL.11-12.1. *Cite strong and thorough textual evidence to support analysis of what the text says explicitly as well as inferences drawn from the text, including determining where the text leaves matters uncertain.*

Following are some notes about this assessment, Handout 21. Preassessment: Evidence and Claims:

- Task 1 asks students to distinguish between evidence and claim (brief matching using Big Idea topic sentences). Task 2 asks students to do an explicit, denotative interpretation of text. Task 3 asks students to draw an inference from the text.
- Task 1 should be accessible to a range of student readiness levels. The task also models evidence and claims, which may help some students complete the subsequent tasks.
- Task 2 tests vocabulary knowledge, analysis of denotation, and analysis of connotation and meaning. This section tests for a range on Bloom's Taxonomy: Remember, Understand, Apply, and Analyze.
- Note how this preassessment not only provides skill practice but also introduces students to names, text, and Big Ideas from the play.

You can find digital copies of these handouts at lynhawks.com/extra macbeth.

Handout 21. Preassessment: Evidence and Claims

Can you tell the difference between evidence and claims? Can you infer claims from evidence? This preassessment will help me prepare lessons to meet you where you are with these skills.

Directions for Task 1: Distinguishing Evidence and Claims.

- Label the sentence pairs below as either evidence or claims.
  - *Evidence:* specific details that could be used as proof for summary, argument, or reasoning: examples, statistics, anecdotes, sensory details, etc.
  - *Claims:* ideas, reasoning, interpretation, summary, argument evaluation that needs proof: a general statement

SENTENCES	EVIDENCE OR CLAIM?
PAIR A: ■ Hecate is manipulative.	
PAIR A: ■ Hecate criticized Bellona's work in front of the teacher, hoping that the teacher would notice Bellona's errors instead of hers.	
SENTENCES	**EVIDENCE OR CLAIM?**
PAIR B: ■ Bellona started the rumor that Hecate was dating Tarquin, citing Hecate's texts and Hecate's conversations.	
PAIR B: ■ Bellona loves to start trouble; she's always getting into other people's business.	
PAIR C: ■ If Neptune is your friend, you could steal all his stuff and he would still support you.	
PAIR C: ■ Neptune is too loyal.	

Directions for Task 2: Explicit Interpretations of Text. Tell Us What's Happening.

Answer the questions about this passage below:

- Context: A bloody, wounded soldier walks up after a battle to Prince Malcolm and his father, King Duncan, who is king of Scotland. King Duncan is at war with those rebelling against him. King Duncan and Prince Malcolm speak.
- Definitions for Shakespeare's diction are starred.

continued on next page

TEXT	DEFINITIONS
Duncan: What bloody man is that? He can report, As seemeth* by his plight,* of the revolt* The newest* state. **Malcolm:** This is the sergeant Who like a good and hardy* soldier fought 'Gainst my captivity. Hail, brave friend; Say to the king the knowledge of the broil* As thou* didst* leave it.	 *seemeth: seems *plight: a dangerous situation *revolt: rebellion *newest: latest *hardy: strong, tough *conflict *thou: you *didst: did

1. Why does King Duncan think the soldier can report on the battle? Write your own sentence (paraphrase what Duncan thinks) while also using the text in your answer. Put quotation marks around whatever part you quote.

2. What does Malcolm think of the soldier? How do you know?

Directions for Task 3: Inferences:
Tell Us What You Might Assume.

Answer the questions below and use evidence from the text to make a claim:

- What is Shakespeare saying about the current state of Scotland? Write a full sentence that draws an inference (your argument and reasoning).
- What evidence do you have for this argument? Give as many examples as you can. You can use bullets and quotations.

CLAIM	EVIDENCE

Answer Key and Rubric for Handout 21. Preassessment: Evidence and Claim

SENTENCES	EVIDENCE OR CLAIM?
PAIR A: ■ Hecate is manipulative.	CLAIM
PAIR A: ■ Hecate criticized Bellona's work in front of the teacher, hoping that the teacher would notice Bellona's errors instead of hers.	EVIDENCE
PAIR B: ■ Bellona started the rumor that Hecate was dating Tarquin, citing Hecate's texts and Hecate's conversations.	EVIDENCE
PAIR B: ■ Bellona loves to start trouble; she's always getting into other people's business.	CLAIM
PAIR C: ■ If Neptune is your friend, you could steal all his stuff and he would still support you.	EVIDENCE
PAIR C: ■ Neptune is too loyal.	CLAIM

Assessment Approaches for Task 2.

1. Why does King Duncan think the soldier can report on the battle? Write your own sentence (paraphrase what Duncan thinks) while also using the text in your answer, and put quotation marks around whatever part you quote.
   a. This OT-ADV task asks students to paraphrase and to quote. Below are some examples of how students might perform:
      i. NOV paraphrase and quote: Is incomplete, misunderstands the context, may misunderstand the question, and/or may struggle to use own words in paraphrasing. May or may not quote directly, or may copy all of Shakespeare's words. Example: *Duncan thinks the soldier is bloody.*
      ii. OT paraphrase and quote: Is complete or partially complete, has a general sense of the context, and can paraphrase using their own words. Quotes at least a word. Example: *Duncan thinks the soldier should talk about the battle because he was in the battle and is a "bloody man."*
      iii. ADV paraphrase and quote: Is complete, acknowledges the context, accurately paraphrases in their own words, and goes beyond with inference. Example: *Duncan thinks the soldier can report because his bleeding wounds ("what bloody man") and his "plight" show he has firsthand knowledge of the battle ("revolt"), which could be key since it's a rebellion.*

2. What does Malcolm think of the soldier? How do you know?
   a. This NOV-OT task also asks students to paraphrase and to quote. Use the same rubric standards above. Many students should be able to articulate with at least one-word quotes that Malcolm is impressed by or likes the soldier, since he uses many positive adjectives.
   b. ADV paraphrase and quote: Is complete, acknowledges the context, and accurately paraphrases in own words. Example: *Malcolm is impressed with the soldier, calling him "good," "hardy," and "brave." He also calls him "friend." Malcolm values this sergeant because he "fought / 'Gainst my captivity," so we can assume Malcolm was captured by the enemy and the soldier freed him.*

Part 3. Here are some sample responses to show the range of analytical depth students may demonstrate in answer to this question that asks for a claim and evidence. Ask yourself how much student responses can move along the spectrum of KNOW → UNDERSTAND → APPLY → ANALYZE → EVALUATE in this task.

- What is Shakespeare saying about the state of Scotland? Write a full sentence that draws an inference (your argument and reasoning).
- What evidence do you have for this argument? Give as many examples as you can. You can use bullets and quotations.

Readiness Level	CLAIM	EVIDENCE
NOV	There are battles and blood. (Student shows comprehension of some events and quotes a few words or phrases.)	■ "Revolt" ■ "Blood" ■ Words or phrases
OT	Scotland has battles and bloodshed and rebellion. Scotland has a lot of problems. The king has a difficult situation to handle. Malcolm is pleased a soldier helped him. (Student shows comprehension of events and character relationships to them and quotes a few words or phrases.)	■ "Revolt" ■ "Blood" ■ "Plight" ■ Words, phrases, or lines
ADV	By showing us a battle, rebellion, and a bloody soldier, Shakespeare shows us a country in chaos. Things are changing so fast that wounded soldiers have to give reports instead of getting the medical help they need. Duncan is waiting for good news, while Malcolm has just been rescued from captivity. (Student shows comprehension of events and character relationships to them, and can draw evaluative conclusions. Student quotes a few words, phrases, or lines and may interpret them in more detail.)	■ "Revolt" ■ "Blood" ■ "Report" ■ "Plight" ■ "Captivity" ■ "Broil" ■ "Newest state" ■ Words, phrases, or lines

In-Process Assessment for Claims and Evidence

Entrance and exit tickets on Essential Questions, characters, and other elements of the play can be efficient samples of growth in student understanding around evidence and claims. Here are some sample questions you can ask students to complete at the beginning or close of a lesson. Students can use any information gleaned from reading or that day's lesson.

Here's a sample of an exit ticket on Big Ideas:

- One Big Idea evident in this scene is ______________.
- I know this because __________________ [claim].
- One piece of evidence to prove this is ______________ [example].
- Citation: [Did you find this on your own in the text, think this on your own, find another source, or hear a classmate or teacher state it?]

Summative Assessment for Claims and Evidence

See the final essay topics in Chapter 11.

Preassessing for Core Content Knowledge: Shakespeare and *Macbeth*

Knowledge of basic dates, biographical information, historical information, and other elements of Shakespeare and *Macbeth* knowledge: this sort of content mastery should be preassessed for students who might qualify for compacting. Highly gifted youth with extensive experience reading Shakespeare prior to your class may enter this unit eager to show that knowledge. Ask such students to complete Handout 22. Preassessment for Shakespeare Knowledge. If you discover students with extensive prior knowledge of Shakespeare and *Macbeth,* meet with them further to explore the potential for compacting. See lynhawks.com/extramacbeth for Project materials and review the section on compacting.

Go to lynhawks.com/extramacbeth for Handout 22. Preassessment for Shakespeare Knowledge.

DYO: Tips for Designing Preassessments

- Choose your macro and micro skills according to student needs. Be very specific in determining what the growth will look like.

- Write the preassessment and postassessment at the same time.
- Preassess core skills and don't worry about others. You can't pretest it all.
- Make the preassessment part of the student portfolio and part of the student's reflection at the end of the unit.
- Name your tiers of handouts and assessments with fun names ("Nerd" and "Sleuth"). Though I have used numbers and letters to cue tiers (where "1" or "A" is NOV–ELL), I also try to mix it up since letters and numbers imply hierarchy and seek instead titles that imply scholarship and intellect.
- Ensure your directions are clear; that your presentation is welcoming and invitational, letting students know your interest in their growth and success; and that the assessment is low stakes.
- Refine your rubrics as you learn about student strengths and skill gaps.

Integrate interests, Big Ideas, and text allusions in your preassessments. The more exposure students get, the better. Just as the best way to learn a foreign language is through immersion in the culture or community, so immersion in Shakespeare's text is the best way to understand his language.

Managing the Paper Trail

Here are some tips for making sure students write early and often and that you are not spending hours and hours with their work.

- Choose only one element of a rubric to grade and pay attention to the micro skills therein. What are students understanding and misunderstanding about this one skill? How can you better coach this skill for each readiness level?
- Keep writing assignments under a certain word count. Approximately 500–650 words is fine for large essays in the first half of a semester; then graduate students to longer forms when they have shown mastery of the key elements of evidence, reasoning, and structure. When their work is stronger and easier to read, make it longer.
- Ask students to write in class for timed periods. Return their drafts to them to revise after a few days away, when they can look again with fresh eyes after your mini-lessons.
- Use highlighters on rubrics. If a student is doing well at something, color it pink or purple. If a student still needs to work on something, highlight it yellow or orange.
- Limit your feedback to:

- one compliment (highly specific);
- one criticism (highly constructive, a specific step for skill development); and
- one question regarding Big Ideas and themes. Challenge critical thinking.

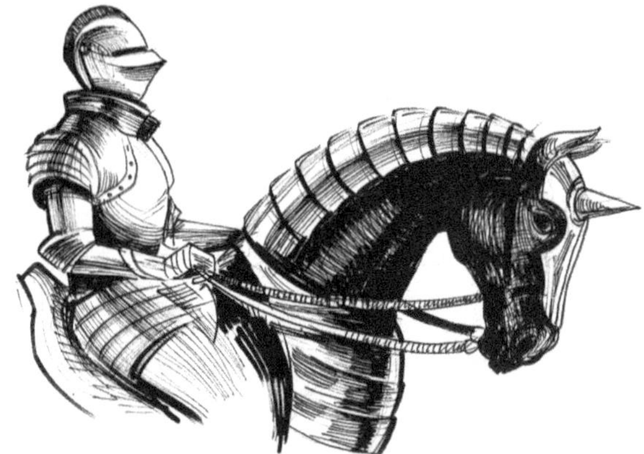

5 Hook Activities

What You Will Find in This Chapter

- A rationale for hook activities
- Hook activities to engage students
- Tips for designing your own
- Ideas for hook lessons you could develop

The Why and How of Hooks

On day one of the *Macbeth* unit, all students can dive right into high-level investigations of Big Ideas and the pursuit of meaningful interests. We can hook 'em at hello with WCAs that are MR activities. These engage student interest by giving them real-world roles, by providing real-world context and skill practice, by raising relevant ideas and themes, and by providing previews and culminations for a unit.

Hooks also create the buy-in you need to spark student interest for CRs and other in-depth analysis of text. By creating a personal connection to issues raised by *Macbeth*, you help students see why this text matters.

Hooks can be ten minutes or a few days of class time. They are part of a differentiated lesson design philosophy that honors a balance of WCA, TR, and MR activities across a unit.

To me, hooks are part theater. So in a few instances, I provide a script, because first impressions for a lesson mean everything.

WCA: Whole-class activities bring the community together to explore universal skills, themes, and concepts.

TR: Tiered-readiness activities let individuals progress in their proximal zone of development.

MR: Mixed-readiness activities let individuals bring their intelligences, interests, and skill strengths to collaborative and cooperative challenges.

These hook activities can be used in conjunction with any lessons in Chapter 6, "Key Scenes to Teach." For the most buy-in, select hooks that match students' interests. See Chapter 4 for the Bardometer student interest survey (Handout 14).

DYO Hook

When designing a hook activity, consider the elements listed below, where I model a full list of these features and then offer notes and essentials for other hook activities.

A great hook is not only fun but also offers rigorous skill and content objectives.

Hook or Wow Factor	What would inspire your students to want to learn more about the skills, concepts, and text?
EQs & Big Ideas	*Essential Questions and Big Ideas.* How will Essential Questions and Big Ideas drive this activity? What are we exploring or investigating together?
SO & CO	*Skill objectives.* What skills should all students be developing? *Content objectives.* What knowledge and information should students master?
I & I	*Interests and intelligences.* What talents, passions, hobbies, and abilities will this activity need and/or develop?
D-C-C	*Discussion-Collaboration-Cooperation.* What activities will get students interacting, using play-related and relevance questions, in order to deepen their exploration and critical thinking?
TA & Handouts	*Text analysis activity, CR, or handouts.* What text and/or information will be needed for close analysis?
Steps	What are the steps of this activity?
HW	*Homework.* What engaging homework will extend the fun of the hook?
ND	*Notes on differentiation.* Which activities should be WCA, TR, or MR? What are the collaboration and cooperation opportunities?

Hook #1: Tell Me Where You Stand

Activity Summary: Students identify their assumptions and beliefs about Big Ideas in *Macbeth* while choosing their guiding question for writing tasks and projects. Students determine where they stand, literally and figuratively, at the beginning of the play, before developing their own interpretations from the text.

Hook or Wow Factor: Students explore and defend their own beliefs about ideas and questions relevant to their lives. You can edit, add, or delete these statements as needed for your community.

EQ & Big Ideas: What do I believe about these Big Ideas?

SO & CO:

- Generalization and summary, claim creation, evidence finding, elaboration, clarifying questions
- The definition and methods of clarifying questions

I & I: Kinesthetic, visual, and interpersonal; debate and discussion

D-C-C: Whole-class discussion, or you can also kick off with pair or small-group discussion before moving to a WCA.

TA & Handouts: Handout 2. Pre- and Post-Play Poll: Where Do You Stand? (page 91) and Handout 3. Let's Clarify: Asking Good Questions (lynhawks .com/extramacbeth/)

Steps:

- Introduction: Preview the most controversial and debatable premises. "In a minute, I'm going to read aloud some debatable and controversial generalizations. I want you to not answer aloud but pay attention to your immediate gut reaction: YES, I AGREE; or NO, I DON'T AGREE; or I DON'T KNOW. What comes to your mind when I say:
    - *Women are more compassionate than men.* Ask yourself, but don't say aloud: Yes, I agree. No, I don't agree. I don't know.
    - *Sometimes you must assassinate a leader to get a better government.* Yes? No? I don't know?
    - *If you see a ghost or hear from a spirit, you'd better listen.* Yes? No? I don't know?
    - Today we will discuss Big Ideas and generalizations like these, ones that relate to the story of *Macbeth.* We will get closer to figuring out what each of us believes or where we have even more questions and need to think further."
- D-C-C or independent work: Give students ten to fifteen minutes to independently complete Handout 2. Pre-Play Poll. For highly active and verbal groups, having pairs or triads debate first is a great option.
- WCA Discussion. Before class starts, select three statements you think students should discuss. You can also have students vote on a few from a smaller list. If you want to reinforce the skill of asking clarifying questions, also distribute Handout 3. Let's Clarify: Asking Good Questions (lynhawks.com/extramacbeth). For more question-building techniques, see the DYO Questions section in Chapter 3.

- Review the rules for listening well and participating respectfully, as well as what constitutes "evidence": any fact from a student's experience or any fact supported by reputable sources.
- If in the classroom, ask volunteers to take their places in a line at the front of the room (or to turn on mics and hold up signs in an online classroom) to indicate their beliefs on the first statement: Agree, Disagree, or Undecided. Tell students these are temporary and not permanent commitments to these beliefs. They can move or create a new sign at any time.
- Ask a student at each position to explain their choice using concrete examples.
- Ask those undecided to pose questions to students who agree or disagree.
- After a few minutes of discussion, invite the rest of the class to help with examples, clarifications, and questions, or invite new students to join the line.
- Ask students to define and clarify ideas, look for similarities and differences, and restate, generalize, and summarize. Your questions might be:
    - *How do you define "a better government"?*
    - *What does "more compassionate" mean to you?*
    - *Brixton, how does your view of "luck" differ from Nadia's for "fate"?*
    - *When you said, "Trust is for losers," how do you define "loser"?*
    - *How might we rewrite the statement to something more neutral?*
- Ask students to use Handout 3. Let's Clarify: Asking Good Questions.
- After discussion, ask if anyone wants to change positions or signs.
- If time, introduce another statement and bring new students up (or on mic).
- Exit ticket option: students can revise generalizations to better express neutrality or a more committed opinion. Post these in a place for all to see, such as on a classroom poster or an online bulletin board such as Padlet.

■ Return to the poll at the end of the unit and see where students stand now. You can also assign an independent reflection followed by a WCA discussion.

- Consider making this a prompt for a final timed summative writing in which students choose a generalization and defend it or make counterclaims.

This lesson can be used as skill practice for identifying claims, reasoning, and evidence for any argument. In literary analysis essays, students must analyze and elaborate on a quote or paraphrased example, providing context and commentary. Model and coach this skill with this activity:

In that quote you gave, what is a key word or phrase that supports your argument? How is the example you gave evidence of your point?

Let students know that answers to these questions are what you want to see in their essays.

HW: Tell students:

- Choose a statement we discussed and write a journal entry expressing your thoughts on the subject. Use Handout 2. Pre- and Post-Play Poll: Where Do You Stand?
- Complete an independent reading activity, linking your text to a statement on Handout 2. Pre- and Post-Play Poll: Where Do You Stand?
- Complete Handout 1. Pick Your Favorite Big Ideas.

See Chapter 10, "Independent Reading," for more homework suggestions.

ND:

- This activity encourages deep critical thinking, challenging students to get beyond gut reactions to pay close attention to each word in a statement before declaring they agree. All students can clarify definitions of nouns, adjectives, and verbs.
- Invite your most extroverted, verbal, and kinesthetic students to kick off the continuum of opinions.
- Consider appointing a Proof Detector who asks during discussion, "Could you give an example?" or "Where'd you get that from?" This role is for students who love to play sergeant at arms. Why not marshal the most interruptive, irrepressible students who love chiming in, giving them a chance to remind their peers to bring the evidence?
- When using Handout 3. Let's Clarify: Asking Good Questions, ask ADV students to model how to ask more detailed, intensive questions.

- Do you have a class of highly vocal debaters? This hook can be used across multiple classes. Choose a new statement every few days as a lesson kickoff, using a warm-up journal entry (5 min.) followed by a timed, briefer debate (15 min.). You can then lead another activity related to relevant Big Ideas: e.g., a CR, a viewing activity, etc.
- Edit the Handout 2. Pre- and Post-Play Poll questions as needed, based on student interests and current events. If you see a thematic connection between the news and *Macbeth*, develop a generalization that gets students discussing the related Big Ideas.

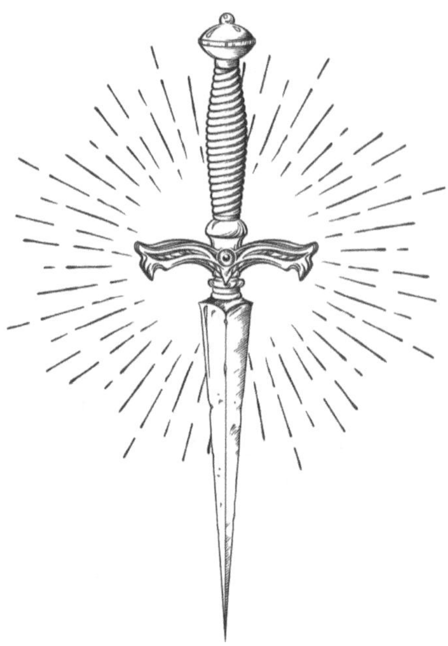

Handout 2. Pre- and Post-Play Poll: Where Do You Stand?

Directions: This poll seeks your opinions. Decide whether you AGREE, DISAGREE, or are UNDECIDED about the following statements, and write A, D, or U next to each statement.

- Before studying *Macbeth*: What do you believe about the statements below, based on your current life experience and learning?
- After studying *Macbeth*: Has our study influenced your beliefs on any of these statements?

1. Sometimes you must assassinate a leader to get a better government.
2. Women are more compassionate than men.
3. If you see a ghost or hear from a spirit, you'd better listen.
4. Power always corrupts.
5. The human imagination is a terrifying thing.
6. Nature seeks order.
7. There are no honest leaders.
8. Ignore your conscience at your peril.
9. Your needs and wants as an individual are more important than those of general society.
10. Sometimes a good leader or politician must lie or dodge the truth.
11. You can't really trust anyone because they might try to take advantage of you.
12. There are forces of good and forces of evil.
13. Violence is acceptable when fighting evil.
14. Despots are always in danger.
15. Listen carefully to those with the gift of prophecy.
16. People are prisoners of their own desires.
17. Always give people the benefit of the doubt.
18. The human imagination is magical.
19. True patriots sacrifice all for their country.
20. Personal ambition always hurts someone.

Hook #2: Shakespeak Trailers: Wordplay and Plot Speculator

Activity Summary: Students learn frequently used Shakespeare words while creating a skit or trailer using *Macbeth* events, speculating on potential plot outcomes.

Hook or Wow Factor: Students love a chance to invent stories with a low-stakes, what-if prompt that allows silly skits and wordplay.

EQ & Big Ideas: What story will we invent using the information we're given?

SO & CO: Cause-and-effect analysis; speculation; character motivation and choices; Big Ideas in *Macbeth*

I & I: Kinesthetic, interpersonal; theater and improvisation; [optional] cinema and filmmaking; group facilitation

D-C-C: Small-group cooperation and WCA performance and discussion

TA: Handout 24. Mini-*Macbeth* and Handout 25. Shakespeak in *Macbeth* (lynhawks.com / extramacbeth)

Steps: Decide prior to this activity whether you will have students perform live or make videos.

- Introduce the storytelling task by letting students know this activity will challenge their creativity as they tell stories from a grab bag of characters, plot events, words, and themes. Tell them Big Ideas will drive their stories. Example: "Can you tell an intriguing story with a brief message in ten minutes? Can you create an interesting character who makes consequential choices? Your Mini-*Macbeth* stories will show your ability to link cause and effect while making an interesting point. Don't research the full story; be creative with what you are given in this grab bag and show us *your* Macbeth."
- Talk about spoilers in Shakespeare's day and how people were comfortable coming to the theater knowing the full story. Explain that Shakespeare also revised some English and Scottish history, taking a lot of license in *Macbeth* with actual events.
- Review the task instructions and rubric using Handout 24. Mini-*Macbeth* (lynhawks.com / extramacbeth). Introduce groups and roles. I recommend assigning MR triads and quads in which students appoint a director and everyone serves as actors.
- When students perform or present their trailers, use the performance rubric as a guide for evaluation, posing rubric elements as questions for other groups to answer. You might ask, Which performance or trailer shows creative risk-taking? Which one made truly unique connections among events? Which one raised interesting questions about a Big Idea?

- After performances or viewings, share the actual plot with students using Handout 26. *Macbeth* Key Events at a Glance (lynhawks.com/extramacbeth). Ask: Did any stories come close? Did anyone follow familiar Western plot structures (e.g., hero's journey, Freytag's plot structure, etc.)?
- Watch the trailers for various film interpretations and ask students which is their favorite and why. See Further Resources at the end of this book for trailer links.

HW: Tell students:

- Write a review of the film trailers and nominate the film you want to see, and why. Explain why you are persuaded to see this film now.
- Write a review evaluating the best student trailer. Analyze cause-and-effect sequences in your independent reading, the result of character choices. How does a character choice change everything in the story? Make this part of your claim and evidence to defend Best Trailer.

ND:

- Expect to see a range of students shine in a variety of interests and intelligences during this MR activity. Note that the rubric doesn't assess excellent acting or filmmaking as much as it assesses storytelling.
- As you circulate to coach, focus on the first elements of the rubric related to character, plot, and Big Ideas as you help students figure out what makes a good story, how cause leads to effect, and how given this detail, what can we assume will happen?

> Trailers teach storytelling skills, a task for many professions. As Will Dunne says in *The Dramatic Writer's Companion*, our job as creators of story is to make readers worry about the outcome of events (269). How do cause and effect get us leaning forward? How does meaning and message (Big Ideas) tug at our heartstrings?

Ideas for Hook Lessons

Whether you're exploring history, manhood, or womanhood, *Macbeth* provides many more ways to engage students. Below are tips for other hooks as you design your own.

Hook #3: Trust Me

See the lesson plan "Reader Idea: Reading 'Macbeth' through the Lens of Ferguson" (Learning Network) and adapt it to your students' needs and interests. This lesson of a few days leads students through several exercises with this driving EQ: "Why do we trust some people over others?"

A shorter lesson you might use with the Big Idea of Trust asks students to first collaboratively populate a Venn diagram called Trust/Trust Not. Ask students, "I want you to list human behaviors that lead to trust or not trusting someone." In the overlapping space, place behaviors that are confusing and "could go either way." What you are seeking for that section are examples of behaviors that are manipulative and "false face" strategies. Then lead a class discussion using the above EQ, followed by an independent journal and reflection assignment. Trust can be a Big Idea for the remainder of the unit and a driving inquiry lens for text annotation.

A follow-up D-C-C activity, journal, or digital tool product can be this task: *Create a meme about trust and share in a project gallery.*

Hook #4: Six Things about 1606

This lesson's EQs ask students to seek the most interesting person or incident from Shakespeare's era. Begin by sharing historical trivia from 1606 and then let students do research to find the most fascinating facts they can while also posing their questions.

Steps:

- Explain to students that Shakespeare lived in chaotic, turbulent times with strife, plague, exploration, innovation, and creativity. They will soon research some fascinating facts and make some connections to our time.
- Share some intriguing facts. Below are lists of historical facts you may wish to incorporate with copyright-free images in a slideshow. See Handout 27. Historical Notes for Shakespeare's Day (lynhawks.com/extramacbeth) for background that will be helpful in asking students more questions as they research. If you create a slideshow, end each slide with a question to spark research curiosity.
    a. On November 5, 1605, a small group of men tried to blow up the English Parliament, the king and his family, the kingdom's chief judges, and more people. Now there's an English national holiday to remember the event: Guy Fawkes Day (Carroll). *What might have motivated such a terror plot? How might government officials and the king's family have felt?*
    b. King James I was fascinated by witches. *Why was he so fascinated by witches?*

c. Elizabethans and people of King James's era were used to bloodshed. Even with constables on the streets of London, it was best to duck if you heard someone holler, "Clubs!" Because that meant a fight, which were frequent. Whether with daggers, or fists, or swords, fights were brutal—as were cockfights, bear baitings, and public executions (Papp and Kirkland). *Why were things so violent then?*

d. Shakespeare wrote sonnets, possibly to a man, while also writing a sonnet about a mistress. But wait, wasn't he married to a woman? *Whom did Shakespeare love? Did anyone in particular inspire his work?*

> Coming as it did so soon after 2001, the [Guy Fawkes] anniversary provided an especially compelling opportunity to think about terrorism. **How do we define it? Who gets to define it? What are the boundaries between terrorism and political opposition, collective violence and individual acts?** . . . There was also an alarming report in circulation at that time that physicists had recently worked out the full extent of the damage to Westminster had the blast gone off. It was illustrated in the press with an ominously large gray circle superimposed on an early map of London.
>
> —Kathleen Lynch, "Remember, Remember, the Fifth of November"

- Let students know their task: build and present slides of Elizabethan and Jamesian trivia to help us better understand the era when Shakespeare made a powerful work of art, *Macbeth,* as well as finding the most fascinating facts they can while also posing more questions to answer. While they are searching and gathering information, they should also pursue these analytical and evaluative EQs:

  e. Who is the most interesting historical figure? Why?

  f. What's the most fascinating fact I can find?

  g. What is a fact that reminds me of our era?

  h. What is a fact that seems very different from our era?

  i. What else do we want to know? What questions might we research further?

- Review resources students can use that describe Elizabethan and Jamesian England, 1564–1616. Work with your media specialist to develop search terms and a list of resources that are most accessible to you and your student population.

- Send students out to research the topics with the EQs above as well as suggested websites and inquiry questions found on Handout 50. Research Activities for Hook 3: 6 Things about 1606 (lynhawks.com/extramacbeth). Check out suggested homework activities available there as well.

> Take a moment to read the ingredients of the Witches' cauldron:
>
> Scale of dragon, tooth of wolf,
> Witches' mummy, maw and gulf
> Of the ravin'd salt-sea shark,
> Root of hemlock digg'd i' the dark,
> Liver of blaspheming Jew,
> Gall of goat, and slips of yew
> Silver'd in the moon's eclipse,
> Nose of Turk and Tartar's lips,
> Finger of birth-strangled babe
> Ditch-deliver'd by a drab,
> Make the gruel thick and slab:
> Add thereto a tiger's chaudron,
> For the ingredients of our cauldron.
> —Third Witch, act 4, scene 1, 22–34
>
> Who is killed to become a soup in this society? Even gruel is based in power and privilege, murder and oppression. What does Shakespeare include that needs context, interrogation, and explanation? What potentially painful references are here needing preparation before sharing with students?

Hook #5: Man Up! It's a Woman's Job!

This activity asks students to question the definitions of *manhood* and *womanhood* while also defining *personhood*. See Chapter 3 for relevance and play-related questions.

Steps:

- Preview the topics of gender identity and expression by telling students that *Macbeth* raises questions in these areas. Let students know this conversation requires respect. Everyone has a right to define and express themselves as they wish. To have a respectful, meaningful discussion, everyone must listen carefully and openly to one another's perspectives. Review the Challenging and Sensitive Subjects section in the introduction before beginning this lesson, and review the Learning for Justice resources on gender and sexual identity (see Further Resources).

- Preview some ways that Big Ideas of Manhood and Womanhood thread throughout *Macbeth*.
    - There are witches who look like men and who also look like women.
    - A woman who desires to be less womanly calls on demons to make her so.
    - A man is criticized by his wife for not being manly enough.
    - One man tells another when he's feeling grief that he needs to "take it like a man," and the second man responds, "First I need to feel it like a man."
    - After the preview of these plot moments, ask students to silently reflect on this question (or journal): Do you think Shakespeare is reinforcing or challenging traditional definitions of *manhood* and *womanhood*?
- Share with students the traditional dictionary definitions (synonyms) of *manhood* and *womanhood*. Note how these are the binary poles of gender identity. You might draw a continuum on the board, a line with one word at either end.

MANHOOD	WOMANHOOD
Macho Male Manly Masculine Strong Tough Virile	Female Feminine Girlish Ladylike Maidenly Maternal Motherly Womanly

- Ask students to define *manhood*, *womanhood*, and *personhood* in a journal reflection, using their own synonyms. You can also assign the plot preview journal at this time.
- One way to begin the conversation is by defining *personhood* together. If students are confused, use terms such as *humanity* or *human beings*, noting that in law and politics, personhood relates to concepts of equality, liberty, and citizenship. Then move to traditional definitions of gender, then to more modern definitions of gender. Use the relevance questions for Manhood and Womanhood from Chapter 3.
- Ask students to track references to Manhood and Womanhood in the play going forward.
- Consider sharing biographies during subsequent days as lesson openers, noting historical individuals who have fought for gender equity and transgender equity. From Alice Paul to Ida

B. Wells to John Rechy to Laverne Cox, there are myriad names worth noting for posing these relevance questions through their activism and their lives.

- Consider showing excerpts of the 1992 movie *Orlando,* directed by Sally Potter and starring Tilda Swinton. This movie is based on Virginia Woolf's novel *Orlando: A Biography* (1928), the story of a male poet who becomes a woman and lives across the centuries, now considered a classic work in feminist literature and transgender studies.
- Consider doing a book talk on David Levithan's *Every Day*, a young adult novel about the character of A, who a spirit that has no choice but to wake up every twenty-four hours in a new body, switching from male to female to male to female every day.
- If students are fascinated by superstition, medieval and Renaissance medicine, and the status of women, read various chapters on those topics found in Joseph Papp and Elizabeth Kirkland's *Shakespeare Alive!*, as well as "'A Strange Infirmity': Lady Macbeth's Amenorrhea" by Jenijoy La Belle, and consider sharing some notes from this scholarship that show how womanhood is equated in the play with childbirth, menstruation, or lack thereof.

Hook #6: Who's Got the Power?

This activity asks students to examine power and privilege in their lives and in the play, plus suggestions for later activities to extend throughout the unit. Consider reading and sharing excerpts of Peggy McIntosh's "White Privilege: Unpacking the Invisible Knapsack" (see Further Resources). Also look at the Power and Privilege relevance questions available in Chapter 3.

Steps:

- Explain to students that *Macbeth* is a historical record. Whether he intended it or not, it's Shakespeare's snapshot of habits, beliefs, practices, relationships, and systems of a particular time in history. Of course, it's his fiction, so it can't be taken as pure historical record, but because it's one of the surviving records, it's an artifact of the times. We have historical records, literature, and drawings done by those with access to paper and writing utensils and the time to use them. (If you have time, reference passages related to Virginia Woolf's *A Room of One's Own*. Who has the time to make art and whose art will be seen or heard or experienced depends not just on creativity and hard work but on several elements, including power and privilege. You can also connect to the #disruptexts and #weneeddiversebooks movements.)

- Therefore, *Macbeth*'s characters carry different amounts of power and privilege, just as we all carry certain amounts. Our first job is to examine our own, and then to track the systems of power in the play and how different people play a role in it.
- Use social- emotional learning practitioner-scholar Dena Simmons's activity with students as a journal entry prompt for the next seven days:
  - "Ask students to play the role of social scientists for a week by observing the world with a racial-justice lens. Ask students to track how different racial groups seem to experience the world. What trends, similarities, and differences do they notice? At the end of the week, lead a reflection where your citizen scientists report their findings and generate questions or theories based on the evidence" (Simmons).
- Ask students to keep a power and privilege tracker in their reading journals, answering these questions about characters in *Macbeth:*
  - Who holds power? How do you know?
  - What privileges do they hold? How do you know?
  - How did they get this power?
  - How do they maintain it?
  - Does their power and privilege exclude others from having the same? How do you know? The smallest references in a play can show racist oppression, religious oppression, and class oppression from a specific time, and all three appear in this play.
  - Refer to the relevance and play-related questions associated with Power and Privilege found in Chapter 3.
  - Throughout the unit, ask students to report in as you work through scenes that raise issues around class (act 3, scene 1) or race and ethnicity (act 4, scene 1). To prepare for these discussions, a compacting student or another student with an interest in history can research any of these topics:
    - Economic class (murderers whom Macbeth hires)
    - The status of Jewish people in England
    - England's trading and political relationship with Turkey
    - England's trading and political relationship with Tartars, "peoples of central Asia such as the Mongols

of Genghis Khan. They were thought to be fierce warriors and great archers" ("Tartar's Bow").

- In the Witches' spell in act 4, there is a lot to unpack, and it's worth a class period. Keep in mind that there is offensive language here to treat with sensitivity. For example, with regard to religious oppression, a "birth-strangled babe" is mentioned in the spell for this reason: "killed right after birth and before baptism, thus making the baby damned like the unbaptized Turk, Tartar and Jew" (Mabillard, [birth-strangled]).
- Note to students that when the Witches use body parts of certain people and not others and link them to animals and other natural elements, assumptions are made. Study the spell to discover:
    - Who is otherized and made less human?
    - What assumptions are made about these people?
    - What interpretations are we to make here? Is it [let students speculate first] *The Witches are evil and wrong for doing this; don't be like them?* Or *Shakespeare's audience had no problem oppressing or killing people who weren't white and Protestant? Something else?*
    - What research would we need to do to develop a more informed opinion? What sources would be good to seek?
    - Record students' questions and talk about Renaissance and Shakespeare scholars, as well as other historians who dig into these types of Essential Questions. Students may not be aware that colleges and other institutions spend money and time debating and researching these topics.

- Share information about white supremacy and colonialism and their roots in English society, as well as the diversity of English society at that time. See the BBC article in Further Resources titled "Britain's First Black Community in Elizabethan London" and consider reading it together. Note that the color black symbolized power and authority, but phrases such as "black magic" and diseases such as the "Black Death" were common, and with these the color black connotes evil and suffering.
- Ask students to track representations of color in the play. Both black and white have positive associations, but black has more negative connotations, and white most often is associated with

beauty and goodness. Ask students to do connotation exercises around color in the play as well as its use in our language today when not describing people. Ask students to look at casting in Shakespeare films and theater productions. This topic can also be the subject of a student's research project.

> How does Shakespeare's work engage with race, racism and people of colour? What was the early modern experience of race? How do modern productions tackle this topic, if at all? . . . From looking closely and more deliberately at the language in Shakespeare's England, particularly in his own work, we can see how binaries of black and white helped create or contributed to concepts of race; we gain a deeper understanding of racial difference today and therefore a deeper awareness of what we are up against in the fight against racism. I think this is one of the chief values of studying Shakespeare and race.
>
> —Farah Karim-Cooper
>
> Shakespeare's plays and other writings of his time show us, as indeed our own world does, that racist ideologies can pick up on somebody's skin colour, body shape, religion, cultural difference, or geographical origins to mark them as *permanently* different or inferior. Thus, as in Shakespeare's day, in our world Muslims, Jews, Blacks, Dalits (or lower-castes), Asians and many other peoples, depending upon the context, are the targets of violence and hate.
>
> —Ania Loomba

Hook #7: Riddle Me This

This activity introduces figurative language or imagery in a fun way, as part of riddling.

- Ask students if they know any riddles and then explain that Witches speak in riddles, or forms of equivocation that are puzzles for Macbeth, codes to crack. Tell them they are about to be riddlers themselves.
- Review figurative language options with students using the answer key for Handout 10. Figurative Language & Sound Devices, Word Nerds, Part 1 (see Chapter 4) as a definitions list for the class.
- You can give students this riddle:

  My ears are big as this room.
  My eyes see all.
  My voice can stretch across a stadium.
  I am important and unimportant, powerful and powerless,

> *impactful and negligible, depending on who's looking.*
> *I am all hands on deck all the time.*
> *What am I?*
> *Answer: a teacher*

- Ask students to find the figurative language first and then try to find the meaning:

> *My ears are big as this room.* (hyperbole)
> *I am all hands on deck all the time.* (synecdoche)
> *I am important and unimportant, powerful and powerless,*
> *impactful and negligible, depending on who's looking.*
> (antithesis)
> *What am I?*

- You may also want to show them other poems such as these at ReadWriteThink: http://www.readwritethink.org/files/resources/lesson_images/lesson169/RiddlePoems.pdf.
- Tell students their task is to create a riddle using a range of figurative language.
- Share poems and see how students can create mystery with language.
- Find your favorite riddling lines from the Witches and preview them for students, telling them to stay on the lookout for mysterious, equivocating language and how characters might be tempted into believing things that aren't quite what they seem.
- For follow-up or hook activities with poetry and exploring its depth and power, connecting to the Big Idea of Power, check out ten young poets featured in Maya Phillips's article, "Young Black Poets: Ten Teenage Writers Show the Future of Poetry."
- Ask students to connect how people today empower themselves through poetry with how Macbeth uses words. Even when he's weak, his language holds him up.

> How do we—the artists, the writers, the ones who are so used to squaring off with the worst of ourselves, our world, our humanity—find a language suitable for our current state of disaster, which is almost biblical in its force and Shakespearean in its unfolding?
>
> The ten young Black writers in this project—talented poets from Oakland, Houston, St. Louis, Chicago, New York, Nashville, New Orleans and Los Angeles—are using the tools at their disposal, whatever they have. There's the "Black vernacular" of Akilah Toney's poem, the unshakable end rhymes of Alora Young, the expansive lines of Nyarae Francis's sestina and the stunning yet harrowing fragments of Samuel Getachew's "justice for —."
>
> These fledgling June Jordans and Robert Haydens, who are youth poets laureate and organizers and rappers, examine and fight back against an America that threatens to swallow them.
>
> —Maya Phillips

For more hooks, head to lynhawks.com/extramacbeth for Handout 48. Hook #8. Culminating Activity: Tell Me What Matters Most and Handout 49. Hook #9. Make a Visual PSA, Bard Style. Instead of a final quiz on passages from the play, consider offering the PSA activity in MR groups.

6 Key Scenes to Teach

What You Will Find in This Chapter

- Suggestions for key scenes to study in depth during class
- A list of characters and plot events (say yes to spoilers!)
- Multiple activities for certain key scenes, modeling how to design your own
- DYO tips

Remember Alicia in Chapter 3? Without time to design lessons for every scene, she skims the play, on the lookout for scenes that fit her skill goals. Where can she best explore translation and annotation, figurative language, and claims and reasoning? That's her first set of filters.

When selecting *your* key scenes—scenes to share with all students—filter by skill goals, student interest and intelligence, and your interest and readiness. Like the three Witches making their magic, there should be a blend of this triad of needs in your scene selection.

Why Key Scenes?

We should read some words of Shakespeare and read them well. We should perform, discuss, and analyze some scenes well too. Then I believe we shouldn't worry about the rest.

Differentiated instruction is about in-depth instruction for all readiness levels rather than mastery of quantities of information. It's about in-depth skill practice for all students so that everyone is making progress at their readiness level.

Class performance and film viewing allow students to experience a play the way it was meant to be. Rather than worrying about recall of events or character lists, let's worry about how students plumb the depths of character hearts, minds, and motivations; how they analyze the consequences of character actions; and how they learn to imitate the poetry on the page. They can craft their own interpretations in critical and creative work based on some of the text, not all of it. If a few excerpts make an impact, students will remember the play, knowing why certain key scenes, characters, and phrases are iconic in Western history, why they have inspired other words, and why an artist who lived hundreds of years ago still has thoughts to share.

So let loose with spoilers! Give students the entire story just as Shakespeare's contemporaries knew it before they saw his work on stage. Rather than quizzing students on recall of plot points, provide reminders and move straight to the higher-level skill activities of analysis, evaluation, and creation.

How Do I Choose? Let Student Interests Be Your Guide

- What do your students love to do?
- Do you have a class full of performers? Artists? Moviemakers?
- Then maybe performance, viewing, film, or art activities are the ones to choose.

How Many, When, and How?

You might select four or five scenes for in-depth study during your unit (see the Suggested Key Scenes in the next section and Handout 26. *Macbeth* Key Events on the website). One per week works well.

You will note there is no recommended time frame for each lesson because depending on student interests and readiness levels, you might expand what could be a one-period activity into three days of study. Since I give you more activities than you have time to implement, treat any of the Lesson Steps as a suggested order or flow if you did all suggested activities over multiple periods.

How Do I Choose? Your Passion and Skills Can Guide

- What are you best at leading? Do you have a passion for theater? Then bring that skill to coaching performance activities.
- Are you a cinema buff? Viewing activities might be a great go-to.
- Are you a game master? Then spend more time on problem-based learning activities.
- Let your students' and your skill strengths and interests help you choose.

List of Key Scenes and Key Scene Lessons

These scenes listed below are some of my favorites for in-depth, in-class exploration.

You will see a highly detailed lesson for act 1, scene 1, including a breakdown of the internal design. I want to showcase the myriad possibilities for teaching a scene. Trust that I haven't even scratched the surface! It's also a format you can keep in mind if you add one new lesson to your repertoire annually. Shorter notes and suggestions follow for remaining scenes, inviting you to arrange various activities in your preferred order for each section of the play.

Suggested Key Scenes

- Act 1, scene 1: Are You a Good Witch or a Bad Witch?
- Act 1, scene 3: Pleased to Meet You and Strange Intelligence
- Act 1, scene 5: Criminal Intent, or Delusional Thoughts?
- Act 1, scene 7: Double Trust and The Rules of Manhood
- Act 2, scene 3: What's the Matter?
- Act 3, scene 1: We Are Men . . . and Dogs
- Act 3, scene 2: Doubtful Joy
- Act 3, scene 4: Most Admir'd Disorder
- Act 4, scene 1: Double, Double Toil and Trouble
- Act 4, scene 2: We Are Traitors
- Act 4, scene 3: Feel It as a Man
- Act 5, scene 1: Out, Damned Spot!

DYO: Elements of a Key Scene Lesson

- Skill objectives should be planned first. What data on skill mastery do you want to retrieve during this lesson? How will activities or assessments you collect be part of a greater portfolio of work? How can you blend fun with skill development?
- Content objectives can be brief. Which definitions, methods, processes, stats, and facts should students commit to memory as required knowledge before skill practice—if any? Which just-in-time content can they find or be given while developing a skill?
- I offer tiered discussion questions for WCA discussions before and after an activity but assume you will offer them to all students. For example, if you ask an OT question, ask yourself whether an ELL or NOV student is ready for that challenge if you provide support. If you ask an ADV question, maybe an OT student could attempt it. Always keep your mind open to both the readiness level needed for a question as well as the

possibility that students are ready to move beyond their readiness level.

- Every Shakespeare unit should include performance activities. Start with Chapter 8, "Performance Activities," for guide recommendations as well as lesson ideas.
- Return annually to revise and refine lessons using student feedback. It's better to do a few long lessons on a few key scenes rather than scattered, disconnected lessons that "cover" a lot of the play. Students disengage when we rush forward for the sake of coverage.

When designing your own key scene lessons, don't forget to differentiate the flow in a given lesson or a given week from WCA to TR/MR to WCA, creating a whole-part-whole flow.

As you think about individual lessons and also the flow of each week, how will you create a ritual of whole-part-whole flow?

WCA: Whole-class activities bring the community together to explore universal skills, themes, and concepts.

TR: Tiered-readiness activities let individuals develop skills and make progress in their proximal zone of development.

MR: Mixed-readiness activities let individuals bring their intelligences, interests, and skill strengths to collaborative and cooperative challenges.

When you design your own key scene lessons, consider a number of these elements:

DYO Key Scene Lesson	
WHY: the lesson's reason for being	**SOs: Skill Objectives.** Which key skills will students practice? Should you preassess for any skills? See Chapter 1 for suggestions on skill sets as well as how to set readiness ranges.
	EQs: Essential Questions. Which Essential Questions rooted in a Big Idea drive activities?
	I & I: Interests and Intelligences. Which interests can students pursue during this scene? What intelligences can students harness through activities?
	SEL: Social and Emotional Learning. What opportunities do we have to build social-emotional skills such as social awareness, self-awareness, self-management, relationship building, and responsible decision making?

WHAT: key information and key activities	**SA: Scene Action.** What key events from the scene should we know?
	SQ: Story Question. What is the driving question for the protagonist and the story action? What is the question of suspense that turns pages?
	COs: Content Objectives. Which definitions, methods, processes, and facts do students need to know?
	DO: Dramatic Opening. Using a hook sentence, image, or action can "set the stage" for student engagement. This can be an alternative to a full hook lesson or part of one. Is there a quotation, image, clip, story, or analogy that quickly engages students?
	H: Hooks. Which hooks might pair nicely with this scene?
	ML: Mini-Lessons. Which mini-lessons might pair nicely with this scene?
	HC: Historical Contexts. Is there any key historical context that helps us understand Shakespeare's era and/or perspective?
	TA: Text Analysis. What brief text analysis could happen, or what Close Reader might be used with this scene?
	D & J: Discussion and Journaling. What are opportunities and strategies for students to think critically about Big Ideas and Essential Questions, using play-related and relevance questions?
	VA: **Viewing Activity.** What should students analyze while watching film interpretations of the play?
	PA: Performance Activity. How might students perform part of this scene?
	HW: Homework Activity. What can students do for homework?
	WA: **Writing Activity.** What creative writing opportunities might work well with this scene?
HOW: the order and flow and key considerations	**Lesson Summary & Steps:** What are outcomes? What are key actions students will take? What is the recommended flow, such as WCA-TR-WCA or WCA-MR-WCA, if you were to attempt all activities in this lesson?
	ND: Notes on Differentiation. Which activities should be WCA, TR, or MR? What are the collaboration and cooperation opportunities?
	CA: Cultural Awareness. What aspects of Western culture must be explained for students to understand the scene? What aspects of others' cultures might be invited into the conversation?

Act 1, Scene 1: Are You a Good Witch or a Bad Witch?

HOW: the order, flow, and key considerations

Lesson Summary & Steps: Students explore the Witches' scene and find evidence to corroborate Big Ideas while doing cinematic viewing analysis, performance, and/or discussion.

Recommended prior lesson: Hook #1: Tell Me Where You Stand (see p. 86)

Consider one or more of these activities:

1. WCA Activity: Students write warm-up journal entries with relevance questions related to witches, magic, and evil (see p. 111 and also Chapter 3).
2. WCA Hook: Welcome to the Film Crew (see Chapter 7, "Film and Graphic Novel Activities").
3. Book Talk: See Chapter 10, "Independent Reading," for recommendations for witchy tales.
4. MR Activity: Cinematic Viewing Activity (see p. 139).
5. WCA Mini-Lesson: Consider designing your own lesson based on guides recommended in Chapter 8, or try the Five Stresses Are All You've Got mini-lesson in *Teaching* Julius Caesar: *A Differentiated Approach* (Hawks). You can also consult guides such as *Shakespeare Set Free* (O'Brien) or *Reading Shakespeare with Young Adults* (Dakin) for performance activities.
6. MR Performance Activity: Where Will You Land? (See Chapter 8.)
7. TR Questions: Incorporate D & J questions throughout as needed, using suggestions from Chapter 3.

ND: This scene is a great WCA opportunity to build community and harness multiple intelligences. The text is short, the EQs are deep, and viewing and performance activities are fun.

- If you want to make the skill competencies of evidence identification and claim creation a priority, consider preassessing a few days before implementing the lesson for evidence identification and claim creation using Handout 21. Preassessment: Evidence and Claims (lynhawks.com/extramacbeth/). In this lesson, the skills are introduced and practiced at a low-stakes level through discussion, cinematic viewing, and performance activities. In subsequent lessons, these skills will be more deeply explored through TR and MR activities.

- The text being read aloud is quite accessible so translation doesn't have to be a priority. Ask a few students to look up words such as *"hurly-burly"* (tumult and turmoil), *"ere"* (before), *"heath"* (wilderness or moorland--open, frequently flooded), and *"anon"* (I'm coming! On my way!). Ask another student to serve as an expert on witches' familiars (e.g., Graymalkin, Paddock). These students can provide the answers when you call on them.
- Note that the EQs below are ADV. All students should be offered the opportunity to attempt them when you are leading the VA, while understanding that they take a higher level of critical thinking and inference to answer.
- **CA:** Western witches (Halloween, Salem Witch trials) loom large in the American cultural psyche because of their dominant narrative in literary, political, religious, and economic establishments. You should assume there are many diverse cultural interpretations of who a witch might be, what a witch can do, and whether a witch is good, evil, or something else entirely. How might students be able to explore these ideas in your class?

WHY: the lesson's reason for being

SOs: Reading, Evidence Identification, Speaking and Performance

- **NOV Standard,** 7th: CCSS.ELA-LITERACY.RL.7.1. *Cite several pieces of textual evidence to support analysis of what the text says explicitly as well as inferences drawn from the text.*
- **OT Standard:** CCSS.ELA-LITERACY.RL.9-10.1. *Cite strong and thorough textual evidence to support analysis of what the text says explicitly as well as inferences drawn from the text.*
- **ADV Standard,** 12th: CCSS.ELA-LITERACY.RL.11-12.1. *Cite strong and thorough textual evidence to support analysis of what the text says explicitly as well as inferences drawn from the text, including determining where the text leaves matters uncertain.*

EQs:

- What is evil?
- How do we see beyond the "fair" to the foul that's hidden?
- What do witches represent in my culture? Evil, Magic, Nature, Power, Prophecy, the Supernatural?

I & I: Visual-Spatial, Interpersonal, Theater, Cinema

SEL: Students explore how prophecy, magic, and evil impact their personal lives and in particular their decision making.

WHAT: key information and key activities

SA: Three witches meet on a stormy battlefield to discuss a future meeting with Macbeth.

SQ: Are these witches foul (evil) or fair (good)?

CO: Students should use or remember this knowledge in order to practice various skills:

- The definition of evidence when doing textual analysis
- The definition of Big Ideas and Essential Questions when doing critical inquiry
- Cinematic terms when doing viewing analysis
- Iambs and trochees when doing textual analysis
- Motifs when doing textual analysis

DO:

Option One: Premonitions of Evil

- Post this Macbeth quote: "Something wicked this way comes" (act 4, scene 1, 45).
- Ask students these discussion questions and invite students to tell any stories. If you have a personal story, share it with students first.
    - Have you ever had a sense that something bad was about to happen? What is your word for that feeling?
    - Did it happen? How do you feel about that premonition or intuition now?
    - Have you ever listened to premonitions and been glad that you did?

Option Two: Fair Is Foul and Foul Is Fair

- Present students with two scenarios. Ask them to choose one, turn to a partner, and make up a story ending.
    - *She seemed like my best friend, but then . . .*
    - *He won the lottery, which seemed like a great situation, but then . . .*
- Ask students to share the "but then" part.
- Explain the many meanings of "*fair*" and "*foul*" in Shakespeare's day. I recommend posting these synonyms for the unit somewhere where students can access them:
    - Fair:
        - "Plausible, flattering, seductive"

        - Or "Virtuous, honorable, upright"
        - Or "clean, unsoiled, not dirty" (Crystal and Crystal 165).
    - Foul:
        - "false, hypocritical, shameful"
        - Or "detestable, vile, loathsome"
        - Or "dirty, miry, muddy" (Crystal and Crystal 186)
- Ask students to explain this line from Shakespeare—"Fair is foul and foul is fair"—using real-life situations, or write an explanation in a journal entry.

Option Three: There Can Be Only One Winner

- Ask students to look at just the characters in Handout 28. *Macbeth* Characters and make predictions. Ask them to take a couple of minutes in pairs to conjecture about the plot of *Macbeth* based on only the characters. Tell them the theme has to be reality show style, based on hierarchy, winning, and competition.

TA: Much of Shakespeare's plays is written in iambic pentameter, including *Macbeth*. But the Witches speak in trochees and much shorter lines. Whatever might that mean?

- To get the definitions, watch videos from the Royal Shakespeare Company(www.youtube.com/watch?v=Ee_M1qUQ9nY) or Shakespeare Coach (www.youtube.com/watch?v=W-tayWCupD8&feature=youtu.be and www.youtube.com/watch?v=9Uieu0AGXXs).
- Give MR student pairs or triads the text of the first scene. Ask them to read it aloud twice and then mark the stresses of trochees.
- Ask them to draw a conclusion: Why do trochees make for better magic?

HC: Shakespeare's historical sources called these witches "the Weird Sisters," or *wyrd* in Anglo-Saxon, meaning fates or destiny (Lipowitz and Conley 7). For more information on witches, see Hook #4: Six Things about 1606 in Chapter 5 and Handout 27. Historical Notes for Shakespeare's Day.

D & J:

- APPEARANCE: How are the Witches shapeshifters? What do you know about shapeshifting?
- MAGIC: Different people and different cultures have different views about witches. How would you feel about a witch wanting to meet with you? What would your questions be and how would you prepare for the meeting?

- PROPHECY: The Witches are fortune-tellers, and their prophecies will impact Macbeth deeply. If you have encountered psychics or mediums, spiritualists, or palm readers, what have they told you or others you know? Reflect on the experience and whether it impacted your decision making. If you have not lived this experience, what are your beliefs about prophecies and predictions based on intuition and/or spiritual guidance? Do you question whether prophecy is possible?
- GOOD and EVIL: What is your belief about witches and the quality of magic? Do you associate magic with good or evil or both? Why do you have these associations?
- See Chapter 3 for more play-related and relevance questions for both discussions and journals: Magic, Evil, Prophecy, and Nature.
- Macbeth is the main character. What might be Shakespeare's reasons for not showing Macbeth's face in the first scene? Why introduce the Witches instead?
- What is fair about the Witches? What is foul?
- Evil is a Big Idea with religious, spiritual, and/or moral resonance for students. Consider making relevance questions related to Evil journal prompts. Tell students that as they study the play's characters and actions, they can point to the nature of Evil as they see it and use their own personal rubric as a set of standards.

VA: View the scene's interpretation from two different films.

- Share Handout 29. Welcome to the Film Crew! before viewing films (lynhawks.com/extramacbeth/). Ask students to take on a preferred role and to take notes while viewing through the lens of that role.
- Ask students to gather in jigsaw triads or quads to share their findings. The guiding EQ might be *How do we all see the Big Idea of Evil play out in this cinematic interpretation of the play?* Depending on the film, replace with other Big Ideas: Terror, Order, Hierarchy, etc.
- Note that the 2011 PBS version sets up Terror, Evil, and Chaos beautifully. From the image of the bloody hand, to black-and-white war footage, to electrical surges in the hospital power grid, to gaping patient wounds on gurneys, there's much for study here. The 2022 Coen version also uses black and white in interesting ways to create a similar tone.

HW:

- Ask students to read Handout 26. *Macbeth* Key Events at a Glance, highlight two or three events most interesting or relevant to them, and list as many Big Ideas they might see in those events.
- Ask students to begin independent reading activities and search in their own texts for answers to EQs about Evil, Prophecy, Magic, Nature, and other BIs.

WA: Most Foul? Most Fair? Most Gray?

Tell students:

- Choose one of the following mediums and prompts as you grapple with the concepts of foul and fair. Interrogate the definitions of *foul* and *fair*. Surprise us with your interpretations.
- Flip the Sitch Script: Flip a situation (real or imagined) from fair to foul or foul to fair.
- Write a poem or story with a fair witch and a foul witch.
- Write foul and fair words of a riddle spoken by a witch speaking in code.
- Design parts of a graphic novella or comic that includes a foul witch or a fair witch.
- Make a rebus, meme, or other visual infographic using the fairest words in the English language as well as the foulest (no curses, please). You can define *fair* and *foul* as you choose.

Next Key Scenes

For the subsequent key scene lesson plans, I offer a shortened version of the lesson plan, including one or more of the following: lesson summary and steps, notes on differentiation, and selected activities.

Act 1, Scene 3: Pleased to Meet You and Strange Intelligence

Lesson Summary: Students explore the Witches' next meeting with one another and then the one with Macbeth and Banquo. Students analyze how each man views the prophecies, weighing character reactions and finding evidence to corroborate Big Ideas while also doing cinematic viewing analysis, performance, and/or discussion.

- EQs: Should I listen to prophecies? Who's in charge: fate or my free will?
- CA: When discussing the Big Ideas of Prophecy, Fate, and Free Will, keep in mind that some students come from cultures and spiritual traditions that value prophecy, and so "fortune-telling" is not an apt description. Some of your students might possess a certain reverence for what is considered a spiritual gift, whereas other students may be dismissive or suspicious of such practices. Ask students to speak from their own experience and not express judgment about others'.
- SO: Reading, Writing, Speaking and Performance, Collaboration and Cooperation
- CO: Dramatic irony. A literary device found in theater in which the story offers the audience more information and understanding than the characters do, creating situations in which characters' words and actions could then carry contradictory meaning and significance for the audience.

ND:

- MR cinematic viewing activities let students with visual-spatial intelligence track Big Ideas.
- TR questions can be posed to all and used to draw out certain students when appropriate.

Steps:

WCA: Invite students to explore Prophecy using relevance questions as journal entry prompts. Discuss student responses using those opening questions:

- Y/N: I do or don't believe in prophecy, prophets, spiritualists, psychics, or fortune-tellers: those who speculate about my future.
- Why are prophecies so tempting and enchanting to us?
- What's one prophecy you would not be able to resist? Why?
- What do you think gets our attention when it comes to predictions? Why do we love pundits, forecasters, and other speculators, whether it's in politics, weather, or sports?
- Help students come up with categories to explain our human desire for foreknowledge of the future. Here are some potential questions that will help you elicit the category names by leading with the italicized expressions.
    - Is it the "Fair" element? As in, *I wish for good Fortune/ Fate too, and really want this to be true!*

- Is it the Supernatural element? As in, *I've got faith that Someone or Something bigger than me knows my future.*
- Is it the Equivocation element—our fascination with mystery? As in, *That prediction is like a riddle; it could be read multiple ways!*
- Is it the Surprise or Oddity element? As in, *I would never have predicted that!*, or *Such a weird thing to imagine!*

TA: See Chapter 9, "Close Readers, Translation, and Annotation."

TR or WCA Mini-Lesson: Focus on evidence identification and claim creation. Design a lesson to help students understand what constitutes substantive evidence and meaningful claims. See Chapters 4 and 11 for ideas.

MR TA: Ask students to be skeptical as they analyze the Witches' riddles, working in pairs or triads to break down all the connotations of their words and the Big Idea of Equivocation. See Handout 30. You Imperfect Speakers (lynhawks.com/extramacbeth) for a guided text annotation and analysis exercise.

- Place students in pairs or triads to complete it. Use the answer key for Handout 30 on page 118 to guide your coaching of students.
- When bringing the class back together, you can ask any of these TR questions, accessible to a range of students, to make sure students are beginning to note key patterns and character trends while tracking the development of Big Ideas.
  - All students: If you could ask the Witches any questions, what would they be?
  - ELL and NOV: Define "*rapt*." If Macbeth is "rapt" and Banquo is not, what is Shakespeare saying about the Witches' different impacts on them?
  - ELL and NOV: How many question marks do you count in Macbeth's words to the Witches, as distinguished from Banquo's words?
  - OT: Find two ways that Banquo is suspicious in this scene and Macbeth is not.
  - OT: How do Banquo's and Macbeth's approaches differ from each other as they hear the Witches' prophecies? Characterize their different approaches.
  - OT: How does the sum total of the prophecies lead a careful listener to question all the Witches' words, taken together—something neither of these men does?

- ADV: How does prior information about the Witches that we have as audience members infuse this scene with dramatic irony?
- ADV: We've met the Witches already, and we've heard Macbeth's résumé. "What's past is prologue" is a famous line from another Shakespeare play, *The Tempest*. In that context, two men plotting murder use it to indicate that prior events have led to the current moment and opportunity. Inscribed on the front of the US National Archives building, this quote is also used by our military to indicate similarities between wars. Taken in the biggest context, this statement might mean that any past behavior dictates current behavior, or past events are leading to these events.
  - If that's true, what do the Witches and Macbeth already seem capable of, and why?
  - What should Banquo and Macbeth be wary of?
  - If you were Duncan, who would you trust, and why?

■ WCA: Can you "catch" evil like a disease? Lady Macbeth uses the word *catch* in an upcoming scene. Is there anything in this scene that suggests evil might be contagious?

Answer Key for Handout 30. You Imperfect Speakers: Connotations, Speculations, Questions

Here are some assumptions the Witches make, as well as the types of questions Macbeth and Banquo maybe ought to ask the Witches:

- *We know that you, Macbeth, are Thane of Glamis.*
    - How do you, the Witches, strangers, already know that?
- *We know you have been promoted to Thane of Glamis.*
    - How do you know about the promotion?
- *We know you will be king "hereafter" (sometime in the future).*
    - When will I get to be king?
    - How will I get to be king?
- *We hail you because that's what you do with powerful people—royalty, etc.*
    - Isn't it treason for me to be talking with you Witches, who hail a person who isn't the real king?
- *We know that you, Banquo, are lesser than Macbeth. You didn't get a promotion like Macbeth did.*
    - Lesser how?
- *We know that you are not as fortunate as Macbeth, yet much more fortunate.*
    - Greater how? Fortunate how? Unfortunate how?
- *We say that you will father kings, but you will never be a king.*
    - Why not? Which of my descendants will be crowned? When?
- *We hail Macbeth first and then Banquo.*
    - Why are you addressing us in different orders?
    - What are you Witches already known for doing? (Go back to act 1, scene 2 to get the witchy résumé.) Why might the Witches' past jobs and references matter here?

MR Activity: Cinematic Viewing:

- Select one or two film versions to view. Give students Handout 29. Welcome to the Film Crew! and this viewing prompt: Imagine the Witches are players in a game with Macbeth and Banquo. Imagine a big football match or chessboard, only we don't really know who's on what team. As the men approach the Witches, who's the smartest player on this dangerous field of fate, a field that just saw a very bloody battle? Tell or ask students:
  - Watch the Witches' predictions using one or more cinematic versions and take notes on any clues you see about Fate, Free Will, Ambition, Prophecy, Evil . . . [name any other Big Ideas key to your class's study].
  - What are three reasons to trust the Witches? What are three reasons not to?
  - What are three reasons to trust Macbeth? Three reasons not to?
  - What are three reasons to trust Banquo? Three reasons not to?
- Show students act 1, scene 3. Have a short discussion about one or more film versions, with the follow-up questions above plus those in the following Discussion and Journaling section.
- Note that Coen's film version uses only one actor instead of three. You can ask students to analyze his reasons for that casting choice.

D & J:

- Free Will: Do you believe you make your own luck? Why or why not?
- Violence: How is the statement "Past is prologue" relevant here when it comes to Macbeth's résumé?
- Ambition: Watch how different film versions have Macbeth deliver these lines: "Two truths are told, / As happy prologues to the swelling act / Of the imperial theme" (act 1, scene 3, 127–29):
  - What is Macbeth weighing here? What metaphor does he use? What are the connotations of "*swelling*" and "*imperial*"?
  - How is Macbeth seeing this prophecy "his way"?
- Evil: Note what Banquo says in lines 122–25: the potential for betrayal by "the instruments of darkness."
  - Journal entry: Has a person, place, situation, or thing ever been an instrument leading you into something you wish you hadn't tried?
  - Journal entry: Is there evil in us or outside us or both? Is evil a presence or entity?

WA: Give students a creative writing task in class or for homework:

- Strange Intelligence: Meet the Witches, Intelligence Operatives. These "imperfect speakers" challenge you to make your own riddle. Make a prophecy to yourself at age ten, predicting your future to your younger self. Use ambiguous and opaque language as you tell yourself the truth of your future while making your younger self guess what will happen. If you can, say things in a way that could be interpreted two different ways; use doublespeak, aka equivocation.
- I Am My Ancestors' Wildest Dreams. You may have seen this statement on T-shirts or social media. Make a prediction, you to your ancestors. Tell them a story, or write them a song, or a poem, or a rap in the magical, imagistic, and fantastical language of dreams. How did they dream of you?
- Handout 31. The Silliest, Most Searching, or Most Sorrowful Soliloquy Ever (lynhawks.com / extramacbeth). Write a speech—as yourself or as a famous character—delivered as a soliloquy.
- MR activity: The Silly Soliloquy, Sestina, or Sonnet. Write a description of yourself or someone you care about using as many Shakespearean words as you can. Use humor, drawings, rhyme, rhythm, repetition, metaphor, simile. Use Handout 25. Shakespeak in *Macbeth* from Chapter 5 (lynhawks.com / extramacbeth).

Notes for Other Lessons

Need some tips for building DYO lessons on the other scenes? See the following topics and suggestions.

Act 1, Scene 2: Macbeth's Résumé: We're in for a Bloody Ride

SA: A warrior whose gaping wounds are bleeding out must first report to King Duncan about the battle's progress, where Macbeth and Banquo get credit for bravery, victory, and violence.

EQ: Leadership. What makes a great leader? Who should lead?

- How did Duncan get to be a leader?
- What types of powers does Duncan seem to have?
- Who will succeed him?
- How will he die?

Use any of these other Big Ideas and their EQs from Chapter 3 that fit: Authority, Betrayal, Compassion, Courage, Cowardice, Cruelty, Disorder, Fortune, Hierarchy, Loss, Loyalty, Power, Privilege, Victory, and Violence. Have students track Big Ideas of interest to them and related motifs.

HC: See the lesson suggestion in Chapter 5 called Six Things about 1606.

PA: Use performance activities and / or a mini-lesson on iambic pentameter to get all students standing and saying a few lines (three to five). Give students the translation.

- Analyze the scene in a WCA with any of these questions:
  - Whose title does Macbeth inherit? Why?
  - What is auspicious and inauspicious about this scene? Is it good or bad luck to inherit a traitor's title? Good or bad luck that his win equals another's loss? Have you ever had a "win" that felt more like a "loss"?
  - What do we already know about Macbeth before we meet him? How do scenes 1 and 2 in act 1 reveal key details? What do we know about Duncan? (Since students might find it upsetting that this messenger might die simply because the king needs news, you may have to note the social hierarchies of the day and how servants lacked many basic rights.)
  - Figurative language was the special effects of Shakespeare's day. How does he preview that we're in for a bloody ride here? How does Shakespeare explore with the power of figurative language Big Ideas such as Violence, Betrayal, Cruelty, Cowardice, Disorder, Courage, Fortune, and Loyalty? What do key words and images in the figurative language connote?
  - What are some assumptions we could make about Duncan's kingdom? About Macbeth's character?
  - Send students on a figurative language hunt for imagery (e.g., allusion, simile, metaphor, personification, hyperbole) and sound devices (e.g., alliteration, cacophony, consonance). Use the information from the answer key in Chapter 4 for Handout 10. Figurative Language & Sound Devices Preassessment, Word Nerds, Part 1 (p. 51) as a handout or definitions list for the class.
  - Another technique Shakespeare uses is *hemistichomythia,* the split-level line. Ask students, Why do these lines get shared among actors?
  - Ask students to answer or pose questions about Duncan's kingdom, about Macbeth, and about Big Ideas. What does the scene show us about Violence? Betrayal? Courage? Ask students to try initial generalizations and encourage them to err on the side of simple. *A former loyalist can become a traitor. These leaders celebrate the brutal violence of their soldiers.* Students can use figura-

tive language as some of the evidence to prove these generalizations are true.

- Ask students if they can find any evidence so far of Macbeth being a leader. What are the required skill sets of leadership?

WA: On Macbeth's Soldier Résumé, it might say, "I'm a nave-to-the-chops kinda guy. I get the job done in battle." But if he wants to be king, what should be on his résumé? Write two drafts of your own résumé: one that is current with skill sets you possess, focusing on skills you have developed in any work you do with extracurricular activities or outside of school, and a second résumé that is five years in the future, called My Ambitious Résumé, listing all the skills and activities you plan to develop in the future.

- Read over some templates for résumés at Ethan Sawyer's College Essay Guy's website: www.collegeessayguy.com/blog/college-resume-templates.
- You can ask students to do multiple drafts of this résumé throughout the unit if you wish and invite guidance and college counselors in for mini-lessons to discuss how to write and revise. Ask experts who visit to coach students in best self-representation, in keeping with themes of the play: not a false or fake face, like the Macbeths, but an honest and "fair" face like Macduff, using best examples and language to emphasize strengths.

ND: The writing activity is a WCA coaching valuable life skills. Revising well to best represent one's self for both college and job applications is worth class and homework time. This task reinforces CCSS standards of claims, evidence, and succinct, clear writing.

Act 1, Scene 4: That Is a Step

EQs: See Chapter 3 for EQs regarding Trust, Betrayal, Evil, and Ambition.

HC: See the Six Things about 1606 lesson in Chapter 5. Discuss succession in Scotland. What are the strengths and flaws of Scottish succession and leadership structure? Ask students to analyze the succession plan before you share "Things about Thanes" in Handout 27. Historical Notes for Shakespeare's Day at lynhawks.com/extramacbeth. Consider making slides of Historical Notes as needed for brief, five-minute mini-lessons on historical context.

Mini-Lesson: Consider taking the following concepts to do a brief mini-lesson on tragedy, asking students to find examples of these "tragedy dos and don'ts" to support Arthur Quiller-Couch's claims, below.

- Ask students to question Quiller-Couch's statement that tragedy, according to ancient Greeks and the Elizabethans, had to include characters who were "highly renowned and prosperous." American tragedies such as Lorraine Hansberry's *A Raisin in the Sun* or Arthur Miller's *Death of Salesman* say differently. This point could lead to an interesting conversation related to Power and Privilege.
- Give students a tracking grid to track these aspects of tragedy in *Macbeth*. Students can also do parallel tracking in the news, determining why we use "*tragic*" there, and noting how the definition in our contemporary conversations is similar to or different from Quiller-Couch's claims. Note that the boldfacing is mine, to call out phrases I see worthy of greater discussion. *Macbeth* presents us a terrifying example of how we, too, with our ambition, imagination, and greed might run amok.

A Definition of Tragedy

Aristotle says this concerning the hero, or protagonist, of tragic drama, and Shakespeare's practice at every point supports him:

(1) A tragedy must not be the spectacle of a perfectly good man brought from prosperity to adversity. For this merely shocks us.

(2) Nor, of course, must it be that of a bad man passing from adversity to prosperity: for that is not tragedy at all, but the perversion of tragedy, and revolts the moral sense.

(3) Nor, again, should it exhibit the downfall of an utter villain: **since pity is aroused by undeserved misfortunes, terror by misfortunes befalling a man like ourselves.**

(4) There remains, then, as the only proper subject for tragedy, **the spectacle of a man not absolutely or eminently good or wise, who is brought to disaster not by sheer depravity but by some error or frailty.**

(5) Lastly, this man must be highly renowned and prosperous—an Oedipus, a Thyestes, or some other illustrious person.

—Sir Arthur Quiller-Couch (qtd. in Lerner 174)

D & J:

- Fate & Free Will. Macbeth is a complicated human being with many facets. What are his many facets here? What is his tragic flaw? Why might he be worthy of a whole play?

- Trust. Duncan says of the prior Thane of Cawdor: "He was a gentleman on whom I built / An absolute trust" (act 1, scene 4, 12–13). Now we learn that Cawdor was a condemned and executed traitor. Has anyone you've trusted let you down? How did you handle this?
- Trust. Have you broken someone's trust? Did you seek to rebuild it? Why or why not?
- Temptation. Have you been tempted to take power or responsibility not yours? How?
- Temptation. How do you resist temptation? How do you delay gratification?
- Power:
    - Have you ever gotten a taste of power and then found yourself unable to handle the responsibility? What happened?
    - Has power ever corrupted you? How?
    - Have you seen others get a taste of power and abuse it? In what ways?
    - Why is power so addictive?

VA: Share clips of the movie *Black Panther* alongside readings of *Macbeth.* Invite students to analyze the characters of N'Jadaka (Killmonger) and T'Challa (Black Panther) for their strengths and flaws, particularly around the choices related to Ambition, Power, and Violence. These can be good hook lessons. Ask students with deep knowledge of the film and/or comics to compare and contrast the plots of *Black Panther* and *Macbeth.*

Act 1, Scene 5: Criminal Intent, or Delusional Thoughts?

Lesson Summary: Students investigate the plotting of a murder by observing Macbeth's and Lady Macbeth's behaviors while exploring Big Ideas such as Evil, Manhood, Womanhood, and Manipulation. Students pursue text analysis, cinematic viewing, and/or discussion. Students also assess the mental states of the Macbeths per the legal definition of murder.

- EQs: Who is leading this murder? Are the Macbeths delusional or completely lucid? Why does Lady Macbeth feel the need for spiritual help?
- CA: Lady Macbeth summons demons. This can be a bit unnerving for some students who have strong feelings about evil spirits. Snakes also get a bad rap.

- SO: Reading, Writing, Speaking and Performance, Collaboration and Cooperation

ND:

- This lesson begins with a TR text activity with WCA and MR interactions.

Steps:

- Book Talk: *Laura Dean Keeps Breaking Up with Me* (Tamaki) or *The Narcissist You Know* (Burgo). These books deal with manipulative, dangerous personality traits that offer important topics for social-emotional learning and development as well as information to enhance psychological analysis of various literary characters.
- TR TA: *Attorneys at Work.* See Chapter 9 for more context and guidance in asking students to play professional roles when analyzing text. Tell students, "This play is about many murders. Does anything happen in this scene that might be evidence used against Macbeth and Lady Macbeth if they are accused of murder later? We have in our hands the letter Macbeth sent his wife after hearing from the Witches, and then the recording of Lady Macbeth's response, in private. Here's what we as attorneys preparing for trial need to analyze:
    - Do we see murderous intent?
    - Is this murder plot his, or hers, or both? Is there a leader with an accessory?
    - Do we see delusion?

Give TR groups Handout 32. Word Nerds and Word Sleuths. Attorneys at Work and Handout 33. Wordsmiths. Attorneys at Work. I recommend reading Chapter 9 first to see CR options as well as strategies. This is a shorter example of a CR.

- TR Group A: OT and ELL-NOV students should read Handout 32 to examine act 1, scene 5, 1–13.
- TR Group B: ADV students should read Handout 33 to examine act 1, scene 5, lines 14–29.

- **WCA discussion:**
    - Who's in charge of this murder? How do you know?
    - Macbeth uses these words to describe the Witches' words to him: "Perfectest report," meaning "most reliable" in the Oxford translation. *Is* the Witches' report reliable, or not so much? (Will students notice that the Witches vanish into air and exhibit other unreliable aspects?)

- If you were in the Macbeths' shoes, what questions would you ask? What do neither question?

Find the following handouts at lynhawks.com/extramacbeth:

- Handout 32. Word Nerds and Word Sleuths. Attorneys at Work.
- Handout 33. Wordsmiths. Attorneys at Work.

WA:

- Split lines, aka *hemistichomythia*. Using split lines, write a scene between partners in which the two people planning something evil or good finish each other's sentences.
- The Manipulator. Lady Macbeth is no average manipulator. She's got plans when she says, "Look like the innocent flower but be the serpent under't" (act 1, scene 5, 64–65). What are the methods and ways of "false faces" who manipulate others?

D & J:

- Have you ever been manipulated by someone? How did they manage to manipulate you?
- Do you manipulate others? What are your strategies for doing so?
- Are there different types of manipulation? Are there fair and foul versions? Is manipulation ever justifiable?

VA: Besides using Handout 29. Welcome to the Film Crew!, you might use EQs related to Manhood and Womanhood. How do actors express these Big Ideas differently across film versions? How is the Macbeth marriage/partnership characterized? Ask students to find adjectives and adverbs to characterize their relationship.

Additional Resources: If students enjoy researching and discussing topics such as law and criminal justice, see Further Resources for the *Macbeth Mock Trial: Shakespeare and Problem-Based Learning* unit (Hawks and Agosta). It offers more legal materials, rubrics, and handouts to coach reading, writing, and speaking skills during a trial simulation.

Act 1, Scene 7: Double Trust and the Rules of Manhood

Book Talk: Consider sharing excerpts of Jason Reynolds's young adult novel *Long Way Down,* and also consider assigning it as a second text for all students to read at night. This verse novel is highly accessible and appropriate for middle and high school students, offering strong connections and parallel themes. Ask students to create a list of rules for each protagonist, Macbeth and Will. What rules guide each character's life? Find similarities and differences between the rules and their connection to Big Ideas such as Loyalty, Manhood, Revenge, and Violence. See more suggestions in Chapter 10.

D &J: Trust. See the quote below for critic Quiller-Couch's interpretation of the ways Macbeth violates trust. Ask questions to see if students can come up with the same as below: whose trust does he violate, and how?

> The more we study Shakespeare as an artist, the more we must worship the splendid audacity of what he did, just here, in this play of *Macbeth*. . . .
>
> Think of it:
>
> He made this man, a sworn soldier, murder Duncan, his liege-lord.
>
> He made this man, a host, murder Duncan, a guest within his gates.
>
> He made this man, strong and hale, murder Duncan, old, weak, asleep, and defenceless.
>
> He made this man commit murder for nothing but his own advancement.
>
> He made this man murder Duncan, who has steadily advanced him hitherto, who had never been aught but trustful, and who (that no detail of reproach might be wanting) had that very night, as he retired, sent, in most kindly thought, the gift of a diamond to his hostess. To sum up, instead of extenuating Macbeth's criminality, Shakespeare doubles and redoubles it.
>
> —Sir Arthur Quiller-Couch (qtd. in Lerner 176)

CR: Consider developing a set of TR or MR CRs on the "If it were done when 'tis done" soliloquy. There is much to investigate here, from the motif of multiplication (doubling), to figurative language (hyperbole, personification, animism), to weighing his logical and emotional reasoning, plus his spiritual concerns. You could make a column of "I Should" and "I Shouldn't" for Macbeth's reasoning. See Chapter 9 for further guidance on developing CRs.

WA: Rules of Manhood and Womanhood. Ask students to examine the master narrative here about what a man or a woman should be. (Also use EQs from Chapter 3.) Then ask students to do some creative writing or journaling, using poetry, prose, or song to write a story that expresses their beliefs and experiences regarding gender identity.

> I invite students to craft counterstories related to gender. It is important for students to understand that prior to crafting a counterstory, they must first understand the master narrative they are seeking to subvert. As such, explicit discussions regarding the dominant stories that each student seeks to debunk must occur. Some male students vocalized feeling ostracized for participating in activities deemed "unmanly"; girls shared instances of extreme sexualization that they had grown to perceive as simply "part of being a girl." Despite vastly different experiences, both groups began to understand—and push back against—the time-honored, traditional master narratives that shaped their gender and associated expectations. I then invited students to create other counterstories based on experiences that might move beyond gender.
>
> —Jeanne Dyches Bissonnette and Jocelyn Glazier (691)

Act 1, Scene 6: Motifs Are a Method to the Madness

Book Talk: How settings are a false face can be a discussion related to the following short stories as well as the scenes in which the Macbeths put on their false faces:

- "The Ones Who Walk Away from Omelas" by Ursula Le Guin
- "The Lottery" by Shirley Jackson
- "Revelation" by Flannery O'Connor

VA: Share a clip of movies such as *The Truman Show, Get Out,* or *Parasite* and pair it with the descriptions in act 1, scene 6, beginning with "This castle hath a pleasant seat." How is setting a lie and hiding the truth of what is truly occurring? See Common Sense Media (www.commonsensemedia.org) for more information on films. *Get Out* or *Parasite* are best for juniors and seniors.

Mini-Lesson: See Chapter 3 for a list of motifs as well as some activities for motif tracking. See the Let's Make a Motif Motto lesson in *Teaching* Julius Caesar: *A Differentiated Approach* (Hawks).

WA: Here are some creative writing activities:

- Setting. Write a setting that seems fair at first but is actually foul, or write a scene in which one or more species (such as birds or plants) establish mood and tone for the scene.
- Character. Explain the premise of Oscar Wilde's novel, *The Picture of Dorian Gray,* in which an attractive but vain man sacrifices his soul to stay as beautiful as he is in his painting. As Dorian does evil things, his portrait decays more and more, showing the true state of his soul.

- Ask students to create two visuals with accompanying captions or paragraphs of a character (self, other, fictional) with two faces. These faces must answer the EQs *What is good about this character?* and *What is evil about this character?* Consider using digital tools such as Voki, ThingLink, Pinterest, or Canva for this.
- Ask students to write two or more monologues from the Better Angel, Badgering Demon, and / or UN Diplomat that might advise them in a moral situation. They can also consider trying this for a favorite character from a book, TV show, game, etc.

Act 1, Scene 7: False Faces. Lies, Lies, Lies

> I love words. I just wish there were fewer anodyne synonyms and euphemisms for LYING. Call it what it is.
>
> —Dan Rather on Twitter, October 28, 2020

Hook: Share the following passage from Clyde Edgerton's novel *Raney*, in which a couple, Charles and Raney, with a baby on the way, fight over what words are appropriate for their child to learn. Ask students to be thinking about "nicer" words their family uses for expressing something uncomfortable, hidden, or deemed "inappropriate." Ask students to also be thinking about why people (and it differs within cultures) have different comfort levels of discussing things such as bodily functions, death, and money. If students are comfortable sharing afterward, have them do so, and you can do the same. Note how in the couple's discussion the idea that inappropriate words are unsuitable for a female come up. Note also that the novel is set in the 1970s South, but it's quite possible you will find plenty of students with similar experiences with this subject.

> "Charles," I said, "there's nothing wrong with that. It's what I grew up with."
>
> "Raney, if what you grew up with was all right for everyone, the world would be quite different."
>
> "I'll say. And for the better."
>
> "What are you going to call the baby's natural functions?"
>
> "Natural functions?"
>
> "Going to the bathroom: urinating and defecating?"
>
> "Defecating?"
>
> "Taking a crap, Raney."
>
> "Well, I'm certainly not going to ask a two-year-old girl with pigtails if she has to go 'take a crap.'"
>
> "What will you ask her?"
>
> "I'll ask her if she wants to go grunt."

"Go *grunt?* Go *grunt?* Raney, that's ridiculous."

"Ridiculous? It certainly is not. What would you say?"

"Well, I don't know; this is not one of the things I've planned out. Maybe I should have. What have you got for urinate?"

"Wee-wee. What else is there?"

"That's what I figured. How about if we compromise and come up with 'pee'?"

"I think we ought to start out with 'wee-wee' and when she gets a little older, 'pee-pee,' and then finally 'pee.'"

"Are you going to start out with 'gruntie-gruntie' and work up to 'grunt'?"

"Well . . . that's doesn't sound like such a bad—"

"*Raney,* I wasn't serious."

"Well, I think you should be serious. This is serious business. We have to call all those things something. And my family must have put a lot of thought into this sort of thing."

"I'll say." (Edgerton 224–25)

- Ask students to read headlines and first paragraphs of editorials and/or news stories to search for euphemisms as well as words that are synonyms for *lying*. Plug in any verb plus a politician's name into a search engine and you are likely to find a bank of headlines from authoritative sources. Two examples are NPR's "Trump Says His Misleading Coronavirus Comments Were Meant to Show 'Strength'" (09/10/20) and the Associated Press's "AP FACT CHECK: Trump distorts record; BLM falsely accused" (08/28/20). You can also share the history of the McCarthy era and how much power Joseph McCarthy wielded before journalists began first verifying his claims. When journalists such as Edward R. Murrow began refusing to run headlines unless the claims McCarthy made were verifiable first, McCarthy's power and reach was suddenly limited, and then his false reporting on many citizens was suddenly called into question.
- Discuss the meaning of *euphemism* vs. *equivocation* vs. *lie,* exploring connotation and denotation. Consider these word banks of verbs and nouns.

VERBS

Beguile	Cozen	Deceive	Delude
Defame	Dissemble	Dissimulate	Distort
Equivocate	Falsify	Feign	Fool
Forge	Forswear	Fudge	Garble
Gull	Hoax	Hoodwink	Kid
Lie	Misguide	Misinform	Mislead
Misrepresent	Misstate	Palter	Perjure
Prevaricate	Snow	Traduce	Trick

NOUNS

Calumny	Deceit	Deception	Defamation
Dishonesty	Disinformation	Distortion	Equivocation
Evasion	Hyberbole	Fable	Fabrication
Falsehood	Falsification	Fib	Fiction
Forgery	Fraud	Guile	Hyperbole
Inaccuracy	Invention	Libel	Lie
Mendacity	Misrepresentation	Misstatement	Mistruth
Myth	Perjury	Prevarication	Scam
Subterfuge	Tall tale	Whopper	Untruth

- Ask students to work in MR pairs to research definitions and then design a visual expressing the range and differences of morality among these words.
  - EQ: Which words are most and least powerful in expressing the fact that lying is wrong? Which words appear to carry the most consequences? Is there a continuum along which some "fudging" or "hedging" is better or worse than "prevaricating" or "lying"?
  - Each pair can choose three to five words, look at denotation and connotation, look at etymology, and choose colors to express their "word identities." Consider using digital tools such as ThingLink, Padlet, Canva, Pinterest, or Venngage.
  - Invite students to do counterstorytelling against the master narrative of "white lies." White lies are deemed more innocent. Ask students to choose different colors to express different layers of nuance for different connotations and denotations. As students suggest new colors, they should develop arguments for how those colors express those nuances better.
- WCA: Groups can share or you can lead students in a consensus-building activity to label and analyze words together. Initiate the WCA by saying, "Now we're going to make our own 'web of lies' to see how strong and powerful some words are when conveying wrongness. We'll place the most powerful at the center of the web and the weakest ones at the outer edge of the web." Use a mind map poster or a digital tool such as EdWordle (www.edwordle.net/) to take notes. When students present, ask them to share their findings on connotation, denotation, and etymology, and then ask the class to vote: What are our top three words with the most power in conveying the wrongness (immorality)?

Which words are euphemisms and more likely to cover up the truth of what is happening?

- Discuss: Is there a time and place for euphemism, equivocation, or fudging? Where do the Macbeths' lies fit on this web?
- Truth Is Physic. Invite students to do the same with a bank of words for truth-telling.

WA: Ask students to share their preferred expressions, slang, and idioms that convey lying. After they've shared, share others they didn't mention: *Blow smoke. Take it a with a grain of salt. Cry wolf. Lie like a rug. Full of hot air. He got taken in. Leading her down the primrose path. Lying through your teeth. Smoke and mirrors. Taken to the cleaners. Pull the wool over your eyes.* Invite students to create visuals for these, with the classic idiom featured prominently, or, for an ADV activity, design new idioms based on inspirations from motifs and other visual ideas you are brainstorming. When students present, conclude the conversation by asking them to pin the idiom tail on the Macbeths' donkey. Which expression fits the Macbeths best?

HW: Ask students to study Snopes, the MediaWise feed on Instagram, AP Fact Check, and other places where false stories are debunked and to bring their findings to class.

Act 2, Scene 1: Dagger Delusion?

PA: Hold "auditions" for the "Is this a dagger . . . ?" speech. Give student MR pairs a range of cue cards that ask some to play Macbeth as paranoid and faltering, some as delusional and confident, and some as violent and immoral.

- Ask students to study the text to determine whether they will use a real prop for a dagger or whether the actor will imagine it. What does the text suggest? Props you might provide include a plastic knife, a plastic bat, or a broom or other random props found around a house that could add some interesting twists. There's nothing to say that Macbeth isn't seeing a dagger in something else.
- See Chapter 8 for a brief note on cue card activities. Watch how one or more film actors handle this scene. Patrick Stewart's and Denzel Washington's are worth a view!

In most of the best contemporary fiction, objects and events aren't usually described from a God-like view, but from the unique perspective of the character. As in life, everything we encounter is a component not of objective external reality, but of that character's inner neural realm—the controlled hallucination that, no matter how real it seems,

> exists only in their head and is, in its own way, wrong. In fiction, it might not be going too far to say *all* description works as a description of character.
>
> —Will Storr, *The Science of Storytelling: Why Stories Make Us Human and How to Tell Them Better* (77)

WA: This character analysis activity uses the literary concept of *endowed object* to express character, where the object takes on qualities or traits, abilities or beliefs, of that character. Ask students to work in MR pairs or triads to describe a person contemplating murder by looking at the murder weapon; however, don't state directly that it's a certain kind of weapon. Instead, tell us:

- What this character wants, as reflected in aspects of the weapon
- What this character believes, as reflected in aspects of the weapon
- What this character may or may not do, as reflected in aspects of the weapon

Character traits and sensory details will make a poetic riddle for readers and listeners, who will guess the following: what the character wants, believes, may do, and what the weapon is.

WCA discussion after students read: What does each character want? Believe? What might they do? What is the weapon? How does their endowed object show character?

WCA Reading and VA:. Read aloud in a round robin Macbeth's "Is this a dagger which I see before me, / The handle toward my hand?" speech (act 2, scene 1, 33–61). On the second read, ask one student to volunteer to read it through with an emotion voted on by the class (fear, loathing, curiosity, desire for violence, etc.). As students listen, ask them to keep an eye out for figurative language and sound devices that emphasize emotion. Then watch some film interpretations and ask students to report back on the key words, phrases, figurative language, and sound devices that struck them.

CR: Use strategies from Chapter 9 to develop TR CRs for this passage.

Act 2, Scene 2: Murder, Directed By . . .

Book Talk:

- If you choose to incorporate Jason Reynolds's *Long Way Down*, you might note how Reynolds uses poetry and multiple motifs (e.g., elevator/direction, teeth, blood) to communicate a young man's moral dilemmas.

- You might note how he converses with ghosts before he contemplates committing murder and compare that to when Macbeth sees ghosts during his descent.
- You can ask students to examine how the depictions of violence are vastly different.
- You can make many connections between these two characters' choices, their descents, and their final choices. Invite students to speculate on Will's future based on what you see him contemplating and because Reynolds leaves the story open-ended. *Macbeth* is considered a tragedy. Is *Long Way Down* also a tragedy? Or should we characterize Reynolds's novel as something else?

TR CRs: The murder is offstage and can be viewed only by our own "horrible imaginings" (act 1, scene 3, 137). Consider developing a set of TR jigsaw CRs per the guidance in Chapter 9. Elements to analyze:

- ELL-NOV CRs: Students can study the text for details about the murder and analyze Macbeth's panic attack versus Lady Macbeth's surreal calm. If you choose a professional role, you can have them analyze this scene through the eyes of a criminologist and a forensics specialist. What would make for a slam dunk conviction? Students can also analyze the themes of Manhood, Womanhood, Guilt, Conscience.
- OT CRs: Students can analyze how, when the stakes get higher in a particular situation, the Bard reaches for multiple metaphors. Images build because figurative language was the special effects of the day. Macbeth murders sleep, so sleep will never be a release for him. He cites six ways sleep is important—and he's killed all of those options for himself! What happens to someone if they murder sleep? The plot will tell us, won't it (Fairchild)? See the "Shakespeare's Metaphors: A Deep Dive with Tenor, Vehicle, and Macbeth" lesson in Further Resources (Hawks and Fairchild) for a full set of materials on this topic.
- ADV TR CRs: The backstory of characters can be raised here, such as the fact that the Macbeths are childless, and it's implied that Lady Macbeth has lost a child. Students also can analyze the rapid-fire exchange between husband and wife in terms of sound and rhythm.

WA: Consider assigning a creative writing scene in which students craft a story of moral dilemma and suspense.

Acts 3–5

For more ideas, consult Chapters 8, 9, and 10 and Handout 44. Projects, Rubric, and Compacting recommendations found at lynhawks.com/extramacbeth.

Problem-Based Learning Project as Unit Conclusion

If you have a group of enthusiastic actors and problem solvers, why not end the unit with a mock trial? In a unit I developed with Vincent Agosta, students can play the professional roles of attorneys, jurors, witnesses, judge, bailiff, and journalists while putting the Macbeths on trial. See Further Resources for "Macbeth Mock Trial: Shakespeare and Problem-Based Learning" (Hawks and Agosta).

For more information on problem-based learning and DYO tips, consult the work of Shelagh Gallagher such as *Problem-Based Learning for Your Classroom.*

7 Film and Graphic Novel Activities

What You Will Find in This Chapter

- A rationale for the use of film and graphic novels
- Recommended film and graphic novel versions
- Tips for viewing and visual analysis activities

The Rationale for and Role of Film and Graphic Novels

We are reading Shakespeare's scripts, and in these actors' lines we can find everything from notes for lighting to stage directions. Viewing and analyzing scenes from excellent film or graphic novel versions should be an essential part of the critical thinking experience. After consulting this chapter, also consider Chapter 8, "Performance Activities."

Viewing and visual analysis activities can be incorporated into a few lessons a week. Consider asking students to compare and contrast clips from different cinematic interpretations of the play or different graphic novels. See Chapter 2 for potential schedules, including one in which cinematic viewing and interpretation kicks off the unit for the first weeks.

Keep captions on for all students, especially ELL students. Don't hesitate to stop a scene after one minute to ask students to repeat back key words, to share what images struck them most, or to note what sounds, special effects, or other cinematic elements leapt out at them. Viewing activities can include quick clips with you or a student facilitator stopping the scene for knowledge and comprehension checks. See Chapter 9, "Close Readers, Translation, and Annotation," and Chapter 6, "Key Scenes to Teach," for suggestions on how to integrate cinematic viewing activities throughout the unit. *Reading Shakespeare Film First* by Mary Ellen Dakin is another excellent resource.

Film Versions

The following versions of *Macbeth* are all excellent. I recommend integrating as many as you can into your lessons. Don't feel obligated to show a full film version, but if you find you have a favorite, you can use it as a baseline film to share regularly.

- **The 2011 PBS film version, recipient of a George Foster Peabody Award and directed by Rupert Goold.** You can't go wrong with Patrick Stewart as Macbeth or with Goold's choice of World War II hospital settings where the Witches are scary army nurses, stark tunnels and bunkers create tension, and allusions to fascism are frequent. The director's intention was to parallel *Macbeth* with Eastern European despotism, such as Ceaușescu's in Romania (Brall). This version is a great inspiration for students who take on projects to reimagine a new world for the setting. As critic Gabrielle Malcolm says,

  > Invention and re-invention accompany Goold's directing style, and there are some excellent set-pieces that surround the different murders. A cramped railway carriage and a bleak locker room provide the settings for the removal of Banquo and Macduff's family, respectively. Goold also blends the presence of the Witches into various scenes throughout to encourage the sense of all-pervasive evil; and in their guise of army nurses equipped with those exquisitely sinister amputation tools and ample plastic sheeting to catch the spatter. Indeed, this version of *Macbeth* injects both modern horror and serial killer chic into the proceedings, to further the reach of this timeless haunting tale.

  Note that Lady Macbeth (Kate Fleetwood) seems to suffer demon possession in her summoning of spirits.
- **The 1971 version directed by Roman Polanski.** Its medieval landscapes and interiors echo the historical references, and we are immediately drawn in by the brutally cold, wet, and wind-battered moors of the British Isles. Read Roger Ebert's review at rogerebert.com in which he alludes to the Manson murders and then concludes, "This is certainly one of the most pessimistic films ever made, and there seems little doubt that Polanski intended his film to be full of sound and fury—which it is, to the brim—and to signify nothing."
- **The 2015 Justin Kurzel film version starring Michael Fassbender.** This is the version to watch for incredible battle scenes and moments with the Witches. However, this version is also quite violent, so you might want to use it sparingly. It's not only the graphic nature of the violence that's a concern; it's the fact that this version shows Duncan's murder, an off-stage event in Shakespeare's play. It's a choice not in keeping with the original

script. The Aristotelian nature of tragedy keeps violence off stage, eliciting pity and fear in the audience. After Duncan's murder, Macbeth's breakdown has the potential to connect with the audience; we almost forget he's a murderer and pity him. By showing us the murder, the director makes redundant the beautiful language that follows, as Macbeth tries to explain to his wife what has happened. We as listeners are denied the horror of our own imaginations—Big Ideas of Imagination, Terror, and Violence—that only we could experience (Fairchild). That said, some viewers may find the violence of Macbeth's character and Scottish society a good match with Kurzel's interpretation.

- **The 1979 Trevor Nunn Royal Shakespeare Company production starring Ian McKellen and Dame Judi Dench.** This videotaped version keeps the original stage production's spareness, including minimal costuming, props, and set elements; the circular set (actors in the round facing one another); black background; and changes of setting marked by lighting changes. This version can be great for listening activities, asking students to pay closer attention to what they hear.
- **The 1983 BBC version directed by Jack Gold.** This *Macbeth* is notable for its staging and speechifying, especially how soliloquies by Macbeth (Nicol Williamson) and Lady Macbeth (Jane Lapotaire) and secondary characters are handled. The way actors interpret lines make them quite clear, and there are some unique moments of blocking and actor interaction. Students may find the staging and costuming both fake and uninspiring, however, so use brief clips as a contrasting method of interpretation. The scene of Lady Macbeth' summoning evil spirits is also quite sexualized.
- **The 2021 Joel Coen version, *The Tragedy of Macbeth,* starring Denzel Washington and Frances McDormand.** This revision has a crime thriller focus and a focus on the Macbeths as an older couple. Coen says, "It's interesting how Shakespeare sort of prefigured certain tropes in American thriller and crime literature that were common in the early part of the 20th century. . . . Which just had to do with, in crime novels, a story centered around a husband and a wife who plotted a murder. . . . I thought it would be interesting to bring certain aspects of that to the production of the movie" (qtd. in Chand). As McDormand notes, "In Joel's adaptation, we are exploring the age of the characters and [in] our adaptation the Macbeths are older. Both Denzel Washington and I are older than what is often cast as the Macbeths. We're postmenopausal, we're past childbearing age. So that puts a pressure on their ambition to have the crown. I think the most important distinction is that it is their last chance for glory" (Chand).

Cinematic Viewing Activities

Here are some suggested WCAs to try with students.

Activity 1: Welcome to the Film Crew (WCA)

Before introducing this cinematic viewing activity, determine your EQs and SQs. For example, during one lesson you might give students the EQ of the day based on a Big Idea and the SQ of the day (*Will Lady Macbeth convince Macbeth to murder Duncan?*). You can also coach students to choose these questions.

Use Handout 29. Welcome to the Film Crew! (lynhawks.com/extramacbeth) for the list of choices students have for cinematic analysis. Tell students they will be viewing and analyzing film as though they were a member of the film crew, thinking like artists who craft a product that provides an emotional experience. For a more involved lesson incorporating research skills, send students in MR groups to research their roles on career search sites. They can act as recruiters, generating a brief pitch for a Career Fair, and then share the details of the role with the class. Vote at the end on who had the most exciting pitch, while also asking students to update the handout definitions you've provided.

Activity 2: Murder She Wrote: With Cruelty or Compassion? (WCA)

Students watch various film portrayals of Lady Macbeth and do a Big Idea–driven character analysis, proven by key words, sound devices, and figurative language.

- Introduce Lady Macbeth as a complex, multifaceted woman. Our task is to see her as a full human being with many traits and to study how actors render that complexity within one performance and also across different performances.
- Ask students to listen as you read Lady Macbeth's soliloquy in act 1 in which Lady Macbeth gathers her will—and demons—to incite her husband to murder Duncan. If possible, give students a copy to annotate. Tell them they will also be seeing professional actors' interpretations shortly. The EQ and the SQ to consider are:
  - SQ: *How will Lady Macbeth handle the news of Macbeth's promotion to Thane of Cawdor, and the prophecies of the Witches?*
  - EQ: *What drives Lady Macbeth?* Ask students to identify key words they think an actor would emphasize most strongly in a performance and to listen for words that exemplify Big Ideas. Use the posted list of Big Ideas or Handout 1. Pick Your Favorite Big Ideas. See Chapter 3 for more guidance.

    - TR: Ask students to listen for and mark sound devices such as consonance and cacophony, and to stress the syllables that iambic pentameter emphasizes. Ask them to look for figurative language such as apostrophe, metaphor, and personification.

- Read aloud Lady Macbeth's soliloquy in act 1, scene 5, 37–53 ("The raven himself . . . 'Hold, hold.'"). As you read, make your own choices for emphasis.
- Ask students to share words that struck them. They might note the following (and keep in mind the importance of synonyms and students naming Big Ideas their own way):
    - The Supernatural: "heaven," "spirits," "hell"
    - Nature: "raven," "croaks," "nature," "thick night," "dunnest smoke," "blanket of the dark"
    - Womanhood: "woman's breasts," "milk," "unsex"
    - Violence: "murd'ring," "wound," "fell," "keen knife"
    - Evil: "direst," "murd'ring ministers," "mischief" (Note that some students will connect "black" and "night" with evil as well, as Shakespeare and other cultures have, and be prepared to restate as "the color black as it appears in nature" to clarify this is not a racial reference.)
    - Conscience: "compunctious visitings of nature," "remorse" "cry, 'Hold, hold.'"
- Ask students to watch two or three different film interpretations. Task: Watch the scene and keep annotating for key words, figurative language, and sound devices.
- After viewing each soliloquy, give students these writing prompts:
    - Now identify three descriptive adjectives (your claims) about Lady Macbeth's *character*, which constitutes her values, beliefs, and morals.
    - Wait till students have completed the prior answer to ask this: Is she a person of Ambition, Compassion, and/or —Cruelty—or something else entirely?
- After viewing the final cinematic version, ask students to decide what is the strongest Big Idea that came through the interpretations. Is there a pattern or a trend across the actors' portrayals, or were these very distinct portrayals? Ask students to report their analyses as a claim. Then ask them to review the text for how the actors used emphasis, cacophony, and/or consonance to get ideas across. You can also bring in other sound devices and, of course, figurative language.
- Suggested film versions:

- Kate Fleetwood in the 2011 PBS version
- Francesca Annis in the 1971 version
- Marion Cotillard in the 2015 version
- Judi Dench in the 1979 version, beginning at 22:09 (See "*Macbeth:* A Production from 1979" in Further Resources for the YouTube link.)
- Frances McDormand in the 2022 version

Activity 3: Murderous Mayhem, or Pity These People? (WCA)

How does Shakespeare create both mayhem and pity on stage? Ask students to view various film versions of act 2, scene 2—Macbeth and Lady Macbeth scrambling post-murder—using the following Big Idea lenses. Different MR pairs or triads can track:

- How Chaos is expressed; which lines stand out because of actor delivery? Which lines are said fastest?
- How Cruelty and Violence are expressed; which lines pop because of actor delivery?
- How Conscience and Guilt are expressed; which lines pop because of actor delivery?

Ask two students who enjoy performance and reading aloud to perform the scene of Macbeth and Lady Macbeth post-murder. The class can act as directors and acting coaches to suggest a unique interpretation through the lens of a particular Big Idea.

Activity 4: Tomorrow and Tomorrow and Tomorrow (WCA)

See Chapter 8 for notes on this most famous soliloquy and use Ian McKellen's interpretation. Use multiple film versions, including Patrick Stewart's.

Graphic Novel Versions

Keeping a class set of graphic novels to use anytime is a great way to help students experience the play visually. You might spend twenty minutes with the graphic novels, and then put those away and move to text only for a conversation.

Classical Comics produces an original-text, hardbound version of Macbeth that might be a great investment. SparkNotes offers their graphic novel illustrations online for free.

Graphic Novel or Comic Panels Analysis

Whenever I teach a graphic novel, I create questions for several visual elements to help students discuss or independently analyze the artistic skill behind rendering a visual story.

You can also adapt many of the activities described above for analyzing a graphic novel, especially where Big Ideas are concerned.

Text

- Devise questions about character development and arc, tracking how visuals and text intersect to demonstrate change.
- Devise questions about use of figurative language and sensory description that intersect with visual elements.
- Devise questions about speech bubbles and how they are used, about boldface type, and about places where text is omitted.

Art and Style

- Devise questions about dominant colors and color palette and how they are used for emphasis, background, etc.
- Devise questions about style (e.g., realist versus abstract). What do you notice about background colors? What is effective or special about these?
- Devise questions about panel size and image size, page layout, page bleed, camera angles, and trends across pages.

For a sample of how you can design journal questions, small-group and whole-class discussion questions, as well as creative expression and graphic novel tasks and projects, check out my unit in *When Stars Are Scattered*, a graphic novel by Victoria Jamieson and Omar Mohamed.

8 Performance Activities

What You Will Find in This Chapter:

- A rationale for performance activities
- Recommended resource guides
- Suggestions for performance activities

Why Perform Shakespeare?

Shakespeare's plays offer fun, kinesthetic, and visual scripts to expand students' vocabulary and deepen critical thinking through acting. Our roles aren't about enforcing perfect pronunciation or pacing; we're here to have fun. Considering how much work it takes a professional actor to learn Shakespeare, we all need to just relax and shout him out as best we can while also seeking out any experts (theater kids) who have some expertise to share too.

Performance activities that use repetition, asking students to re-read a passage in order to perform it, are great ways to improve reading comprehension. As senior education correspondent Emily Hanford notes about the science of reading, "stuff . . . gets stored in your brain through processing a word several times through its phonology and through its orthography, . . . the way it sounds and the way it's spelled. . . . You do that a few times and it's mapped into your memory as a word that you know on sight in the future" (qtd. in Loewus). Kicking off class with a quick read-aloud of a few lines, repeated several times until everyone can say it faster and faster, can be a fun vocal warm-up before class begins. By repeating and sounding out words and phrases, students will get comfortable with saying Shakespeare aloud.

What's Your Readiness Level?

Are you an actor or director? Were you a theater kid? An avid theatergoer? If yes, you probably don't need this chapter, because let me guess: you already tend to get kids on their feet, in front of the mic, or on camera performing in class. Consider skipping ahead to performance activities.

If the idea of performing or speaking publicly beyond your students sets your knees quaking, then remember this: Speaking Shakespeare is like dressing up for Spirit Day. Everyone's going to look and sound goofy, and that's okay. In this chapter, you'll find some low-stakes ways to build up to more comfort with language and performance. This is a great area for us to grow in the same way we challenge students and to improve our coaching performance. Each week there might be some sort of on-your-feet or recording moment when tongues get tangled, but eventually the sound and imagery will begin to click, and students will understand what Shakespeare meant. Words will make their mark and get clearer with each moment spent with the play.

Recommended Resource Guides

My favorite teaching guides are the Folger Shakespeare Library's *Shakespeare Set Free: Teaching* Romeo & Juliet, Macbeth, A Midsummer Night's Dream by Peggy O'Brien and *Reading Shakespeare with Young Adults* by Mary Ellen Dakin. Their stellar activities combine close reading and theater, and in Dakin's book writing tasks as well, in playful, rigorous ways.

The following websites are also helpful, with tons of resources to help you teach everything from iambic pentameter to providing different acting interpretations:

- American Shakespeare Center (Teach & Learn section): https://americanshakespearecenter.com/
- Royal Shakespeare Company: https://www.rsc.org.uk/shakespeare-learning-zone/macbeth
    - View the video on iambic pentameter and try this exercise with your students: https://www.rsc.org.uk/shakespeare-learning-zone/macbeth/language/key-terms#

Activity Ideas

Low-Stakes Recitation: Spice It Up!

This activity allows you to integrate figurative language and sound devices while helping coach students in performance. You also model your own risk-taking along with your students. You can pair this activity with any scene, particularly those in act 1.

- You can begin with everyone saying lines aloud. Gather all the most powerful quotations from the play (no more than four lines) and assign them randomly. Give yourself an assignment as well. You might model for students how to deliver the lines clearly and smoothly without much emotion; the goal on first try is "finding a flow" to say each line. Tell students that this is intentional because everyone will learn in the next practice how to use figurative language and sound devices to "spice up" the line delivery. Reassure your introverts that this is not about performance prowess but instead about articulating clearly and hearing the beauty of the language.

- Let students know that you want them to practice memorizing the lines without trying to understand them. Their homework is to memorize two to four lines. They can go online to hear pronunciations of words, but they will not be expected to explain any words or meanings; their listeners will. Reciters will be asked after the performance, however, which was their favorite word or phrase and what was hardest to remember.
- The next day in class, place students in MR pairs, ideally extroverts and introverts matched and theater aficionados and experts spread across pairings. If possible, partner with a student or join a pair to become a triad. Here are the jobs of listeners:
    - Listen to the recitation twice. Give any feedback if you have some for greater clarity and flow. For example, you can tell a partner to stress a particular word.
    - Research the meaning of the line together.
    - Now that you know meanings, advise your fellow performer on the following:
        - Which key words (nouns, verbs, adjectives) should you emphasize?
        - Which figurative language (metaphor, simile, personification) is a cue for you to emphasize a word or phrase? See the answer key for Handout 10. Figurative Language & Sound Devices Preassessment, Word Nerds, Part 1 in Chapter 4 (p. 53), for a full list of definitions.
        - Which sound devices (alliteration, internal rhyme, consonance, assonance, stresses in iambic pentameter, etc.) are cues for the speaker to emphasize a word or phrase? See the the same answer key for a full list of definitions.
    - Practice a few more times.
    - Ask one partner from each pair to perform. The rest of the class should give compliments on the emphasis and clarity achieved. Ask students about their favorite and most difficult parts of their lines.
    - See *Teaching* Julius Caesar: *A Differentiated Approach* (Hawks) for the Recitation Regulars assignment if you would like to repeat this activity throughout the unit.

Where Will You Land? Performance Activity of Act 1, Scene 1

There are many ways to teach students the importance of stresses and beats. *Macbeth* Lesson 4, "Is Execution Done on Cawdor" for act 1, scene 4 (O'Brien) is a great lesson in stress and inflection. In *Teaching* Romeo and Juliet: *A Differentiated Approach* (DeCourcy et al.), I and my coauthors offer a lesson called How Many Ways Can You Say Goodbye that uses stress and inflection to create a tone and various meanings and subtexts. Dakin shares wonderful activities in *Reading Shakespeare with Young Adults*; check out her chapter "HeartSpeak: A Tone Vocabulary," in which she has great insights keeping ELL students in mind and getting all students comfortable with emphasis.

- Offer a mini-lesson to teach how tone can be dramatically different depending on where emphasis lands, and to show students there are a lot of ways to read and play the characters in Shakespeare. You can do fun experimentation with Macbeth in the scene where we first meet him and Banquo. Ask students, How many ways can we play these men? Which are the most reasonable performances, based on the language?
- First practice with regular old English. Ask students to read aloud with you these lines (shared on a board or screen):
    - Person #1:
        - ***Who*** do you think you are?
        - Who ***do*** you think you are?
        - Who do ***you*** think you are?
        - Who do you ***think*** you are?
        - Who do you think ***you*** are?
        - Who do you think you ***are?***
    - Person #2:
        - ***I*** did not steal your cupcake.
        - I ***did*** not steal your cupcake.
        - I did ***not*** steal your cupcake.
        - I did not ***steal*** your cupcake.
        - I did not steal ***your*** cupcake.
        - I did not steal your ***cupcake.***
- Tell students their challenge will be to tell an intriguing story in two sentences. They will use volume, emphasis, pacing, pitch, and pronunciation to create different characters with different tones.
- Ask students to form pairs to present a scene, deciding their preferred emphasis on one of these sets of lines, and being ready

to explain why the emphasis is important to the backstory. They don't have to emphasize only one word; they can use multiple stresses.

- While three to four pairs present, call out the differences between performances in **volume, emphasis, pacing, pitch,** and **pronunciation**. Ask for more presentations till you see a demonstration of a few of these strategies. List these strategies for students.
- Tell students they will now do this activity with two lines from *Macbeth,* and in doing so, explore all the ways to play a character, as well as the mixed emotions that motivate a person. Cue cards, an activity in *Teaching* Julius Caesar (Hawks), is adapted here. You can give students tone words such as the following: Agitated, Aloof, Fearful, Compassionate, Depressed, Guilty, Jovial, Insistent, Irate, Loving, Paranoid, Solemn, Tyrannical, etc. They can work with partners to practice delivery with their assigned emotion. You can also use the emotions listed in Handout 15. Creative Writing: Soundscapes (lynhawks.com / extramacbeth).
- Students will perform these two lines, emphasizing one or more words:
    - Macbeth: "So foul and fair a day I have not seen." (act 1, scene 3, 36)
    - Banquo: "What are these / So wither'd and so wild in their attire . . . ?" (act 1, scene 3, 37–38)
    - After each pair presents, ask:
        - What is the key emotion being expressed? How did you know?
        - How did emphasis, pacing, volume, etc. contribute to this interpretation?
    - After at least four teams have presented, ask students which characterization seems most appropriate to Macbeth, and why they think so.
    - WCA: What do these opening lines from these men tell us about how things will go for them in the rest of the play? (If you are already several scenes or acts in, say, "How are these opening lines emblematic of these men's characters?")

Tomorrow and Tomorrow and Tomorrow: Meet the Saddest Person

You can introduce Macbeth's most famous speech long before he says it. There's a strong argument for having students study and perform it before you reach the end of the play. Students not only have an opportunity to creatively explore strong, relatable emotions—depression, nihilism, and ennui—but they can also see how Shakespeare's poetry handles these feelings, which could build a deeper connection with his work. By the time they see Patrick Stewart or Denzel Washington or Ian McKellen perform the soliloquy, they will be invested and also ready to listen in a different way.

- Ask students to write a brief poem that they will not have to share with the class, just with you. They can complete the following sentences as a prose poem, or write a poem with their own words, answering these three prompts:
    - *Depression is like* __________.
    - *Listlessness is like* __________.
    - *Pessimism is like* __________.
- Ask students to use their best powers of simile, extended metaphor, and other tools of figurative language to respond to these prompts.
- Tell students you are about to read the speech of a listless, depressed, pessimistic man. Ask students to close their eyes as you read. You might also play an audio recording of an actor, but refrain from any video. Explain to students that in an aural society such as Shakespeare's, listeners and theatergoers could take in a lot of imagery. As a playwright, you had to build worlds for listeners using the power of your voice. So when the stakes are high, one image isn't enough; Shakespeare gives us several (Fairchild).
- Read aloud or play audio for act 5, scene 5, 17–27.
- Ask students to silently annotate the text.
    - What line strikes you as effective for describing depression, pessimism, or listlessness? Highlight that.
    - How do figurative language and sound devices create a tone of sadness?
- WCA discussion:
    - Why are some people unmoved by death?
    - What is nihilism and its consequences?
    - Why should two murderers (the Macbeths) elicit our pity and concern?
    - What are triggers for suicide? How do we prevent them?
    - If you were to interview Shakespeare about what he really felt about depression and Macbeth's situation, what do you think he might say?
    - How does Shakespeare make depression sound both beautiful and horrible? How can you explain that paradox?
    - Macbeth sums up his misery thanks to Shakespeare's

beautiful words. But what about the depression of Lady Macbeth? Some critics says she's forgotten as a character because her death is but a tiny moment before Macbeth has his say. Yet we had premonitions of her problems in act 5, scene 1. Why do you think Macbeth missed Lady Macbeth's unwellness?

- If you didn't lead students through act 5, scene 1, consider returning to it with the Jigsaw CRs for Act 5, Scene 1 handout (lynhawks.com/extramacbeth). Ask students to rethink how they feel about Macbeth's woe in light of how he responded to the woe of his wife.
- If you are doing this activity toward the end of the unit, play film clips of the scene. Consider using the last minutes of the following video of Ian McKellen's 1979 performance. For a wonderful breakdown of what Shakespeare is doing, listen to Ian McKellen's analysis first before he performs: https://www.youtube.com/watch?v=zGbZCgHQ9m8. You will see resonance and important history and context in words such as *today, tomorrow,* and *yesterday,* as well as in *fool, out,* and *candle.* You can convert McKellen's insights into discussion questions to ask students about patterns and images. See if they can elicit these meanings themselves. Give students the historical context McKellen provides.

Final Projects

If you want to make theater production a big part of your unit and something all students attempt, ideally because you have an enthusiastic bunch of players in your class, consider giving the Production Skills and Interest Inventory I provide in my *Macbeth* unit in ASCD's *Differentiation in Practice: A Resource Guide for Differentiating Curriculum* (Tomlinson and Strickland).

Consider activities such as Shakespeare, Inc.: An Experiment in Theater and Finance, a detailed theater project offered in *Teaching* Romeo and Juliet (DeCourcy et al.), in which students present their proposal to produce the play on a certain budget. You can also assign scenelets, in which student groups take on the performance of brief excerpts of text or do video productions. In the years I've asked students to make films of a key scene, they have produced a tremendous range of creative interpretations, from a *Sopranos* spin to historically accurate renderings.

9 Close Readers, Translation, and Annotation

What You Will Find in This Chapter

- A rationale for CRs
- How to introduce and assess CRs
- TR and MR CRs

Why Use Close Readers?

What if students read, understand, and analyze a few words of Shakespeare well rather than skimming several words poorly or not at all? Close readers allow students to practice skills of translation, annotation, and literary analysis. CRs are more than handouts; they are the questions you pose to individuals and groups to get them investigating the text.

CRs can help students practice any of the skills noted under Reading in Chapter 1. In particular

- translation
- annotation
- text analysis for denotation, connotation, key words, figurative language, and meter
- evidence identification
- claim creation
- text analysis to interpret character, plot, setting, theme, tone, and style

CRs show you how your students comprehend reading passages, and they show you their powers of analysis, evaluation, and creation to make even deeper meaning. You can use flexible grouping structures to bring the best parts of many minds together as students solve the Shakespearean textual puzzle.

I offer a full tiered readiness (TR) CR with text included below and then offer tips on how you can create the core element, the questions, for other CRs you wish to develop.

Cryptography and Role-Play

Close readers are both cryptography and role-play when done well. This chapter offers TR CRs that ask students to "crack the code" of the Bard's language, while mixed readiness (MR) CRs invite students to take the role of a professional career such as psychologist, journalist, or diplomat.

> More than any work of literature in the secondary classroom, reading Shakespeare is what Louise Rosenblatt calls "a doing, a making, a combustion fed by the coming together" of particular readers with a particular text at a particular time (xvi). . . . [W]e must always be building a theatre in our minds, and to do that we must frequently interrupt ourselves to comment, question, clarify, connect, summarize, and predict.
>
> —Mary Ellen Dakin, *Reading Shakespeare with Young Adults* (122)

Consider using both CR types, whether cryptography or role-plays. Depending on your goals for students and depth of skill practice needed, you might give a few TR CRs in the first weeks and then switch to MR CRs, then back to TR CRs as needed. Vary groups and allow different interests, intelligences, and skill sets to shine.

Paper or Paperless?

Don't think of these as handouts as much as interchangeable, three-part activities that can be paper or paperless. The argument for paper would be for step 1 (see below), which is all about translation. Students can focus on the text without any distractions and work at the skills of decoding and making sense of words from context and provided definitions. Steps 2 and 3 of any CR might be easily moved to online spaces such as shared documents, electronic bulletin boards or galleries, or discussion boards.

How to Introduce and Use TR CRs

TR CRs are best presented as analytical small-group discussions completed prior to a larger WCA discussion. If used as independent homework or treated as independent worksheets, CRs will not have the same context or purpose. How should you introduce TR CRs to students? Try these strategies:

- Ask students if they've ever heard this phrase, "Read the fine print," and what it means to them. What might happen if we don't "read the fine print"? Explain how CRs teach the skill of close reading, crucial not only to standardized tests but also to multiple careers, never mind democratic citizenry.
- Preview the EQs and/or professional roles you plan to use for the CRs so that students know the relevance to them as individuals. For example, with the first sample CRs I provide, you might say: "You're about to meet some fascinating witches. Just how evil are these witches? What gives them their power?" Or you might discuss the nature of work done by psychologists, criminologists, or forensic scientists before inviting students to take on such roles.
- If using the TR CRs, explain that you will be using preassessment data as well as interest inventories to determine activities. Tell students that if anyone feels ready for more or less of a challenge, you invite them to approach you to discuss. Explain that there are also MR CRs and that you will change things up, so students will switch groups.
- Explain that when using CRs, there are these key steps:

Key Steps to a CR

- Step 1: Read Shakespeare's words and crack the code (translation tasks).
- Step 2: Interpret Shakespeare's words (annotation tasks, including paraphrase and summary).
- Step 3: Make meaning of these words (create something new—anchoring activities using interests and intelligences).
- Use Handout 34. Tips for Tackling Translation (lynhawks.com/extramacbeth) as you work.

- Explain that each TR CR group is doing critical thinking at the highest levels: evaluative, analytical, and creative work. Each group will report back to the whole class because you have given them different lenses through which to view the scene.
- There's no way to prevent students from using other sources and translations, whether in or out of class. So how do you introduce and explain the need for translation skills when anyone can hop over to No Fear Shakespeare? In what real-world context does translation matter?
    - Tell students that each CR contains an EQ and that EQs require students to think critically. Note how the Analyze and Evaluate questions on each CR require a student to

go back to the text, whether translated solo or with support. Remind them that a habit of carefully circling back to reread is needed for most serious things in life: reading prescription directions; buying a home, car, or anything expensive; or signing a contract. If they think the questions you're asking are easily Googleable, they are not. Students will have to reread and think.

- Explain that in order to play the role of psychologist, for example, you need to know the basic meaning of the text first. If you trust only the secondhand version of translation, and don't attempt to dig into what's on the page, you may not get wholly accurate information. In other words, psychoanalyze what Lady Macbeth is saying, not what someone else says she's saying. You might miss something rich. Tell students to keep these principles in mind:
    - *Every translation is an interpretation. It's not THE interpretation.*
    - *Study Shakespeare's actual words through your own lens and do research.*
    - *Use that information to fully play your role.*
    - *You still have to read the text to answer an Essential Question.*

- Set the scene. What historical context might be helpful, just a few bits of trivia, before students embark on a scene? For example, with the first TR CRs, you might ask students what they know about witches or ships in the 1600s. If they don't know anything—such as that many people believed in witches, or that sailors used compasses and star charts to navigate the seas—give them that information. See Handout 27. Historical Notes for Shakespeare's Day for further information (lynhawks.com/extramacbeth).

> [T]he small percentage of Shakespeare's archaic words is surrounded by recognizable, modern words; . . . [C]ontext clues and vocal inflection are natural tools for understanding them. ELL students survive this way, hungrily gleaning the page for sound and context clues. . . . Shakespeare is the great equalizer in the language arts classroom in that his text is new and strange to all of our students. Instead of skipping over "the hard stuff," we should encourage our students to embrace it.
>
> —Mary Ellen Dakin, *Reading Shakespeare with Young Adults* (18)

How to Use CRs

- For the best assessment of skill knowledge, use CRs only in class.
- When first introducing CRs, use groups often. Move to independent, timed CR work and individual CR assessment in the final weeks of the unit.
- The first time you introduce CRs, model work to be done with a mini-lesson that demonstrates how to translate three to four lines of *Macbeth*. See Handout 34. Tips for Tackling Translation (lynhawks.com/extramacbeth).
- Preview the different Evaluate and Create tasks each group will complete so students are excited. For example, you might introduce the first TR CRs below, Word Nerd, Word Sleuth, and Wordsmith handouts, What Can Witches Do? this way: "Today some of you get to measure just how evil these witches are. Meanwhile, some of you are going to figure out where witches get their power, aka their power source. And others will figure out how witches cast their spells with words."
- Talk about key words with your students. All students need to be familiar with how to hunt for these in any Shakespeare passage.

> *Key word:* An important conceptual word with resonant connotations and thematic possibilities. It might also be the root word of an Essential Understanding, Essential Question, or theme. Ask students: *Which words seem most important here? How do you know?* Start with key nouns and verbs, and then move to adjectives and adverbs.

- If time permits in your unit, use Dakin's Chapter 9 strategy in which she forms literature circles, called "companies," and teaches students a range of roles (*Reading Shakespeare with Young Adults*, pp. 102–32). This strategy is most helpful if you plan to use this reading strategy across multiple texts all year, for as Dakin says, this method takes time and training for students to develop skill.
- Previewing options of text before asking students to do a CR, including the following:
    - Read a scene aloud or listen to a recording. Giving students audio access before or during any CR activity is ideal.
    - Watch a film version of the scene first without trying to explain anything to students; then send them into groups to complete a CR.

- Share in class the Spark Notes graphic novel (https://www.sparknotes.com/shakespeare/macbeth/graphic-novel/) and have willing students come forward to narrate the voices as the class looks at pictures.
- Have students review the graphic novel for homework before starting CR work.

- After CR groups do their work, have different groups report in. When using TR groups, you will see their CRs are designed in such a way that every group's report is essential for the class to fully understand the scene.

You might try this lesson flow for a unit, spending one day a week on these various activities.

Day	Activities
Week 1	■ Kick off with independent reading book talks (5–10 min.) in which students share analyses of passages or pitches from thematically related books (if Terror is the day's topic, someone reading horror might be a great impromptu speaker). See Chapter 10, "Independent Reading," for more suggestions on how to create an investigative, celebratory culture around reading that extends to the reading of Shakespeare. ■ Hook students with the Socratic EQ (relevance questions) and allow journal and/or discussion time. ■ Ask students to start TR CR work in pairs and triads. Assign the TR CRs.
Week 1	■ Ask students to complete CR work in pairs and triads. ■ Report and discuss through WCAs, with all TR CRs reporting their findings.
Week 2	■ Hold independent reading book talks. ■ Do MR CRs around professional roles.
Week 2	■ Hold independent reading book talks. ■ Return to TR CRs in pairs (same as week 1). Assign TRs.
Week 3	■ Hold independent reading book talks. ■ Offer independent TR CRs in class, timed. Allow students to choose. Mark this as a key formative assessment for you to review.
Week 4	■ Hold independent reading book talks. ■ Do MR CRs around professional roles.
Weeks 5 on	■ Hold independent reading book talks. ■ Return to TR CRs in pairs; allow students to choose. ■ Do MR CRs around professional roles. ■ Offer independent TR CRs in class, timed. Allow students to choose. ■ Consider giving all class time for students who finish early to do independent reading and/or anchoring activities. ■ Give a summative CR assessment.

Tips for Tackling Translation

You can do a mini-lesson on text decoding. Remind students that this text is more than four hundred years old. It's why all of us need help, with at least a handout! Give students Handout 34. Tips for Tackling Translation (lynhawks.com/extramacbeth). Refer to it as you go through a text decoding exercise, modeling for students how you ask these questions of the text. Call for students to assist you as needed.

- You might do this lesson in two phases: fifteen minutes using strategies 1–5 on the text, and then another mini-lesson the next day to teach advanced strategies, 6–9. As students volunteer to help, or as you see what students say when called on, you'll get a sense of how hard this task might be for this group.
- This handout is structured by increasing levels of skill. As you model and discuss use of the strategies, point these layers out to students. Celebrate anyone who answers any level and celebrate students who move within and beyond their zone of proximal development to think at higher levels of Bloom's Taxonomy. I recommend you use act 1, scene 1, for its short lines and witches; if you've already done a fun hook too, students may be more engaged in the subject matter and willing to assist you.

How to Assess CRs

Give students full credit on CRs. CRs are formative skill practice and formative demonstrations of skill knowledge. Consider these readings and annotations as part of the writer's or reader's portfolio.

Make rounds of CRs focused on a few skill sets that you deliver over weeks. Round 1 is for observation; 2, for group trend analysis; and 3, for individual student analysis.

- Round 1: The first CRs you give should be formative in the fullest sense: low-stakes, authentic practice of translation, annotation, and literary analysis skills. Grab a few from the first student round of forays and review to see how different tiered groups are doing.
- Round 2: The second time you give CRs, collect all students' work and study the patterns and trends within each tier. What percentage of students are showing gaps in content or skill knowledge? For example, is there widespread confusion about the difference between a subject and a verb? Do too many students not understand how to provide evidence for a claim? Make some notes and observations about where students need mini-lessons or other types of support.

- Round 3 or 4: Ask students to complete CRs independently, and group student work by ELL-NOV (need a mini-lesson and practice); OT (need a little more practice); ADV (doesn't need practice; can do an anchoring or extension activity). Design WCA or tiered mini-lessons as needed to address any skill gaps while providing anchoring activities such as projects or independent reading to students already demonstrating mastery. As always, these should be flexible groupings. A student whom you thought might be ADV at making claims and finding motifs might actually need some remediation. You might witness an ELL student who has never spoken up in your class conversing animatedly in a group discussion about the nature of the Witches' evil, making a highly analytical claim. Keep your mind and eyes open to all possibilities for each student.

DYO CRs

Here are some guiding questions as you design your own CRs:

- *What passages intrigue me?* Pick passages of text you are excited about discussing. Students will feed off your excitement.
- *How much text will we use?* Make sure the text is short, under fifty lines, and preferably under twenty-five whenever you give individual CR work.
- *How will students annotate?* Decide whether you will do online annotation (on a Google doc, for example) or print handouts using highlighters and other writing tools.
- *How will students find definitions?* Will you provide definitions or have students look at a translation? I prefer to provide definitions so students stay with the text before them.
- *What questions will they answer?* Create Big Idea questions using tips from the DYO Questions section of Chapter 3 and also by using the strategies from Handout 34. Tips for Tackling Translation (lynhawks.com/extramacbeth). Make sure steps 2 and 3 ask students to use higher levels of Bloom's Taxonomy: analysis, evaluation, and creation. Root the EQ for the creation task in a Big Idea relevant to students.

Make sure the task or role is meaningful for each tier and the EQ is interesting. Students shouldn't be able to listen in on others' tasks and wonder why they're not getting to do something deep or creative.

TR Code-Cracking CRs

The following sample CRs, for use as TR activities in pairs or triads, ask students to translate, to annotate, and then to make meaning in some creative way. You will find one example of a same-scene CR and one example of a jigsaw CR.

You might want to use only a few questions off of my sample CRs. I give you more than you need for each; since there are so many Big Ideas and EQs, you could make these pages long!

> Word Nerds are ELL-NOV code crackers.
> Word Sleuths are OT code crackers.
> Wordsmiths are ADV code crackers.

Place students in pairs or triads to complete the work. Each TR pair is part of a larger group that can report back to the class. For example, in a class of thirty students, you might have five to ten ELL-NOV students in groups, the same for your five to fifteen OT students, and then two groups of five or fewer ADV students.

Each group must report back to the class to share their findings, jigsaw style, for the entire scene to be understood.

Each tiered CR has three parts:

Step 1. Crack the Code: translation tasks using one or more of strategies 1–4 on Handout 34. Tips for Tackling Translation (lynhawks.com/extramacbeth)—identifying parts of speech, summarizing via images or paraphrase, and creating images.

Step 2. Interpret the Code: annotation tasks, including paraphrase and summary, using one or more of strategies 6–9 on the handout.

Step 3. Expose the Code: anchoring creation activities using interests and intelligences, in which students create deeper meaning inspired by the text. These tasks are driven by EQs and other open-ended questions. See DYO Essential Questions in Chapter 3 to learn more about building your own. This step is also an opportunity to integrate digital tools and offer product options using materials or tools available to you.

For each set of CRs, you will find a set of class discussion questions to guide the WCA discussion and bring all parts together, eliciting wisdom from each group.

> Students enjoy creating images and layouts with digital tools. Note that the Create tasks in the Step 3: Expose the Code section (see pp. 163, 166, and 170) are a chance for students to be makers using these types of formats.

- How might the visual be an interactive or dynamic image using tools such as ThingLink or Canva, allowing students to add captions, icons, images, animation, and weblinks to an image?
- How might the visual use a well-designed template to build a poster, social media post, or pamphlet using tools such as Canva?

Digital tools are opportunities for engaging formative and summative assessment.

Same Scene CR Sample: Act 1, Scene 3, 1–35

A same-scene CR asks all students, no matter what the readiness levels, to read the same scene from different angles. ELL-NOV students may receive slightly fewer lines. Find Handouts 35, 36, and 37 on the following pages and at lynhawks.com / extramacbeth.

Handout 35. Word Nerds: What Can Witches Do? Act 1, Scene 3, Lines 1–28

Directions: Read the text as a group one time. Play the parts with witchy voices. Check the definitions below as you read. Complete steps 1–3 to crack this code of the Witches' evil.

Step 1: CRACK THE CODE	
The heath:* thunder. Enter the three Witches. *moorland, wilderness **First Witch:** Where hast* thou* been, sister? **have *you* Second Witch: Killing swine.* **pigs* **Third Witch:** Sister, where thou? **First Witch:** A sailor's wife had chestnuts in her lap And munch'd, and munch'd, and munch'd. 'Give me,' quoth* I. **said* 'Aroint* thee, witch', the rump-fed runnion* cries. **Get away *fat-bottomed woman* Her husband's to Aleppo* gone, master o'the'Tiger:* **Syrian trading city *ship name* But in a sieve* I'll thither* sail, **basket *there* And like a rat without a tail, I'll do,* I'll do, and I'll do. **have sex* **Second Witch:** I'll give thee* a wind. **you* First Witch: Thou'rt* kind. **you are* **Third Witch:** And I another. **First Witch:** I myself have all the other.* **other winds* And the very ports* they blow, **ports were supposed to be safer from winds* All the quarters* that they know **directions* I'th'* shipman's card.* **in the *card compass or chart used to direct ships* I'll drain him dry as hay: Sleep shall neither night nor day Hang upon his penthouse lid;* **eyelid* He shall live a man forbid.* **cursed* Weary sennights* nine times nine, **weeks (short for seven nights)* Shall he dwindle,* peak,* and pine. **diminish in strength, size, or amount *waste away*	**Translation:** ■ Find 1 full sentence and mark the subject with a circle and the verb with a box. ■ Highlight all the words that rhyme. ■ What are three things the Witches do to people? ■ What do you think the underlined sentence means? Find synonyms and translate into your own words. ■ Draw one key image from this passage and be ready to explain it to the class. Challenge: make that image a symbol—a thing (living or not) that best represents the Witches. Label the image to explain why this is a good image for the Witches. **Our Answers:** *continued on next page*

Though his bark* cannot be lost, **ship* Yet it shall be tempest*-toss'd. **storm* Look what I have. **Second Witch** Show me, show me. **First Witch** Here I have a pilot's thumb, Wreck'd as homeward he did come.	

OUR IMAGE	

Step 2: INTERPRET THE CODE	
▪ ANALYZE: Why does the First Witch go after the "rump-fed runnion"? How does she get revenge on her? ▪ ANALYZE: Find three or four key words that are related to the Big Idea of Evil. Explain how these words connect to Evil. ▪ ANALYZE: How is the Witches' magic evil? ▪ EVALUATE: Which magic seems most evil, and why? What's the worst thing they can do? Why?	
OUR ANSWER:	ANALYSIS of Why and How of Revenge: EVALUATION: Most Evil Magic: Because:

continued on next page

<table>
<tr><th colspan="2">Step 3: EXPOSE THE CODE</th></tr>
<tr><td>EVALUATE in a group discussion:</td><td>
■ What if Shakespeare is warning Macbeth—or us—what to look for in a witch? Who or what in this play should watch their back around a witch? Why?
■ How evil are these Witches? Discuss on a scale of 1–10, 10 being "Most Evil" and 1 being "A Tiny Bit Evil." Be ready to explain your reasoning with examples from the text.
• If you have a better way to measure evil (such as a thermometer, or a weight scale—whatever way you would like to measure), use that instead.

Write your notes below.</td></tr>
</table>

CREATE your answer to the above questions using:

- a visual image of the scale of the Witches' evil (you might use images from the text), or
- a warning poem/rap/song about the scale of the Witches' evil. A scale can be numeric, as in a 1–5 or 1–10, or it might be like a thermometer, or a weight scale—whatever way you would like to measure evil.

Address your message to characters in the play, including Macbeth.

Brainstorming:

Handout 36: Word Sleuths: These Weird Sisters. Act 1, Scene 3, Lines 1–35

Directions: Read the text as a group one time. Play the parts with witchy and sisterly voices, as if these three are somehow related. Check definitions as you read. Complete steps 1–3 to crack this code of the Witches' relationship to one another and understand the depth of their powers.

Step 1: CRACK THE CODE	
The heath:* thunder. Enter the three Witches. *moorland, wilderness **First Witch:** Where hast* thou* been, sister? **have *you* **Second Witch:** Killing swine.* **pigs* **Third Witch:** Sister, where thou? **First Witch:** A sailor's wife had chestnuts in her lap And munch'd, and munch'd, and munch'd. 'Give me,' quoth* I. **said* 'Aroint* thee, witch', the rump-fed runnion* cries. **Get away *fat-bottomed woman* Her husband's to Aleppo* gone, master o'the'Tiger:* **Syrian trading city *ship name* But in a sieve* I'll thither* sail, **basket *there* And like a rat without a tail, I'll do,* I'll do, and I'll do. **have sex* **Second Witch:** I'll give thee* a wind. **you* **First Witch:** Thou'rt* kind. **you are* **Third Witch:** And I another. **First Witch:** I myself have all the other.* **other winds* And the very ports* they blow, **ports were supposed to be safer from winds* All the quarters* that they know **directions* I'th'* shipman's card.* **in the *card compass or chart used to direct ships* I'll drain him dry as hay: Sleep shall neither night nor day Hang upon his penthouse lid;* **eyelid* He shall live a man forbid.* **cursed*	**Translation:** ■ Find two key words that are related to Loyalty. Highlight them. ■ Find two key words that are related to Magic or the Supernatural. Star them. ■ Find two pieces of evidence that the Witches help each other or work together. ■ Underline all sections where you think the Witches are showing a kind of connection, symmetry, or unity. How do you know the Witches are "on the same page"? ■ Circle places where you see evidence of the Witches interacting with the rest of the world. **Our Answers:** *continued on next page*

Weary sennights* nine times nine, **weeks (short for seven nights)* Shall he dwindle,* peak,* and pine. **diminish in strength, size, or amount *waste away* Though his bark* cannot be lost, **ship* Yet it shall be tempest*-toss'd. **storm* Look what I have. **Second Witch** Show me, show me. **First Witch** Here I have a pilot's thumb, Wreck'd as homeward he did come. *Drum within* **Third Witch** A drum, a drum; Macbeth doth* come. **does* **All** The weird* sisters, hand in hand, **mystic, fateful, supernatural* Posters* of the sea and land, **travellers* Thus do go, about, about, Thrice* to thine,* and thrice to mine, **three times *yours* And thrice again, to make up nine. Peace,* the charm's wound up. **be still, be silent, be calm*	

Step 2: INTERPRET THE CODE

ANALYZE:
- Dissect: How do the Witches help each other? How does their power depend on each other?
- Categorize: What are the Witches able to do? What types of power do the Witches hold?

OUR ANSWERS:	

Step 3: EXPOSE THE CODE	
ANALYZE in a group discussion:	■ How do the Witches' spells work? What can their spells do? ■ The Witches have their own special math. According to Shakespeare Online, "The numbers seven and nine were mystical to almost every civilization in history, but nine is particularly important to the forces of evil. The Witches, followers of Satan, would delight in inverting and reversing numbers and symbols, and 9 would invert to 6. Three sixes are, of course, the number of the beast." How do the Witches use numbers to cast their spells?
OUR ANSWER:	

CREATE your answer to the above questions using:

- a visual image or poem/rap of the way the Witches' spells work, using symbols from the text, or
- a visual image or poem/rap of the way the Witches relate to one another, using symbols from the text

Address your message as a how-to manual to instruct other witches or to help people spot a witch.

Brainstorming:

Handout 37. Wordsmiths: These Witches Have a Way with Words. Act 1, Scene 3, Lines 1–35

Directions: Read the text as a group one time. Play the parts with ominous and conniving voices, as if these three are weaving a trap. Check definitions as you read. Complete steps 1–3 to crack this code of the Witches' magic and understand how they harness language to cast spells.

<table>
<tr><th colspan="2">Step 1: CRACK THE CODE</th></tr>
<tr><td rowspan="3">The heath:* thunder. Enter the three Witches.
*moorland, wilderness

First Witch:
Where hast* thou* been, sister? *have
*you
Second Witch:
Killing swine*. *pigs
Third Witch:
Sister, where thou?
First Witch:
A sailor's wife had chestnuts in her lap
And munch'd, and munch'd, and munch'd.
'Give me,' quoth* I. *said
'Aroint* thee, witch,' the rump-fed runnion* cries. *Get away *fat-bottomed woman
Her husband's to Aleppo* gone, master o'the'Tiger:* *Syrian trading city *ship name
But in a sieve* I'll thither* sail, *basket *there
And like a rat without a tail,
I'll do,* I'll do, and I'll do. *have sex
Second Witch:
I'll give thee* a wind. *you
First Witch:
Thou'rt* kind. *you are
Third Witch:
And I another.
First Witch:
I myself have all the other.* *other winds
And the very ports* they blow, *ports were supposed to be safer from winds
All the quarters* that they know *directions
I'th'* shipman's card.* *in the *card compass or chart used to direct ships
I'll drain him dry as hay:
Sleep shall neither night nor day
Hang upon his penthouse lid;* *eyelid
He shall live a man forbid.* *cursed</td>
<td>Translation:
■ Find two key words that are related to Magic or the Supernatural. Star them.
■ Find two key words that are related to curses, as those curses relate to creating any of these Big Ideas: Chaos, Fear, Terror, or Violence. Highlight them.
■ Find evidence that the Witches are casting some sort of spell. Circle the elements of the spell.
■ List the order, method, and ingredients necessary for spell casting (steps, rules, and/or parts).
■ Count the number of beats per line. Where does the emphasis fall? Put slash marks above the places (syllables or words) where you think the stresses should be.
■ Mark all the rhyming couplets; in the same color, highlight all end words that rhyme.
■ Find any shared or split lines where half a line (five stresses) is one Witch's and the other half (five stresses) is the other's. Link these with arrows.</td></tr>
<tr><td>Our Answers:</td></tr>
<tr><td></td></tr>
</table>

Weary sennights* nine times nine, **weeks (short for seven nights)* Shall he dwindle,* peak,* and pine. **diminish in strength, size, or amount *waste away* Though his bark* cannot be lost, **ship* Yet it shall be tempest*-toss'd. **storm* Look what I have. **Second Witch** Show me, show me. **First Witch** Here I have a pilot's thumb, Wreck'd as homeward he did come. *Drum within* **Third Witch** A drum, a drum; Macbeth doth* come. **does* **All** The weird* sisters, hand in hand, **mystic, fateful, supernatural* Posters* of the sea and land, **travelers* Thus do go, about, about, Thrice* to thine,* and thrice to mine, **three times *yours* And thrice again, to make up nine. Peace,* the charm's wound up. **be still, be silent, be calm*	*continued on next page*

<table>
<tr><th colspan="2">Step 2: INTERPRET THE CODE</th></tr>
<tr><td colspan="2">ANALYZE:
■ Dissect: Shared or split lines are a feature of the Witches' speech, also known as hemistichomythia. What do the Witches discuss when splitting lines?
■ Dissect: Rhyming couplets tend to appear when people are "leaving and loving" in Shakespeare plays, typically at the end of scenes, or between romantic couples, or for manipulations (Morris). Assuming the Witches aren't in the process of leaving just yet, and they're not really in love with anyone we can see, that leaves us with manipulation. Find rhyming words and re-see them through the lens of Manipulation. What might be manipulative about these rhyming words?
■ Dissect: The Witches' speeches follow a rhythm called trochaic tetrameter, which consists of stressed syllables followed by unstressed, and only four beats per line. Meanwhile, other characters in Macbeth speak in iambic pentameter, which is five stressed syllables per line (ten total), alternating stressed and unstressed. Return to some of the Witches' lines and reread, making sure your stresses hit on the first syllable of words.
• Example: A sáilor's wífe had chéstnuts ín her láp
■ Cause and Effect:
• Now discuss the impact of stressing the first syllable. How does that change the delivery? What words are now key words?
• How would you categorize the mood created by this type of rhythm? Use descriptive words that relate to tone, feeling, and emotion.</td></tr>
<tr><td>OUR ANSWERS:</td><td></td></tr>
</table>

Step 3: EXPOSE THE CODE	
ANALYZE in a group discussion:	▪ Why would Shakespeare split or share the Witches' lines? Devise a theory, make a claim, and prove it using the text. ▪ Why would Shakespeare emphasize certain words through rhyming couplets? ▪ Why would Shakespeare emphasize certain syllables through trochaic tetrameter?
OUR ANSWER:	
ANALYZE: How do these sound devices give these Witches Power, Magic, or some other Big Idea?	
CREATE your answer to the above question using: • a visual image of the Witches' language, using symbols to teach the different sound devices you have learned, or • a poem that explains and dissects the Witches' power (methods, sources, etc.) using devices such as split lines, rhyming couplets, and trochaic tetrameter. Write this poem to an audience of other witches who need to learn the proper way to create incantations. *Brainstorming:*	

WCA Discussion on CRs for Act 1, Scene 3, Lines 1–35

Here is a range of questions all groups or TR groups can answer after tiered groups have done their CR work.

Preview for students: "Now that you have studied this scene in depth, we are going to discuss the nature of Evil, Power, Magic, and other Big Ideas. Some of you will tell us just how evil these Witches are, while others will tell us the source of the Witches' power, and others yet will tell us how witches cast spells with their words."

- Key Words from All Tiers:
  - Let's hear the key nouns and verbs you found. Give me a one sentence explanation sharing why you think the noun or verb is "key."
  - If you are building word families with students, take a moment to generate synonyms for Big Ideas on a poster or electronic bulletin board such as Padlet. Word clouds and mind maps can build throughout the unit and be useful to students when they need a range of synonyms for their summative writing.

ANSWER KEY	■ Key words: any nouns with powerful connotations that might associate those words with the Big Ideas, such as *sister* (Womanhood) or *wind* (Nature), and any verbs, such as *dwindle, peak,* and *pine* (Cruelty, Failure, Loss). If a connection can reasonably be made between the textual evidence and a Big Idea, let students make the argument and speculate at this stage. ■ If you can make word clouds and mind maps with multiple synonyms for each Big Idea, and keep those posted on physical or electronic spaces, students will generate rich language for later writing.

- Word Nerds [ELL-NOV]: Raise your hand if you had to analyze the Witches' magic and depth of their evil.
  - Tell us: Who or what in this play should watch their back around a witch? Why? Tell us how evil they are using evidence from the text.
  - How evil are these Witches? Share your creative rendering of your evaluation with us.

ANSWER KEY	■ Rump-fed runnions, married women, sailors, and swine ■ The Witches seem to be able to hurt people but not kill them. They can drain energy from people and wreck ships and steal husbands. Powered by revenge and vindictiveness, they can create tremendous chaos. Let students reason out how evil this might be, and use standards of reasoning to argue which constitutes the worst evil. As with all answers, and no matter which readiness level, be sure to ask students how they know their answer to be true and what in the text supports their interpretation.

- Word Sleuths [OT]: Raise your hand if you had to analyze the Witches' relationships as three sisters and how much power they have.
  - Tell us the nature of that relationship using the evidence from the text.
  - Show us about the depth of the Witches' power and what numbers mean to them.
  - How do the Witches' spells work and how do these Witches work together? Share your creative explanation with us.
  - ANALYZE (Compare): How do the Witches relate to other people, as compared to each other? How do you know?
  - SPECULATE: What might these Witches be able to accomplish together or apart?
  - EVALUATE: If the Witches are one way with each other and another way with others, are they Good or Evil . . . or something else? Find another adjective for them if you like.

ANSWER KEY	■ The Witches are quite supportive, supplying each other tools they need, such as wind. They call each other "sister" and they work "hand in hand."

- Wordsmiths [ADV]: Raise your hand if you had to analyze the Witches' language.
  - Teach us about trochaic tetrameter, rhyming couplets, and split lines, and tell us why these matter.
  - Tell us about the mood or feeling when the Witches talk.
  - Some critics have called them an "unholy trinity." Use the evidence you found to agree, disagree, and/or elaborate on this statement. (Atherton)

ANSWER KEY	■ The mood is trancelike, incantatory, and ominous. Something wicked this way comes. . . .

Jigsaw CRs

Jigsaw TR CRs break up a scene into multiple parts and hand them to students of different readiness levels, so reporting back from all groups is crucial for understanding the entire scene. There is more weight to each TR group's role since not everyone has read the same passages closely.

Note how Big Ideas differ across the following three CRs as each TR group takes a different thematic lens to study the scene. Imagine as the students return to the WCA that they are building a patchwork quilt of interpretation of Shakespeare's multifaceted, multithemed characters and their actions. His work is chameleon and kaleidoscopic, allowing many students to approach it.

You can show a cinematic scene or play audio of a scene while everyone reads it together before moving students into TR CR groups.

Here are suggested questions and activities for act 1, scene 3, lines 102–42:

<table>
<tr><th colspan="2">Word Nerds: But These Robes Are Borrowed!</th></tr>
<tr><td colspan="2">Text: Act 1, Scene 3, Lines 102–15</td></tr>
<tr><td colspan="2">Story Action: Macbeth and Banquo just met the Witches, who make big predictions about the men's futures: that Macbeth will become Thane of Cawdor, and that Banquo's children will be kings. Then Ross and Angus arrive with thanks from King Duncan for Macbeth's courage in battle and share exciting news: Macbeth is now promoted to Thane of Cawdor.</td></tr>
<tr><td colspan="2">Big Ideas: Loyalty, Victory, Loss, Evil</td></tr>
<tr><td>Step 1: Crack the Code</td><td>■ Find the sentence where Ross gives Macbeth a gift (honor) from the King. What is the gift?
■ Find 1 full sentence and mark the subject with a circle and the verb with a box.
■ Find two reasons in the text the Thane of Cawdor is guilty of "treasons capital." (Look up the word treason.)
■ Draw one key image from this passage and be ready to explain it to the class.</td></tr>
<tr><td>Step 2: Interpret the Code</td><td>■ ANALYZE: Why does Banquo mention the "devil" and "truth"? What is he remembering?
■ ANALYZE: Why doesn't Macbeth want to accept the gift at first? Why does he use the phrase "borrowed robes"?</td></tr>
<tr><td>Step 3: Expose the Code</td><td>■ ANALYZE: There's a winner and a loser here in this passage. Find evidence to prove there's a winner and a loser.
• Challenge: Make a claim about this part of the story, answering this question: How does this scene show us a moment of VICTORY and LOSS in the play?
■ EVALUATE in a group discussion: You are a headhunter, also known as a job recruiter. You try to find the right people for jobs. Counsel him: Should Macbeth take the job? Is there any reason Macbeth should look twice before accepting?
• Create a text message, meme, or some other message that only Macbeth can see and use emojis and words to ask him questions and give him advice regarding this job.</td></tr>
</table>

<table>
<tr><th colspan="2">Word Sleuths: Might I Murder?</th></tr>
<tr><td colspan="2">Text: Act 1, Scene 3, Lines 116–41</td></tr>
<tr><td colspan="2">Story Action: Macbeth and Banquo just met the Witches, who make big predictions about the men's futures: that Macbeth will become Thane of Cawdor and that Banquo's children will be kings. Then Ross and Angus arrive with thanks from King Duncan for Macbeth's courage in battle and share exciting news of a promotion: Macbeth, who was Thane of Glamis, is now Thane of Cawdor. Macbeth and Banquo discuss the prophecy and whether to believe it. Macbeth weighs how to handle this "supernatural soliciting."</td></tr>
<tr><td colspan="2">Big Ideas: Imagination, Delusion, Ambition, Evil, Victory, Loss</td></tr>
<tr><td>Step 1: Crack the Code</td><td>■ Find two keywords in Macbeth's lines in this passage proving that Macbeth believes the Witches' prophecies. Circle them.
■ But Banquo says the Witches might be "instruments of darkness" by possibly doing what to them?
■ Where else have you seen the Witches act like "instruments of darkness"? Find evidence from another passage in the play. Draw that image.</td></tr>
<tr><td>Step 2: Interpret the Code</td><td>■ ANALYZE: Macbeth says something "aside" so only the audience can hear. What is it, and why might it matter that he says it aside?
■ ANALYZE: Can you tell anything about Macbeth and Banquo's relationship here? What types of information do they share with each other—and what types do they not?
■ ANALYZE: Iambic pentameter is ten beats per line, unstressed and then a stressed syllable. Read lines 130–41 and hit all stressed syllables.
• Mark the lines where there are more or fewer than ten beats or lines.
• Mark the lines where it's hard to stress every second syllable and it gets awkward to do so.
• Challenge: Why might Shakespeare be breaking the rhythm in these lines?</td></tr>
<tr><td>Step 3: Expose the Code</td><td>Evaluate in a group discussion: Is the devil or Macbeth's imagination persuading Macbeth to murder? Who or what is tempting Macbeth toward murder?
■ You are Macbeth's spiritual counselor or psychologist. He's tormented with strange thoughts and needs some help. Talk about his moral and spiritual side with him and help him see where these messages are coming from.
■ Create a visual map of all the forces influencing him right now so you can explain it to him in session.</td></tr>
</table>

<table>
<tr><th colspan="2">Wordsmiths</th></tr>
<tr><td colspan="2">Text: Act 1, Scene 3, Lines 116–58</td></tr>
<tr><td colspan="2">Story Action: Macbeth and Banquo just met the Witches, who make big predictions about the men's futures: that Macbeth will become Thane of Cawdor and that Banquo's children will be kings. Then Ross and Angus arrive with thanks from King Duncan for Macbeth's courage in battle and share exciting news of a promotion: Macbeth, who was Thane of Glamis, is now Thane of Cawdor. Macbeth and Banquo discuss the prophecy and whether to believe it. Macbeth weighs how to handle this "supernatural soliciting."</td></tr>
<tr><td colspan="2">Big Ideas: Imagination, Delusion, Ambition, Evil, Prophecy, the Supernatural, Power, Appearance, Victory, Loss</td></tr>
<tr><td>Step 1: Crack the Code</td><td>■ Find keywords related to Big Ideas, such as Evil, the Supernatural, Power, Imagination, and/or Appearance.
■ Macbeth gives reasons to see the Witches' prophecies two ways: either "good" or "ill." List the reasons for both views.
■ What's the strongest visual image? What figurative language there makes it so visual? Draw it and caption it with the language.</td></tr>
<tr><td>Step 2: Interpret the Code</td><td>■ ANALYZE: Compare Banquo's and Macbeth's reactions to the Witches' prophecies. Who is acting most rationally, and how do you know?
■ ANALYZE: Macbeth himself says he is experiencing "horrible imaginings." What do you speculate might be running through his head?
■ ANALYZE: Note the two faces of Macbeth—in his private thoughts and then in his speech to Banquo, Ross, and Angus. Identify the differences.</td></tr>
<tr><td>Step 3: Expose the Code</td><td>Evaluate in a group discussion: Should Macbeth sit still or take action, based on what he's heard so far?
■ You are Macbeth's life coach. You want him to walk away with a couple of go-to sayings or mantras from your counseling. Make a life coach set of memes for Macbeth based on all you know so far of his situation.
■ Keep in mind what you know of Macbeth's character already and make sure you are giving him the best coaching for his situation and his character and personality.
■ Write Macbeth's résumé and try to match him to new jobs. Try to help him find another avenue in life.</td></tr>
</table>

WCA for Act 1, Scene 3, Lines 102–42

- Word Nerds [ELL- NOV]: Let's hear from the headhunters (job recruiters). (Historical context: You couldn't refuse a gift from the king, but let's say you could.). Should Macbeth take the job? Is there any reason Macbeth should look twice before accepting?

- Word Sleuths [OT]: Let's hear from the spiritual counselors or psychologists. Is the devil or his imagination persuading Macbeth to murder? Who or what is tempting Macbeth toward murder? Have the Witches shown the power or potential to make him do it?
- Wordsmiths [ADV]: Let's hear from the life coaches. Should Macbeth sit still or take action, based on what he's heard? Why or why not? Use evidence to explain your claim. What in his résumé might make him a better fit for another career?
- All students: ANALYZE & EVALUATE: (Dissect) How close are Banquo and Macbeth? How do you know?
- All students: ANALYZE: (Speculate) Do you think the shoe (borrowed robes) will eventually fit? In other words, will Macbeth be a good Thane of Cawdor? How do you know?
- All students: ANALYZE: (Cause and Effect) What seems to be Macbeth's primary motivation to be king?
- All students: ANALYZE: (Dissect) What mood do you see in the figurative language Macbeth uses (metaphors) or the adjectives he uses?
- All students: EVALUATE: How fair or foul is this situation?

Handout 51. Jigsaw CRs for Act 3, Scene 4, Lines 1–123: A Banquet Gone Bad

In this set of CRs, ones for act 3, I've also added Big Ideas and motifs to consider while asking all students to consider which Big Ideas drive the scene. There is no one right answer, of course. As noted in the party planner role, there are a range of "vibes"!

TR CRs are always works in progress. I provide you more material than you need. Select a few questions you are ready to supervise, and feel free to mix and match across tiers. For a shorter CR lesson, you might take any of the step 3 Expose the Code steps and offer them as WCA final activities (student choice) or as homework.

Or you might remove step 3 entirely from all CRs and frame this lesson through the lens of a party planner or ghost hunter who is trying to gain control of the situation, or through the lens of a horror filmmaker trying to make the audience feel what Macbeth feels. Have TR groups complete steps 1 and 2 and report back in a WCA, and then ask students to write for five minutes at the end of class an exit ticket: it could be an apology for not being able to handle the situation better, or it could be a list of the filmmaker's best ideas for "gory lock"-d ghost special effects.

More CRs

Head to lynhawks.com / extramacbeth for these jigsaw CRs and follow-up WCA questions:

- Handout 51. A Banquet Gone Bad. Act 3, Scene 4, 38–123
- Handout 52. Get That Spot Out, Now! Act 5, Scene 2, 1–85.

> When the ghost of Banquo seats itself at that dreadful supper, who sees it? Not the company. Not even Lady Macbeth. Those who see it are Macbeth and you and I. Those into whom it strikes terror are Macbeth and you and I. Those whom it accuses are Macbeth and you and I. And what it accuses is what, of Macbeth, you and I are hiding in our own breasts.
>
> —Sir Arthur Quiller-Couch, "The Capital Difficulty of Macbeth," qtd. in Lerner

Professional Role CRs

In their book *Making Curriculum Pop: Developing Literacies in All Content Areas*, Pam and Ryan R. Goble offer Learning Experience Organizers (LEOs) as part of their differentiated, constructivist, and problem-based learning approach. This inspirational guide is worth the investment if you would like to expand this approach with both CRs and projects in your classroom. You might bring in roles such as Gamer, Data Analyst, Rhetorician, Predictor, Numerist, and Truthiness Detector, taking my suggestions that follow even further.

Below I have adapted the Gobles' approach within my suggested CRs, expanding the list of career roles that students can take on to plumb the text for evidence and gray areas using that lens. Students will provide evidence and elaboration and / or digital tool products. The goal is always close reading of text.

- **Option #1: Welcome to the Film Crew.** Students take on the roles of a film crew and use a specific professional lens to analyze one or more cinematic interpretations of *Macbeth*. See Chapter 7 and the Handout 29. Welcome to the Film Crew! assignment (lynhawks.com / extramacbeth). Students use an EQ guiding question to find text and cinematic evidence to make a thematic statement. Note in these sample questions for the Director what is required when it comes to close reading, rendered in italics:
  - **DIRECTOR:** How does the director's vision—choice of time period, direction of the actors, choice of shots, and

specific scene actions—answer our EQ or SQ? *What in the text might have inspired this choice?* How would I do it differently?

- If students suggest another choice, which lines influenced their choice, and why?
- Students' ideas can be shared on a physical bulletin board or an electronic bulletin board such as a Padlet. Task: *Submit one or more lines from the scene that justify your choice to handle your cinematic element differently. Elaborate on this evidence to explain how you would change the cinematic element based on diction, rhythm, figurative language, or other aspect of Shakespeare's writing.*

■ **Option #2. I'm Here to Help.** When leading students through key scenes (see Chapter 6), you can create a Help Wanted competition that lets students investigate text through the lens of professional roles. See Handout 38. How Can I Help? (lynhawks .com/extramacbeth) to select tasks that match students' needs and interests.

- You might kick off the activity with a simulation prompt: "Who can help these tragedy-plagued characters? You can! Fortunately, we have resident experts, such as a Criminologist, a Psychologist, a Journalist, etc." Pick four or five roles for students to try per lesson, or as many as you feel comfortable monitoring. Tell students the EQ they will be answering is *How might your expertise be of use here?* Tell students, "Think about how you can help these characters. Find the parts of the text where you might have an opinion or help to give."
- Give the time and rules of the competition: twenty minutes career research, twenty minutes text research, then outlining as a group. By the end of class, each group must create a rough outline. The visual product can be completed in the next class period.
- Form game teams of pairs or triads in which students research the role—find three job responsibilities and three skills this career requires, read assigned text through that lens of choice, and report back to the class.
- Give students a few reputable career sites, such as Linked In, Glassdoor, CareerBuilder, Indeed, etc.) and also point them to university websites and/or your school's career center materials.
- Product: Each student group must create a digital product or a physical poster outline with two to three pieces of evidence from the text (paraphrases and quotes), plus elaborations that prove the career role has something to

observe, advise, assist with, or remedy in this scene. Students must also generate role questions they would ask characters at the scene. Consider tools such as ThingLink, Canva, Padlet, or Venngage, or use poster paper and markers.

- Next is a list of suggested roles suitable to *Macbeth* as well as some suggested scene pairings that you might ask students to review and render an expert opinion on.
- Note: Journalists work for every scene. Why? Because they are the ultimate gadflies, asking the questions that demand full disclosure, truth, and no equivocation. You might assign Journalists, Paparazzi, and Propagandists all working the same scene, then discuss how these roles differ.
- Consider creating a posted public list (physical or virtual document) where student groups continue to add job responsibilities and skill sets throughout the unit. New student groups tackling roles may deliver new insights. Take student suggestions and add other careers to this list too.
- Consider a shorter version of this activity, such as for act 1, scene 6, where you might need only three roles: an Ornithologist, a Party Planner, and a Forensic Psychophysiologist (polygraph examiner). In this scene, students can analyze birds, since every bird matters to the Bard; we watch Lady Macbeth equivocate, so why not have her submit to a polygraph; and two murderers host a party, so there's an interesting vendor contract! Give students limited time to do career research and hand them reputable sites; require them to accurately paraphrase, practicing rules of academic honesty; and then tell them to put on their role hats. What are the habits of these birds, how do polygraphs work, and what's the most distracting type of party games and favors if you're plotting a murder? Coach students to apply their newfound knowledge to the scene.

■ **Option #3: DYO.** Study scenes and brainstorm your own roles. What roles can you create for students that match their needs and interests? See the list of roles below and add to it as you see fit, or maybe enlist student help. Check out Chapters 5 and 6, as well as the projects recommendations (Handout 44) at lynhawks.com/extramacbeth, for more ideas and matches. For scenes such as the ones with the Witches and Hecate (act 3, scene 5), it might be fun to have a spiritualist/psychic grill the Witches, or a detective seek information from them. However you use professional roles, make sure to have fun!

- What if the Naturalist used the Elizabethan concepts of

natural and unnatural to identify environmentally sound and unsound practices? What if the Naturalist used herbal guides and remedies for characters, firmly set in the seventeenth century? What if this Naturalist is also an ecologist who wants to warn characters about the environmentally unsound practices of the time?

- What if the Meteorologist created weather reports to match the mood, tone, and season of certain scenes?
- What if the Chief of Staff brings Macbeth sample policy scenarios (Bay of Pigs, Pearl Harbor, Iraq War, or other domestic and foreign policy scenarios from history) as advice to get Macbeth to handle his rule differently?
- What if you make up new roles? Could there be a Poet in Charge of Special Effects, an author role to point out all the pyrotechnics of figurative language in each scene, since it was the special effects of the day?

<table>
<tr><th colspan="2">Roles</th></tr>
<tr><td>Body Linguist
Career Coach
Chief of Staff
Coroner
Crime Scene Investigator
Criminologist
Detective
Diplomat
Forensics Expert
Forensic Psychophysiologist (polygraph examiner)
General/Battle Strategist
Ghost Hunter
Grief Counselor
Journalist
Leadership Consultant/Management Consultant
Marriage Counselor
Mediator
Messenger</td><td>Meteorologist
Naturalist
Nurse
Ornithologist
Paparazzi
Party Planner
Personal Assistant (maidservant back in the day)
Personal Security Guard
Physician
Probation Officer
Propagandist
Psychologist
Psychiatrist
Recruiter
Server
Soldier
Spiritualist/Psychic
Sports Commentator
Substance Abuse Counselor
Surgeon</td></tr>
</table>

For jigsaw CRs for act 5, use Handout 52. Jigsaw CRs for Act 5, Scene 1, Lines 1–85: Get That Spot Out, Now! at lynhawks.com/extramacbeth.

Act, Scene	**Help Wanted:** *How might your expertise be of use here? How can you help these characters? Find the text where you might have an opinion or help to give.*
act 1, scene 2	Chief of Staff General/Battle Strategist Leadership Consultant Nurse Surgeon Journalist Diplomat
act 1, scene 3	Spiritualist/Psychic Career Coach Psychologist Journalist
act 1, scene 4	
act 1, scene 5	
act 1, scene 6	Ornithologist Forensic Psychophysiologist Party Planner Journalist Paparazzi Propagandist
act 1, scene 7	
act 2, scene 1	
act 2, scene 2	

act 2, scene 3	Body Linguist Career Coach Coroner Forensic Scientist Detective Grief Counselor Personal Security Guard Substance Abuse Counselor Journalist Propagandist Paparazzi
act 2, scene 4	
act 3, scene 1	Probation Officer Career Counselor Coroner Criminologist Detective Psychiatrist
act 3, scene 2	
act 3, scene 3	
act 3, scene 4	Marriage Counselor Party Planner Psychiatrist Server Spiritualist/Psychic
act 3, scene 5	
act 3, scene 6	

act 4, scene 1	
act 4, scene 2 act 4, scene 3	 Diplomat Recruiter
act 5, scene 1	Physician (sleep disorders) Psychiatrist Personal Assistant
act 5, scenes 2–7	General/Battle Strategist Leadership Consultant Chief of Staff Psychiatrist Soldier

10 Independent Reading

What You Will Find in This Chapter

- A rationale for integrating independent reading activities
- Independent reading titles that match Big Ideas in *Macbeth*
- How to introduce independent reading
- Assignment and project ideas
- Lesson ideas for independent reading texts

Why Independent Reading?

What if all our students wanted to do their reading homework? That's what an independent reading plan strives to do. What might your students read on their own, and what books can you reference in class besides *Macbeth*? How might you connect other great reads to the work of the Bard?

Picture the end of the first day of the *Macbeth* unit. "Don't forget your homework!" you holler as students leave your classroom or Zoom session. What's on deck for tonight?

- Nadia, an ELL reader recently arrived in the US, has in hand *Zoey and Sassafras: Unicorns and Germs* by Asia Cistro (grades K–5). Big Ideas: Magic, Medicine, Systems, Empathy. Her list for next week will include picture books from the list you gave her at the Nerdy Book Club blog post by Keila V. Dawson, "10 Picture Books to Introduce Young Readers to Activism." When you and the media specialist found *Malala's Magic Pencil* by Malala Yousafzai, she lit up, because Nadia also hails from Pakistan. You plan to call on her when you talk about Lady Macbeth's handling of power and ambition and ask Nadia to talk about Malala's work as a powerful woman.
- Page, who is an NOV reader with deep emotional intelligence, is often late to class thanks to the impromptu counseling services to peers they provide in the hallway. They have selected *Laura Dean Keeps Breaking Up with Me* by Mariko Tamaki, a graphic novella. Big Ideas: Temptation, Manipulation, Womanhood. You and the media specialist are also building a list of books on emotional intelligence, psychology, interpersonal communications, and mediation since Page is interested in these topics. You plan to call on Page to do their book talk when you address

Lady Macbeth and Macbeth's marriage partnership and how these partners treat each other versus characters' relationships in the novella.

- Lakeisha, who is an ADV reader, is simultaneously reading the essay "The Case for Reparations" by Ta-Nehisi Coates and *Their Eyes Were Watching God* by Zora Neale Hurston. Big Ideas: Power, Womanhood, Manhood, Privilege, Systems, Individuality. She says she can't wait to also read *Dig* by A. S. King and *Dear Martin* by Nic Stone. Lakeisha has volunteered to provide the class with historical information about the range of cultures intermingling in Shakespeare's London and how royalty reinforced its reign of terror on some races and religions in particular. She is already naming a project she wants to do about colonial powers' first designations of racial differences when enslaving people, because she's listening to the historical podcast "Seeing White—Scene on Radio."
- Arabella, an ADV reader just returned from a long personal absence, has shown a flicker of interest in Mindy McGinnis's *The Female of the Species* and asked you more about Roxane Gay's work when you mentioned it in class. You are hopeful that she will read some pages of one of these works by unit's end.
- Blaise, an ADV thinker who does no homework and hates fiction, has just started Martha Brockenbrough's *Unpresidented* while seeming mildly interested in Jon Krakauer's *Into the Wild*. You have just heard from the guidance counselor that Blaise's family is now without an address, so you are navigating with the school psychologist what would be a reasonable amount of reading for him to accomplish by the end of the unit.

For a detailed set of reading suggestions, please see Handout 53. *Macbeth* Independent Reading Suggestions at lynhawks.com/extramacbeth.

Reading Is for All of Us

I love teaching Shakespeare plays. I love finding props like posterboard and capes so one student can ripple a huge board to make thunder while the students playing the Witches cackle and caw on stage. I love leading acting exercises, getting kids on their feet stamping out iambic pentameter or trochaic tetrameter. I love stopping a cinematic clip to give the mic to a student to come forward and analyze the scene. I love waking up every single kid in my class. But I have never figured out a way to follow any student home to make sure they read the play. My enthusiasm hasn't always carried past the classroom door.

So when I think about how much heavy lifting it takes for some of my students to get excited about Shakespeare, and how I want students to work and read as rigorously as I do, I think: *Isn't it better to find readings and reading tasks that guarantee my students will work?* If our goal is to develop lifelong reading habits and critical inquiry skills, then we should let students choose texts suited to their interests as often as we can.

Pairing student-selected texts with *Macbeth* opens up a critical thinking opportunity to consider how authors explore Big Ideas. Pairing student-selected texts with *Macbeth* also increases the chances that most students read something—and with interest—during this unit.

As English teachers, whenever we become book matchmakers and guides (Buehler), we tell students that we trust them to make good choices. When we challenge them with open-ended Socratic questions regarding the literature that interests them, we help them dig deep, make connections, develop arguments, and develop empathy. When excited students begin sharing their findings, we have ourselves a reading community. Suddenly, the authors they admire have something in common with the faraway Bard, who—guess what!—was trying to say something too.

Share Your Reading Joy

What books do you adore? What books stick with you today that you read eons ago? Why? Go ahead and share your reading joy with your students, and be a role model. Wax rhapsodic over lines you love. Let's say you love young adult contemporary novels and feminist essays. Maybe one day you open a class by reading an excerpt from Jason Reynolds's YA contemporary verse novel *Long Way Down*, and another day you read an excerpt from Virginia Woolf's *A Room of One's Own*. Whether it's a book about a young man's descent through fear, guilt, and revenge and ascent through love and loyalty, or a woman's nonfiction meditation on the power and privilege granted female artists, you might frame the entire *Macbeth* conversation through one of these pairings, or one like them. Reynolds's masterful use of white space, punctuation, and rhythm can be compared and contrasted with the Bard's poetry so that students can see an old and a contemporary artist wrestling with the same skill, ideas, and magic.

For more theory and strategies, read the work of Nancie Atwell, Donalyn Miller and Susan Kelly, Penny Kittle, and Rudine Sims Bishop to understand better how student-selected, multicultural readings develop lifelong reading habits, agency, and empowerment in our students.

Teaching the Whole of Literary History: The Abundant Canon

Letting students read deeply and widely is also part of antiracist education. If your curriculum is limited to a few voices, it's imperative that students get chances to explore stories, perspectives, and other visions of the world. As Dena Simmons asks, "Do you and the academic materials you use uphold whiteness or lift up the voices and experiences of people of color?" So what does an inclusive, diverse reading list look like, and how many different views of the world will students experience by the end of the year? Let your media specialist and students support that search.

> We need diverse books in which children can find reflections of themselves. . . .[B]ooks can also be windows. You can look through and see other worlds and see how they match up or don't match up to your own. But the sliding glass door allows you to enter that world as well. So that's the reason that the diversity needs to go both ways. It's not just children who have been underrepresented and marginalized who need these books; it's also the children who always find their mirrors in the books and therefore get an exaggerated sense of their own self-worth and a false sense of what the world is like, because it's becoming more and more colorful and diverse as time goes on.
>
> —Rudine Sims Bishop, "Mirrors, Windows and Sliding Glass Doors"

What Is Canon?

Let's go ahead and say it: there may be pressure within your school or even within you to place only the Bard on an uninterrupted, no-competition pedestal during this unit. And while there is an argument to be made for doing only one thing at a time, I will fall back on my favorite paraphrase from St. Paul when it comes to teachers' roles: We need to be all things to all people.

You may have strong feelings about what constitutes "classic" literature and what ought to be read in schools. I bring to this book my filter as a YA author with years of working with teens and a deep love of what I call the *abundant canon*. It's my belief that classic literature exists across age groups, genres, and forms. I stand with members of NCTE, the ALAN Workshop, and many researchers across the last few decades asserting that the classics are not the purview of only a few works of literature or voices. Why can't Lorraine Hansberry converse with the Bard, who converses with Justin Reynolds and Elizabeth Acevedo, all in the same unit?

Inviting students to interrogate what is "canon" is key. Thanks to the #disruptexts and #WeNeedDiverseBooks movements, which echo, deepen, and innovate upon the movements of the 1980s for multicultural literature, our reading lists grow richer by the day and allow us to redefine what is canon. Our students crave agency and autonomy in their reading and their storytelling. Let's give them space for it.

Writing Activities: Common Core and Counterstorytelling

What reading and writing skills can students develop during independent reading study? Consider taking one of the standards below and making it a skill focus for students' reading notebooks, reading portfolio, and/or related writing assignments. Follow the steps I recommend in Chapter 1 to tier the micro skills within each skill.

CCSS ELA Standard	Details
CCSS.ELA-LITERACY.W.9-10.2	Write informative/explanatory texts to examine and convey complex ideas, concepts, and information clearly and accurately through the effective selection, organization, and analysis of content.
CCSS.ELA-LITERACY.W.9-10.2.B	Develop the topic with well-chosen, relevant, and sufficient facts, extended definitions, concrete details, quotations, or other information and examples appropriate to the audience's knowledge of the topic.

Reading notebooks, portfolios, or journals can serve as a safe space for students to catalog their questions, reactions, and epiphanies to teacher-selected and student-selected texts. I recommend these writing activities to do what authors and educators Jeanne Dyches Bissnonette and Jocelyn Glazier recommend: "[C]reate opportunities that provide students, particularly those from historically marginalized backgrounds, with a space in which they can express themselves, share their lived experiences, discuss their realties, and actively engage in critical reading, thinking, writing, and speaking skills. Counterstorytelling promises such an experience" (686).

For a detailed set of reading suggestions, please see Handout 53. *Macbeth* Independent Reading Suggestions at lynhawks.com/extramacbeth.

Build Your Stack

Your media specialist can be your best friend in creating stacks of texts for students. As my colleague and friend Gordon Jack, media specialist at Los Altos High School in Los Altos, California, says, "Basically, your Librarian and/or Media Specialist is EAGER to collaborate on projects like this. Their job is to stay informed on current YA releases to better recommend titles to students and staff. Another collaborator you might want to consider are local public libraries and bookstores. Depending on your community, they are a great source of knowledge. I rely on people from Linden Tree and Keplers a lot for recommendations as they read even more than me."

Don't go this alone; find help, because you and your students deserve to build stacks with support. I have begun this work with the recommended readings on Handout 53. *Macbeth* Independent Reading Suggestions, but of course there is more in heaven and earth than these!

> Your face, my thane, is as a book where men
> May read strange matters.
>
> —Lady Macbeth to Macbeth
> (act 1, scene 5, 51–52)

Suggested Readings

At lynhawks.com/extramacbeth you will find many independent reading suggestions connected to Big Ideas and based on these categories: young adult literature, adult literature, middle grade books, chapter books, picture books, contemporary retellings of *Macbeth*, historical fiction books set in Shakespeare's time period, nonfiction, poetry, and plays.

Ask your media specialist to help you expand this list. Asks might include:

- How can we address a range of reading levels?
- Can we find more contemporary fiction and nonfiction with connections to *Macbeth*: thematic connections, antiheroes, magical forces, and murder and revenge plots?

- Can you give me a multigenre list spanning interests and reading levels, based on this list of Big Ideas that *Macbeth* addresses? Share Handout 1. Pick Your Favorite Big Ideas (lynhawks.com/extramacbeth).
- How can we both offer and promote readings for all students that lift up the voices and experiences of people of color? (Simmons).

Picture books and chapter books support ELL and/or NOV students as they explore both *Macbeth* and Big Ideas in books at their reading level. Ask ELL-NOV students to read more than a few picture and chapter books during the unit. For example, you might have a student look at how suspense is created in picture books and then compare how suspense is created in *Macbeth*. See the list in the picture books section of Handout 53. *Macbeth* Independent Reading Suggestions at lynhawks.com/extramacbeth.

Give students time and opportunity at the media center and in class to select their next read, and give students time before the *Macbeth* unit begins to make their choices.

How to Introduce Independent Reading: Share the Vision

Explain to students that independent reading is an opportunity for everyone to love something they read. Describe for students your vision for the classroom as a community of readers, one where:

- everyone chooses, enjoys, and finishes at least one if not several books they care about, about issues and topics and characters of interest;
- where everyone expands their knowledge, empathy, and perspective;
- where readers recommend new readings to one another;
- where readers connect shared class readings to what they read independently; and
- where everyone thinks deeply and critically about texts they consume.

Explain to students that no matter what the type or level of reading, the critical thinking can go deep. Everyone can pursue exciting questions and make interesting connections. Let students know the range of genres, styles, and forms of reading they have as options.

When preparing students for a media center visit, ask them to bring their favorite Big Ideas and questions (see Chapter 3). You might say, "Are you curious about sleep? Leadership? Magic? Witches? Guilt? Tyrants? Narcissists? What subjects would you like to explore?"

Model for students how you think about books when you're not reading; talk with them about how stories capture your heart. Show them your reading life beyond the classroom.

Because many English teachers don't have time to be voracious readers on top of mountains of papers, virtual or print, and albatrosses of grading, emails, etc., know that any reading counts as the subject of a book talk. Podcasts and articles count! Any words you consume with passion count. Let's say you love debating a topic such as basketball's GOAT (LeBron vs. MJ). That topic connects to Power, Ambition, and Leadership. So read aloud an excerpt of your favorite sports columnist to model your passion to your students. Whatever has argument, rhetoric, claims, evidence, figurative language, and story—it counts!

We also don't have to have read students' books to supervise independent reading. We are experts in the inquiry and thinking processes we coach, as well as the shared texts we teach.

- Book Talks. Model the joy of reading by doing quick, one-minute book or reading talks as often as you can. Take a minute to kick off class with sentences such as, "I was really struck by this novel . . ." or "I was reading this article and was really excited when . . ."
- If you teach a large range of reading levels, honor the creativity and difficulty in writing all levels of books. It's not easier to write a picture book than a novel; both are extremely challenging. In your talks, showcase a range of books from every age level, pointing out the artistry and craft. Make your classroom a safe space where no one judges that Joe has a picture book and Jamila has a 500-page epic YA fantasy novel. Read from picture-only books, text-and-picture books, chapter books, middle grade books, young adult books, and adult books. Read from nonfiction and literature. Model that all books are welcome.

Independent Reading Tasks

The purpose of independent reading tasks can include:

- Teaching annotation and close reading of a text
- Inspiring deep inquiry where students explore Big Ideas in a text and between texts
- Encouraging pattern and trend analysis of characterization, plot, and setting in a text and between texts
- Encouraging analysis of literary elements such as motifs, figurative language, and sound devices in a text and between texts

One of your primary tasks as reading teacher is helping students develop inquiry skills. If students can ask great questions, they have a powerful life skill. Teach mini-lessons to help students understand the difference between analytical, evaluation, and synthesis questions. See the DYO section of Chapter 3 for more guidance.

The formative tasks listed in the next section allow you to track—and give basic credit for—students making progress in their reading. You can keep observational notes about the growth of student thinking depending on the reading skill sets you hope to nurture in a student portfolio or other assessment space. There are many excellent active reading strategies, annotation journals, dialectical journals, and other ways to let students demonstrate understanding of independent reading. No doubt you already use several strategies. Suggestions below help you monitor and encourage critical thinking about independent reading while teaching *Macbeth*.

Monitoring and Check-Ins of Reading Progress

Entrance and Exit Tickets

- Whether you use online checks or index cards, ask for five minutes of student feedback as class begins or ends on a specific topic. You might consider having students retrieve these details during a summative writing assessment.
    - Point students to the Big Ideas posted in your classroom or shared digital space, and ask for one example of how the author explores this Big Idea. Students must paraphrase or quote a detail and provide context and commentary linking the Big Idea.
        - Challenge levels for formative feedback:
            - Word Nerd: Did you include a specific detail—a quotation or paraphrase of text—that is related to the Big Idea?
            - Word Sleuth: Did you include a specific detail—a quotation or paraphrase of text—that is related to the Big Idea while also noting some element of character, plot, or setting? Is there either clarifying context or explanatory commentary related to the Big Idea?
            - Wordsmith: Did you include a specific detail—a quotation or paraphrase of text—that is related to the Big Idea while going beyond character, plot, and setting to include diction, figurative

language, sound devices, or other stylistic elements? Is there insightful context and explanatory commentary related to the Big Idea?

- Ask for a Q&A Report—a Question and Answer Report—in which the student poses a Socratic query and answers it using their independent reading. The student must paraphrase or quote a specific detail in the answer.
    - Students may select EQs from the list in Chapter 3 or create their own.
    - Challenge levels for formative feedback:
        - Word Nerd: Is the question open-ended? Does the answer contain one specific detail, either quoted or paraphrased, from the text?
        - Word Sleuth: Is the question open-ended? Does the answer contain one or more specific details, either quoted or paraphrased, from the text? Is there anything insightful or surprising about this question or answer?
        - Wordsmith: Is the question open-ended? Does the answer contain specific details, either quoted or paraphrased, from the text? Is there anything insightful or surprising about this question or answer? Is there a creative interpretation and argument developing?

Assessment of Understanding: Journal Entries

Consider using relevance questions in Chapter 3 as guiding questions for students to answer in their nightly reading.

Give extra praise or bonus points for students who can craft text-related inquiry questions. Model questions based on *Macbeth* and then ask students to develop their own.

Assessment of Understanding—Characterization

Six Threads of Character—Digital Tool Gallery

- EQ Options:
    - Why is this character or narrator compelling to me? Why do I want to read more about them? Identify specific character elements that are intriguing to you.
    - Why does this character or narrator irritate me? Why do I want to tell them what to do? Identify specific character elements that frustrate you.
    - Create your own EQ and answer it with details from the text.

- Ask students to visually present their characters using digital tools such as Canva, ThingLink, or Venngage that allows them to show two to three character elements supporting a claim about the character. Elements include character physicality, character family background and history (backstory), character speech, character thoughts, and what others say or think about the character. If the work is nonfiction, you can adapt this assignment to ask students to provide biographical details in the text.
- Formative assessment feedback (use CR readiness levels):
    - Word Nerd: Did you identify one to three elements? Do you support a claim that contains at least one adjective about the character, or do the elements cohere in some fashion even if the claim isn't directly stated? Do visuals match the elements and / or claim?
    - Word Sleuth: Did you identify two to three elements? Do you support a claim that contains at least one adjective or other topical subgroup about the character and make a coherent argument? Do visuals match and enhance the elements and / or claim?
    - Wordsmith: Did you identify three or more elements? Do you offer insightful topical subgroups and evidence, while visuals are a coherent, aesthetically pleasing part of the argument?
- Create a gallery to showcase student discoveries about character or narrator. Invite one student to report in per day.

Connection Journals

Set a schedule for students to share reading discoveries using reading notebooks or your other preferred methods. Ask students to track their reactions and interpretations to their text(s) through four lenses: Personal Relevance, Arts, *Macbeth,* and News & Current Events. Ideally, all students would connect their reading to *Macbeth,* but if your primary goal is to ensure in-depth independent reading, then we don't need our ambitions to vault any higher. For a model of connections I made to *Macbeth* and to help students with their independent reading analysis, go to lynhawks.com / extramacbeth for Handout 39. Making Literary Connections.

11 Summative Assessments

What You Will Find in This Chapter

- A definition of summative assessments
- A rationale for summative assessments
- Sample summative assessments
- Sample rubrics

A Definition of Summative Assessments

How will you assess your students' mastery of knowledge and skills? What authentic products can help students share interests as well as in-depth discoveries about Big Ideas?

Remember Alicia? Here's how she assesses her students' mastery of translation and annotation, use of figurative language and sound devices, and use of claims, evidence, and reasoning.

- After four formative CRs, she gives the fifth and final CR, assessing it as part of the writing portfolio.
- After several discussions and brief creative writing activities using figurative language and sound devices, students do the Poetry Gallery and Peer Review (see p. 204). She assesses the Poem and Peer Review as summative.
- She uses this guide's recommended persuasive writing activities and then gives a timed persuasive writing piece as the summative writing assessment.
- Throughout the unit, students have pursued independent mini-projects centered on a Big Idea, and the culminating activity is creative writing in answer to an EQ: a poem, song, comic, or story, due a week after the unit is over.
- Alicia has read some research showing that even the preparation to teach content to peers benefits students' memory and comprehension of facts (Guerrero and Wiley). So Alicia will also offer students some new summative activity options on the last day of the unit: teach two-minute mini-lessons on figurative language and argument strategies.

- Next year Alicia wants to frame the unit with a new angle—who writes history, and why?—so she is already planning a future class project called History, Written by the Victors?, which will include a persuasive writing activity as the culminating project.

This is how Alicia knows her students are progressing toward these three skills.

In *Strategies for Differentiating Instruction: Best Practices for the Classroom*, Julia L. Roberts and Tracy F. Inman offer several helpful suggestions for designing meaningful products, performances, and tools for assessment, in particular the DAP Tool, which allows you to assess content, presentation, creativity, and reflection (179–82). They offer six levels on their performance scale. I have designed three products or performances using English language arts skills and Roberts and Inman's DAP Tool as models for what you might offer as prompts and assessment rubrics: a poster, a podcast, and an essay.

If this is your first time teaching *Macbeth*, you might begin with the poster product; then move to the podcast, which involves longer writing and a script; and then to an essay involving another text. In future years, you can offer all three simultaneously. The poster product allows students to do a succinct outline (topic sentences and evidence); the podcast involves a more developed outline and scripting through paragraphs; and the essay constitutes, of course, multiparagraph pages.

Note that these prompts can be read purely as essay prompts but can also be converted into more detailed poster and podcast prompts with planning guides.

One of the key skills mentioned in preassessment—persuasive writing—appears in this DAP Tool. You can find more excellent rubrics for speeches, storytelling, and other ELA-related tasks in *Assessing Differentiated Student Products: A Protocol for Development and Evaluation* (Roberts and Inman).

This Is Not a Test: The Writer's Portfolio

If Alicia keeps to her plan for a five- to eight-week Shakespeare unit, students might be generating two to three pieces of writing a week. While we want students to generate a lot of writing and engage regularly in reflective, metacognitive analysis of their growth as writers, the teacher can read only so much. Have students maintain a folder of work where they submit selected works. By selected, I mean "student choice." Which of the three formative writing assessments per week will you look at? The student chooses the one to submit to you.

By the end of the unit, give students a poll or a timed writing prompt to answer specific reflective questions. Here is a sample of what Alicia might design for students to answer:

- *Figurative Language.* Select your best creative work. In 50–100 words, tell me why you believe this is your best creative work. Please provide the link.
- *Close Reading* (Translation and Annotation). Select your best close reading assignment. In 50–100 words, tell me why you believe this is your best close reading work. Please provide the link.
- *Persuasive Writing.* Select your best persuasive writing assignment. In 50–100 words, tell me why you believe this is your best persuasive work. Please provide the link.
- *Strengths.* Name some writing skills you have practiced these last weeks, ones where you see growth and developing strengths.
- *Areas for Improvement.* Name one or more writing skills that you would like to see more growth in. What do you think it will take to get there?
- Anything else you would like to tell me about your writing progress?

Student insight into and ownership of their skill growth can also be quoted in quarterly and semester reports to families and in parent-teacher conferences.

Students might feel better about a formative than a summative assessment, and that's fine. It should be their job to keep track of growth, too, and let you know where they feel they shine. While you ultimately choose what marks progress at the end of a unit, it's worth noting which assessments, formative or summative, truly engage them.

As you examine student work, ask yourself how your next unit's mini-lessons can address areas for student growth.

DYO Essay Prompts

Essays can be inspirational and engaging. If we design meaningful prompts and provide writing workshop structure, we can help our students achieve strong writing. Which Big Ideas, EQs, and play-related or relevance questions sparked most interest in your students? Those can help you design essay prompts that work for your classroom. Students can also propose their own prompts to match the formats I offer below.

Literary and Professional Role Summative Assignments

We can challenge students at varying readiness levels with what I call literary-professional writing assignments—writing tasks that approximate professional roles while harnessing literary analysis skills. You can be a forensics expert while combing the textual evidence of the Macbeths' crime scene. You can serve as a psychiatrist while parsing the lines of Lady Macbeth's sleepwalking soliloquy.

See sample product prompts for essays, podcasts, or posters (Word Nerd, Word Sleuth, and Wordsmith) below. See how I've taken Big Ideas and EQs and scaffolded the critical analysis needed. Use my structure to build your own using play-related or relevance questions you like.

Product Prompts

These prompts are scaled by writing complexity, left to right. While writing an excellent thesis or caption for a poster isn't easy, the poster product is an outline, whereas the podcast is an interview and script, and the essay is a fully developed multipage writing product. You should note your students' prior readiness levels when you assign or choose a product. An ADV student who chooses to do a poster should be performing at a 6 level. ADV students should have the option across units to try something other than essays as well, just as ELL, NOV, and OT students should be allowed diversity in product choices.

For EQs other than the prompts and roles that follow, see Chapter 3, where you'll also find play-related and relevance questions.

The Poster	The Podcast	The Essay
Create an informative and analytical poster for your professional role that answers a key EQ with claims and reasoning. Examples: ■ the criminologist's report ■ the forensic expert's report ■ the psychiatrist's report Must include ■ a thesis ■ topic sentences ■ evidence via images ■ captions with context and commentary	Create an informative and analytical podcast that hosts one or more professionals to answer a key EQ with claims and reasoning. Interview any of the following professionals: ■ a criminologist ■ a forensics expert ■ a psychiatrist Must include ■ a thesis, topic sentences, evidence from each guest, with context and commentary ■ questions from the host	Create an analytical or evaluative essay that explores a professional angle on a key EQ with claims and reasoning. Take the perspective of any of the following professionals: ■ a criminologist ■ a forensics expert ■ a psychiatrist Must include ■ a thesis statement ■ topic sentences ■ evidence ■ context ■ commentary

You can take the above prompts and rewrite the essay prompts in Handout 40. Word Nerd, Word Sleuth, and Wordsmith Prompts for *Macbeth* as needed to feature the poster and podcast products. Where it says "essay" or "paragraph," replace with "poster topic sentence" or "caption" for the poster, or "script topic sentence" or "host question" for the podcast.

The Writing Process

Make time to model the writing process, from prewriting to drafting to revision to editing. Give enough class time for each phase of the process. If you use writing workshops, ask students to submit work by the end of each period in a portfolio system, each draft labeled by a number. If you use electronic documents, ask students to use the Suggesting function and/or review Version History or Comments History to see the changes draft to draft.

Integrate tiered mini-lessons as needed after you review drafts.

Prewriting involves

- prompt selection,
- evidence-gathering (details or significant particulars), and
- topical subgroup development.

Drafting involves

- mapping or outlining,
- topic sentence development from topical subgroups, and
- first-draft writing.

Editing involves

- peer and/or teacher review,
- further revision (more drafts), and
- grammar and mechanics proofing.

Publication involves

- sharing with an audience and
- inviting commentary by an audience.

What will happen at publication? Will students present essays as speeches or post in a gallery? Will students perform their podcasts or present their posters?

Reflection involves

- independent reflection on writing and presentation strengths and areas for growth
- and reflection on and response to (optional) feedback from peers and teacher and other audience members.

How long should you give to the writing process? You can schedule drafting of essays, podcast transcripts, or poster captions for in-class time, while devoting homework and class time to culling substantive details and significant particulars, development of precise topical subgroups, and development of clear and summative topic sentences. You may opt to do all drafting in class.

Decide how long you need to check in with students individually through writing conferences and/or targeted mini-lessons.

TR Essay Prompts: Short, "Perfect Paragraph" Character Analysis Essays

Summative writing assessments don't have to be long. Writing what I call a "perfect paragraph" (can you produce a topic sentence, three examples, and context and commentary?) is a worthy writing assessment. You can take a class period to ask students to analyze a character from *Macbeth* or independent reading texts. Use Handout 19. Expository Writing Rubric (lynhawks.com/extramacbeth).

I also like offering this type of timed writing after students have worked in MR groups to do metaphor posters, where they identify a metaphor to describe a character and find three examples. Students are welcome to consult the posters hanging in the classroom and reuse examples and commentary from their group discussions. They can cite their peers.

Keep assessment goals simple for timed writings. For example: (a) do students understand this passage?, (b) can they find the details?, (c) can they draw a conclusion from these details? Even a student who hasn't read the whole play can write an effective analysis of a *Macbeth* passage.

As Andrea Lunsford et al. argue in *Everything's an Argument*, any writing prompt you assign assumes a purpose of persuasion and proof. What I am most interested in as a writing teacher is not perfect flow, diction, or transitions, but rather can students pull together a coherent argument or exposition under pressure. As long as standardized, timed tests are with us, as well as professional roles that require rapid delivery of emails, meeting summaries and agendas, and other documents, we can treat timed writing as opportunities to practice claims and evidence.

> Lunsford et al. clarify that "the point of argument is to discover some version of the truth, using evidence and reasons. . . . The aim of persuasion is to change a point of view or to move others

from conviction to action" (7). If you need to prioritize and scaffold writing skills, make sure students can (a) see the specifics in the text as evidence and (b) extrapolate topical subgroups to build topic sentences.

For a fun culminating activity, have students take character analysis paragraphs and work in pairs or triads to identify a theme song for their character (*Macbeth* or independent reading) and create a music video (using a platform such as TikTok). You can use a character analysis paragraph by either partner, or have students take the best paragraphs posted in a class gallery as the inspiration for the videos. Students must find a setting or costume or prop to represent the character in the brief video, and song lyrics must match the character's personality and, ideally, Big Ideas. You might frame the character analysis paragraphs as a competition, where the best are used as video inspirations.

TR Essay Prompts: Long-Form Essays

You can revise, mix, and match the following ideas and prompts as needed. You know best what your students are ready to do. See Handout 40. Word Nerd, Word Sleuth, and Wordsmith Essay Prompts for *Macbeth* (lynhawks.com/extramacbeth) for a range of TR writing assignments and Handout 19. Expository Writing Rubric. Note that options within each level increase in challenge.

- Word Nerd Option #1 will not require as many layers of decision making for the student writer as will Word Nerd and Word Sleuth Option #2 and Word Sleuth Option #3.
- Word Nerd and Word Sleuth prompts are highly structured, pushing the five-paragraph outline/structure, whereas levels B and C are less detailed and prescriptive.
- Need more essay prompts? Please see my *Macbeth* unit in Carol Ann Tomlinson and Cindy A. Strickland's *Differentiation in Practice: A Resource Guide for Differentiating Curriculum, Grades 9–12.*

If this is your first time offering TR essay prompts, be selective. Choose a few prompts for your first year, and then offer more as you gain confidence in providing feedback. Some classes are so heterogeneous that all three levels are required, while some classes would be fine with a few choices. An honors course at the high school level can use the most advanced options from Word Sleuths and Wordsmiths. You also may not want to have to consider the great variety as you assess. For more thoughts on assessment, see Appendix B, "Grading in a Differentiated Classroom," in *Teaching* Julius Caesar: *A Differentiated Approach* (Hawks).

Summative Assessment: Persuasion

Here are a few options for assessing skills of argumentation through claims, reasoning, evidence, and rhetorical strategies. You might assign these as TR options or let students choose. If you use these as a TR option, note they are provided in ascending order of complexity: ELL-NOV, OT, and ADV. Use the rubric for Handout 9. Preassessment: Write a Persuasive Message provided in Chapter 4 (see pp. 66–67). I recommend making these in-class assignments over a period of days.

- **Option #1: Revision of "Write a Persuasive Message"** (see Chapter 4). Ask students to revise to ensure they use well-reasoned claims, substantive evidence, and effective rhetorical strategies.
- **Option #2: MacBetter Careers.** You are the headhunter/lead recruiter for a company called Might, Ambition, or Justice. Choose your company and recruit a *Macbeth* character using persuasive techniques learned during this unit.
- **Option #3: Equality for Some.** Persuade us that *Macbeth* is an early argument for the paradox stated in George Orwell's *Animal Farm*: "All animals are equal, but some are **more equal** than others." How does this equivocation connect with *Macbeth*?

For Handout 42. Persuasive Poster Rubric and Handout 43. Persuasive Podcast Rubric, head to lynhawks.com/extramacbeth.

Persuasive Essay: College Prep

In my work with students preparing their college admissions essays, one of the most difficult tasks they encounter is the "Why Us" supplemental essays (often under 400 words) in which they must persuade the school that they and the school are a match. I help students see how providing specific examples isn't bragging when you talk about yourself, and how you need to talk specifically about how a school matches you. These short essays need many drafts for students to find specific personal examples that "match" the school.

If you teach juniors and seniors, consider using free model essays and pointers from Ethan Sawyer, the College Essay Guy (see Further Resources). You can also use my Handout 9. Preassessment: Write a Persuasive Message rubric (see pp. 66–67) and modify it by removing the reference to counterclaims. This can be a formative assessment that students practice a few times until they have a final revision, and it can become a major feature of the writing portfolio. Even if a student doesn't apply to a particular school, the exercise trains them for what admissions officers want.

I often assigned creative nonfiction/memoir writing. The following tasks are excellent practice for the narratives students write for personal statements found in the Coalition App, Common App, and other schools' and scholarships' application requirements. I explain to students that there is a subtle art of persuasion because you are (a) selecting a showcase narrative, something that expresses your uniqueness as an individual while (b) persuading the school that this story (or stories) proves your uniqueness and key elements of your character—elements a school would like to see in its student population. For a full narrative-persuasive rubric, my Great Essay Rubric, see Further Resources (Hawks, "What Makes"). If students don't yet know where they want to apply, you can modify this essay prompt to identify career interests or potential job matches.

Experimental Poetry Gallery and Peer Review

In these summative assessments for the *Macbeth* unit (see Handouts 41 and 57), students showcase their knowledge of figurative language through either creative writing or analysis and application of figurative language in Macbeth's final soliloquy. Poems are posted in a gallery and students write a peer review, focusing on the effectiveness and resonance of the figurative language and sound devices.

Handout 41. Experimental Poetry Gallery

Experimental Poetry Prompt

Write a poem on a topic of your choosing. Use figurative language and sound devices.

Your work will be assessed based on effective use of images and devices, as well as creativity.

- *Unique and Experimental.* The student thinks outside the box with original pairings of images to ideas.
- *Elaborative.* The student goes above and beyond to create an example, such as using a range of details or sound repetitions.
- *Complexity of Thought.* The student wrangles complex, interesting ideas, casting a new light or taking a new perspective.

Peer Review

Find an instance of figurative language and an instance of a sound device and offer specific compliments and elaborations, connecting the author's work to a Big Idea.

- The compliment must be specific, quoting part of the line (up to 100 words).
- The elaboration on the figurative language or sound device notes key words, connotations, denotations, repetitions, and other elements of the image or device that contribute to making meaning (100–250 words).
- The peer reviewer offers a topic sentence making an argument for the presence of a Big Idea.

Handout 57. Figurative Language and Sound Devices Summative Assessment

Directions:

- Read the speech below and find examples of figurative language and sound devices. Highlight or underline figurative language and circle or stress sound devices.
- Choose either an image or a sound and write three to seven sentences explaining why one or more devices enhance the point Macbeth is making.
- Challenge: Explain how figurative language and sound devices lend power to poetry.

Macbeth's Soliloquy, Act 5, Scene 5, Lines 18–27	Device
Tomorrow, and tomorrow, and tomorrow, Creeps in this petty pace from day to day To the last syllable of recorded time, And all our yesterdays have lighted fools The way to dusty death. Out, out, brief candle! Life's but a walking shadow, a poor player That struts and frets his hour upon the stage And then is heard no more: it is a tale Told by an idiot, full of sound and fury, Signifying nothing.	

How an image or sound enhance the point Macbeth is making	

Class Project: History, Written by the Victors?

Was Macbeth a good king, a bad king, or something else? Depends on who writes history, right? What if the class created a Patchwork Quilt of History to represent how varied perspectives are in finding the truth of history, whether in fiction or nonfiction, and how the chroniclers of history often invent their own facts? For more reflection and thematic exploration of America's complex relationship with historical truth, check out *The Atlantic*'s Inheritance series and Clint Smith's reporting on nostalgia for the Confederacy (see Further Resources). Here's an example of one you might modify or use as a model to create your own. Partnering with a history teacher and/or media specialist might take this project to a whole new level.

- *Prompt:* Tell the story of *Macbeth* from one character's perspective. Imagine that you are a descendant of one of the play's characters and you want your family to look good in the eyes of history. Win the history textbook contract to ensure you get to tell your family's version of events. Collaborate with classmates who have similar interests and find proof as you annotate and explain the play from one perspective, using your team's color.
    - Join a team that represents one family's perspective. Your team will choose facts from the play selectively to tell people how to view the events. Create a visual, colorful outline of three examples, with three elaborations (a brief paragraph of commentary), explaining through your character's perspective how these text examples prove one of these arguments, or one you create: Macbeth was a tyrant (color code, Team Yellow, Duncan's Crew or Banquo's Crew); Macbeth was both a good and a bad king (Team Purple, Witches); Macbeth was a good king (Team Green, the Macbeths). (If you have another argument, come up with a team of characters and a color to represent it.) On each team, members should find different facts so everyone on the team has something unique to argue.
    - The rubric for assessment will include (a) the quality of evidence and elaboration, (b) contributions to the class Socratic discussion, and (c) the ability to spot "facts" inserted by classmates that don't fit the play.
    - If you have a large group of ADV students, consider working with your media specialist to have them do research on historical records of Macbeth, such as Holinshed (see references in the Oxford version of *Macbeth* [Gill]), and compare and contrast Shakespeare's fiction with those records.

- *Materials:* Provide students with colored paper, markers, and other ways to create a mixed-media representation of their argument in one "patch" of the Patchwork Quilt of History. Each student can bring an 8.5" × 11" patch of argument to the quilt, which can be a big piece of poster paper representing the varied perspectives. There can be a yellow, green, and purple row, followed by more rows of color depending on new arguments students bring.
- *Socratic Discussion:*
    - Each team will have a few minutes to present their argument and one fact; each student who steps up should say something new.
    - Then lead a class discussion:
        - Whose facts were most compelling and why?
        - Who bent, spun, misread, or just plain made up facts from the play? How do you know?
        - Whose argument was most persuasive, even if inaccurate?
        - Let's look again at our Patchwork Quilt of Macbeth's History. If you wanted to write the most accurate, fair, objective portrayal of Macbeth, name the facts from the play (actual text) that must make the cut.
    - One goal could be for all teams to make such good arguments that it's a tie for the history textbook contract and everyone gets a piece of the print real estate. Or you can play by kingly rules and require that there can be only one winner. Be sure to explain why only one version gets to be told and ask students how they feel about that in further discussion. You might also use songs from the musical *Hamilton*—"The Story of Tonight," "The Schuyler Sisters," and "History Has Its Eyes on You" (Miranda) to explore these themes in more depth.

For more than fifty handouts you can adapt for your classroom, go to lynhawks.com/extramacbeth and log in for exclusive content with the password wyrdsisters.

Glossary for Differentiated Instruction

Advanced student (ADV): A student gifted in a particular core competency or knowledge base, performing with a level of sophistication in that area. A preassessment of the skill area should determine student ability, not prior labels, as activities in this unit might elicit unnoted talents or skills that can be challenged further.

Anchoring activities: Ongoing, independent activities driven by choice that students may pursue throughout a unit; go-to assignments when a student finishes a task early.

Big Idea: A timeless, one-word concept appearing across art, media, and text. Abstract and ill-structured, a Big Idea such as LOYALTY, EVIL, or WOMANHOOD invites Essential Questions and asks students to analyze and evaluate in order to further define it.

Close reader (CR): Reading guides that help students translate, analyze, and question text.

Common Core State Standards (CCSS): National standards for English language arts.

Compacting: Assignments for ADV students who demonstrate prior knowledge and mastery of grade-level content and skills, and who can learn more quickly, deeply, and/or independently.

Cooperative and collaborative learning: While both are opportunities for in-depth teamwork, cooperative learning is led by the teacher, who determines the purpose and matches students in groups to bring their individual strengths to the task. In collaborative learning, the purpose originates with the students' interests and needs, and the group generates new knowledge with student-driven products or performances (Goble and Goble 7–8).

Engagement preference: The mode through which a student prefers to process and construct knowledge and skill, such as aural, kinesthetic, interpersonal, intrapersonal, verbal, or visual means. I use this interchangeably with *learning preference* and *intelligence*.

English language learner (ELL): A student who is a nonnative speaker and who needs support in meeting grade-level expectations in reading, writing, and/or speaking. This student may also be gifted or need remediation in certain competencies outside of English language knowledge.

Essential Question (EQ): A thematic, investigative, open-ended question that directs a unit, assignments and assessments, and discussion by centering the engaging dilemmas, paradoxes, and potential explorations of a discipline (Wiggins and McTighe 28–29).

Essential Understanding (EU): A fundamental principle, theme, or generalization derived or arrived at during the learning experience, or derived from content and skills of the discipline. Engaging, central, and enduring, these understandings are often answers to an Essential Question (Wiggins and McTighe).

Flexible grouping: A grouping strategy based on the results of preassessment data that places students in temporary groups for tasks related to specific skill-building. In this guide, this practice is related to tiered readiness activities. These groups should change as students and their knowledge and skills evolve and be balanced with interest-driven activities students choose.

Hook activity: A whole-class activity (WCA) designed to engage as many students as possible, inviting all students to explore a Big Idea driving the text or an intriguing window into content.

Intelligence: Intelligences such as logical/mathematical, linguistic, musical, spatial, bodily-kinesthetic, naturalist, interpersonal, and intrapersonal, as defined by Howard Gardner.

Interest area: Student interests such as talents, skills, hobbies, expertise, and career preferences.

Key word: A conceptual word in text that elicits resonant connotations and themes. It might also be the root word of an Essential Understanding, Essential Question, or theme.

Macro skill: The skill or standard with multiple layers of skill, appearing across grade levels as a core skill to master.

Micro skill: The subskills within a macro skill, required in order to master the macro skill.

Mixed readiness (MR): A descriptor for activities or assignments in which students of varying interests, engagement preferences, and readiness levels complete a complex task.

Novice student (NOV): A student who performs below grade-level expectations in a certain area of knowledge or skill and demonstrates a need for remediation and support. This student may also be gifted or need remediation in certain competencies outside of English language knowledge.

On-target student (OT): A student who performs at or close to grade-level expectations in a certain element of knowledge or skill. This student may also be gifted or need remediation in certain competencies outside of English language knowledge.

Preassessment: Assignments, activities, or assessments measuring grade-level knowledge and skill, indicating whether a student's prior knowledge and skill is ELL, NOV, OT, or ADV.

Problem-based learning (PBL): An engaging activity posing an ill-structured, open-ended problem for students to solve collaboratively.

Project: A student's multistep creation of a product or performance, directed by interest, an inquiry question, and research and maker strategies required by the subject and question.

Readiness: A student's knowledge or skill in a particular area and level of preparedness to complete assignments (ELL, NOV, OT, and ADV).

Skills: Core competencies, as stated by district, state, or national standards.

Skill strand activities: English language arts interest area activities and projects asking students to demonstrate proficiencies in areas such as dramatic performance, creative writing, cinematic analysis, and more.

Story Question: The driving question for the story's protagonist and the story action in a scene; the question of suspense that turns pages.

Theme: Interpretations or arguments expressed in full sentences, as in essential understandings, generalizations, or thesis statements, derived from a Big Idea or key word.

Tiered readiness (TR): Questions differentiated by readiness level and Bloom's Taxonomy.

Whole-class activity (WCA): A multiple-intelligence activity exploring EQs, designed to inspire, challenge, and motivate several students while emphasizing grade-level content and skills.

Works Cited

Adler, Mortimer J. Introduction and Preface. *The Paideia Program: An Educational Syllabus.* Macmillan, 1984.

Anderson, Scott. "2022–2023 CommonApp Essay Prompts." *Common App,* 27 Jan. 2022, commonapp.org / blog / 2022-2023-common-app-essay-prompts.

Atherton, Carol. "Character Analysis: The Witches in Macbeth." *The British Library,* The British Library, 19 May 2017, https: / / www.bl.uk / shakespeare / articles / witches-in-macbeth.

Bishop, Rudine Sims. "Mirrors, Windows and Sliding Glass Doors." *Reading Rockets,* 30 Jan. 2015, *YouTube,* https: / / www.youtube.com / watch? v=_AAu58SNSyc.

Bissonnette, Jeanne Dyches, and Jocelyn Glazier. "A Counterstory of One's Own: Using Counterstorytelling to Engage Students with the British Canon." *Journal of Adolescent & Adult Literacy,* vol. 59, no. 6, 2016, pp. 685–94, doi:10.1002 / jaal.486.

Bloom, Harold. *Shakespeare: The Invention of the Human.* Riverhead Books, 1999.

Brall, Susan. "Theatre Review: PBS's Film on Stage Presents Shakespeare's 'Macbeth' Starring Patrick Stewart." *MD Theatre Guide,* 27 May 2020, https: / / mdtheatreguide.com / 2020 / 05 / theatre-review-pbss-film-on-stage-presents-shakespeares-macbeth-starring-patrick-stewart / .

Buehler, Jennifer. *Teaching Reading with YA Literature: Complex Texts, Complex Lives.* National Council of Teachers of English, 2016.

Carroll, William C., editor. *William Shakespeare: Macbeth: Texts and Contexts.* Bedford / St. Martin's, 1999.

Chand, Neeraj. "Denzel Washington's *Macbeth* Will Be a Thriller with an Age Twist." *Movieweb,* 14 Apr. 2020, movieweb.com / macbeth-movie-2020-thriller-update-joel- coen / .

Coen, Joel, director. *The Tragedy of Macbeth.* A24 · IAC Films, 2021.

Cohen, Sacha Baron. "The Greatest Propaganda Machine in History." *The Independent,* 29 Oct. 2020. *Facebook,* https: / / www.facebook.com / TheIndependentOnline / videos / 3022782667948920.

Crystal, David, and Ben Crystal. *Shakespeare's Words: A Glossary and Language Companion.* Penguin, 2002.

Dakin, Mary Ellen. *Reading Shakespeare with Young Adults.* National Council of Teachers of English, 2009.

———. *Reading Shakespeare Film First.* National Council of Teachers of English, 2012.

DeCourcy, Delia, Lyn Fairchild, and Robin Follet. *Teaching* Romeo and Juliet: *A Differentiated Approach*. National Council of Teachers of English. 2007.

Dunne, Will. *The Dramatic Writer's Companion: Tools to Develop Characters, Cause Scenes, and Build Stories*. 2nd ed., U of Chicago P, 2017.

Ebarvia, Tricia [@triciaebarvia]. "#DisruptTexts: a primer! 1." Excerpt from an *English Journal* article. *Twitter*, 20 Nov. 2020, https://twitter.com/triciaebarvia/status/1329923631531646983.

Ebert, Roger. "Macbeth." Movie review and film summary. *Roger Ebert*, 1 Jan. 1971, www.rogerebert.com/reviews/macbeth-1971.

Fairchild, Antonia. Personal interview. 24 July 2020.

"The Fourteenth Amendment Due Process Clause." *National Constitution Center, Interactive Constitution*, n.d., constitutioncenter.org/interactive-constitution/interpretation/amendment-xiv/clauses/701.

Gardner, Howard. *Frames of the Mind: The Theory of Multiple Intelligences*. Basic Books, 1983.

Germán, Lorena. "Disrupting Shakespeare." *#Disrupttexts*, 2 Sept. 2019, disrupttexts.org/2018/10/25/5-disrupting-shakespeare/.

Gill, Roma, editor. *Macbeth*. Oxford School Shakespeare. Oxford UP, 2001.

Goble, Pam B., and Ryan R. Goble. *Making Curriculum Pop: Developing Literacies in All Content Areas*. Free Spirit Publishing and NCTE, 2016.

Gold, Jack, director. *Macbeth*. British Broadcasting Corporation, Time-Life Films, 1982.

Goold, Rupert, director. *Macbeth*. British Broadcasting Corporation Great Performances Series, PBS Distribution, 2010.

Guerrero, Tricia A., and Jennifer Wiley. "Expecting to Teach Affects Learning during Study of Expository Texts." *Journal of Educational Psychology*, vol. 113, no. 7, 2021, pp. 1281–1303, https://doi.org/10.1037/edu0000657

Hawks, Lyn Fairchild. *Teaching* Julius Caesar: *A Differentiated Approach*. National Council of Teachers of English, 2010.

Hawks, Lyn Fairchild, and Antonia Fairchild. "Shakespeare's Metaphors: A Deep Dive with Tenor, Vehicle, and Macbeth." *Teachers Pay Teachers*, https://www.teacherspayteachers.com/Product/Shakespeares-Metaphors-A-Deep-Dive-with-Tenor-Vehicle-and-Macbeth-6749310

Jack, Gordon. Email to the author. 10 Oct. 2020.

Karim-Cooper, Farah. "Anti-racist Shakespeare." *Shakespeare's Globe*, www.shakespearesglobe.com/discover/blogs-and-features/2020/05/26/anti-racist-shakespeare/.

Kay, Matthew R. *Not Light, but Fire: How to Lead Meaningful Race Conversations in the Classroom*. Stenhouse, 2018.

Kratz, Jessie. "A Prologue to Prologue." *Prologue Magazine*, vol. 49, no. 4, Winter 2017–18, https://www.archives.gov/publications/prologue/2017/winter/historian-winter-2017.

Kurzel, Justin, director. *Macbeth*. The Weinstein Company, Anchor Bay Entertainment, 2015.

La Belle, Jenijoy. "'A Strange Infirmity': Lady Macbeth's Amenorrhea." *Shakespeare Quarterly*, vol. 31, no. 3, Autumn 1980, pp. 381–86, https://www.jstor.org/stable/2869201.

Lamott, Anne. *Bird by Bird*. Anchor Books, 1997.

The Learning Network. "Reader Idea | Reading 'Macbeth' through the Lens of Ferguson." *The New York Times*, 11 Feb. 2016, learning.blogs.nytimes.com/2016/02/11/reader-idea-reading-macbeth-through-the-lens-of-ferguson/.

Lerner, Laurence, editor. *Shakespeare's Tragedies: An Anthology of Modern Criticism*. Penguin, 1964.

Levithan, David. *Every Day*. Knopf, 2012.

Lipowitz, Daniel G., and James M. Conley. *Advanced Placement Classroom:* Macbeth. Routledge, 2021.

Loewus, Liana. "What Teachers Should Know about the Science of Reading." *Education Week*, 12 Mar. 2019, https://www.edweek.org/teaching-learning/video-what-teachers-should-know-about-the-science-of-reading/2019/03.

Loomba, Ania. "Shakespeare and Race: A Personal Story." *Shakespeare's Globe*, 13 Aug. 2018, medium.com/@shakespearesglobe/shakespeare-and-race-a-personal-story-e998feae257.

Lunsford, Andrea A., John J. Ruszkiewicz, and Keith Walters. *Everything's an Argument: With Readings*. 3rd ed., Bedford/St. Martin's, 2004.

Lynch, Kathleen. "Remember, Remember, the Fifth of November." *The Collation*, Folger Shakespeare Library, 7 Nov. 2011, collation.folger.edu/2011/11/remember-remember-the-fifth-of-november/.

Mabillard, Amanda. "*Macbeth* Glossary [birth-strangled]." *Shakespeare Online*, http://www.shakespeare-online.com/plays/macbeth/macbethglossary/macbeth1_1/macbethglos_births.html.

"*Macbeth*: A Conjuring." *Shakespeare's Globe*, www.shakespearesglobe.com/whats-on/macbeth-a-conjuring-2020/.

Malcolm, Gabrielle. "'Saw' Points: Patrick Stewart in *Macbeth*." *PopMatters*, 24 July 2011, www.popmatters.com/144920-macbeth-by-william-shakespeare-2495984477.html.

Morris, Sylvia. "Shakespeare's Rhyming Couplets." *The Shakespeare blog*, 17 Oct. 2012, http://theshakespeareblog.com/2012/10/shakespeares-rhyming-couplets/.

Nunn, Trevor, director and producer. *Macbeth*. Royal Shakespeare Company, Thames Television, HBO Video, 1978.

O'Brien, Peggy, editor. *Shakespeare Set Free: Teaching* Romeo and Juliet, Macbeth, *and* A Midsummer Night's Dream. Washington Square Press, 1993.

Orlando. Directed by Sally Potter, Mikado Film, 1992.

O'Rourke, John. "Huntington Restages *A Raisin in the Sun*." *BU Today* [Boston University], 13 Mar. 2013, www.bu.edu/articles/2013/huntington-restages-a-raisin-in-the-sun/.

Pan, Steven C., and Faria Sana. "Pretesting versus Posttesting: Comparing the Pedagogical Benefits of Errorful Generation and Retrieval Practice." *Journal of Experimental Psychology: Applied*, vol. 27, no. 2, 2021, pp. 237–57, https://doi.org/10.1037/xap0000345.

Papp, Joseph, and Elizabeth Kirkland. *Shakespeare Alive!* Bantam, 1988.

Pendergrass, Emily. "Differentiation: It Starts with Pre-Assessment." *Educational Leadership*, vol. 71, no. 4, 2013.

Polanski, Roman, director. *The Tragedy of Macbeth*. Playboy Productions and Columbia Pictures, 1971.

Roberts, Julia L., and Tracy F. Inman. *Strategies for Differentiating Instruction: Best Practices for the Classroom*. 3rd ed., Prufrock Press, 2015.

Salesses, Matthew. *Craft in the Real World: Rethinking Fiction Writing and Workshopping*. Catapult, 2021.

Sawyer, Ethan. *College Essay Essentials: A Step-by-Step Guide to Writing a Successful College Admissions Essay*. Sourcebooks, 2016.

Simmons, Dena. "How to Be an Antiracist Educator" *ASCD*, 1 Oct. 2019, www.ascd.org/publications/newsletters/education-update/oct19/vol61/num10/How-to-Be-an- Antiracist-Educator.aspx.

Storr, Will. *The Science of Storytelling: Why Stories Make Us Human and How to Tell Them Better*. William Collins, 2020.

"Tartar's Bow." Popup note index item for Act 3, Scene 2, *A Midsummer Night's Dream*. *myShakespeare*, myshakespeare.com/midsummer-nights-dream/act-3-scene-2-popup-note-index-item-tartar-s-bow.

Tomlinson, Carol Ann, and Cindy A. Strickland, editors. *Differentiation in Practice: A Resource Guide for Differentiating Curriculum, Grades 9–12*. ASCD, 2005.

VanTassel-Baska, Joyce, and Catherine A. Little, editors. *Content-Based Curriculum for High-Ability Learners*. 2nd ed., Prufrock Press, 2010.

Wiggins, Grant, and Jay McTighe. 2nd ed., *Understanding by Design*. Pearson/Merrill Prentice Hall, 2005.

Woolf, Virginia. *Orlando: A Biography*. Hogarth Press, 1928.

———. *A Room of One's Own*. Penguin, 2019.

Further Resources

Allison, Alexis. "How to Write a College Resume (+ Example Templates)." *College Essay Guy*, www.collegeessayguy.com/blog/college-resume-templates.

"American Shakespeare Center." americanshakespearecenter.com/.

Amichai, Yehuda. "In the Middle of This Century." Translated by Assia Gutmann, *Poetry Foundation*, 2015, www.poetryfoundation.org/poems/58625/in-the-middle-of-this-century.

Atwell, Nancie, and Anne Atwell Markel. *The Reading Zone: How to Help Kids Become Passionate, Skilled, Habitual, Critical Readers*. 2nd ed., Scholastic, 2016.

Benthall, R. A. *The Bounding Outline: A Writer's Guide to Form and Power.* Chapel Hill: Atlantic Meridian Press, 1996.

"Britain's First Black Community in Elizabethan London." *BBC News*, BBC, 20 July 2012, www.bbc.com/news/magazine-18903391.

Broadribb, Ben. "'Nor Knows He How to Live but by the Spoil': Spoiler Culture, Trailers and Selling Shakespearean Cinema." *Medium*, "Action Is Eloquence": Rethinking Shakespeare, 21 Jan. 2020, medium.com/action-is-eloquence-re-thinking-shakespeare/nor-knows-he-how-to-live-but-by-the- spoil-spoiler-culture-trailers-and-selling-shakespearean-8c087819a2f.

Brockenbrough, Martha. *Unpresidented: A biography of Donald Trump*. Feiwel and Friends, 2018.

Brooks, Gwendolyn. "Boy Breaking Glass." *Poetry Foundation*, 1987, www.poetryfoundation.org/poems/43322/boy-breaking-glass.

Burgo, Joseph. *The Narcissist You Know*. Touchstone Books, 2015.

Coates, Ta-Nehisi. "The Case for Reparations." *The Atlantic*, June 2014, www.theatlantic.com/magazine/archive/2014/06/the-case-for-reparations/361631/.

Common Sense Media. https://www.commonsensemedia.org/.

Dawson, Keila V. "10 Picture Books to Introduce Young Readers to Activism." *Nerdy Book Club*, 30 Oct. 2020, nerdybookclub.wordpress.com/2020/10/30/10-picture-books-to-introduce-young-readers-to-activism-by-keila-v-dawson/.

Dusinberre, Juliet. "Wilfred Owen and *Macbeth*." *Borrowers and Lenders: The Journal of Shakespeare and Appropriation*, vol. 6, no. 2, 2011, https://openjournals.libs.uga.edu/borrowers/article/view/2354.

Edgerton, Clyde. *Raney*. Algonquin Books, 1985.

Ensminger, David. "Black Light Panthers: The Politics of Fluorescence." *Art in Print*, vol. 5, no. 2, 2015, pp. 16–19, https://www.jstor.org/stable/26350859.

Fairchild, Lyn. "Which Comes First, The Individual or Society? An English and Humanities Unit on *Macbeth*." *Differentiation in Practice: A Resource Guide for Differentiating Curriculum, Grades 9–12* edited by Carol Ann Tomlinson and Cindy A. Strickland, ASCD, 2005.

Gallagher, Shelagh A. *Problem-Based Learning for Your Classroom.* Royal Fireworks Publishing, 2012.

Gardner, Howard. *MI Oasis*, www.multipleintelligencesoasis.org/.

Graphic novel of *Macbeth. SparkNotes*, www.sparknotes.com/shakespeare/macbeth/graphic-novel/.

Hawks, Lyn Fairchild. "What Makes a Great Personal Statement?" *Success Story: Write Your Future Now*, https://lynhawks.com/wp-content/uploads/2020/06/Great-Essay-Rubric-Success-Story.pdf.

———. "When Stars Are Scattered - Graphic Novel Study - The Abundant Canon." *Teachers Pay Teachers*, www.teacherspayteachers.com/Product/When-Stars-Are-Scattered-Graphic-Novel-Study-The-Abundant-Canon-6555664.

Hawks, Lyn Fairchild, and Vincent Agosta. "Macbeth Mock Trial: Shakespeare and Problem-Based Learning." *Teachers Pay Teachers*, https://www.teacherspayteachers.com/Product/Macbeth-Mock-Trial-Shakespeare-and-Problem-Based-Learning-6539384.

"How Courts Work." *American Bar Association*, 3 Sept. 2019, www.americanbar.org/groups/public_education/resources/law_related_education_network/how_courts_work/juryinstruct/.

Hurston, Zora Neale. *Their Eyes Were Watching God.* J. B. Lippincott, 1937.

"Inheritance: A Project about American History, Black Life, and the Resilience of Memory." *The Atlantic.* https://www.theatlantic.com/inheritance/.

Jackson, Shirley. "The Lottery." *The New Yorker*, 26 June 1948.

Jamieson, Victoria, and Omar Mohamed. *When Stars Are Scattered* [Novel study]. Teachers Pay Teachers, 2021.

King, A. S. *Dig*. Dutton Books, 2019.

Kittle, Penny. *Book Love: Developing Depth, Stamina, and Passion in Adolescent Readers.* Heinemann, 2013.

Klepper, David, Josh Boak, and Amanda Seitz. "AP FACT CHECK: Trump Distorts Record; BLM Falsely Accused." *The Associated Press*, 28 Aug. 2020, https://apnews.com/article/virus-outbreak-election-2020-ap-top-news-race-and-ethnicity-health-699e0c893bfbd986cea11b6f403beb3e.

Krakauer, Jon. *Into the Wild.* Anchor Books, 1996.

Lafayette Public Library. *Facebook*, 3 Mar. 2020, www.facebook.com/LafayettePublicLibrary/photos/a.432009312783/10159153477807784/?type=3.

Learning for Justice. "Gender & Sexual Identity." *Learning for Justice*, https://www.learningforjustice.org/topics/gender-sexual-identity.

LeGuin, Ursula. "The Ones Who Walk Away from Omelas." *New Dimensions 3*, edited by Robert Silverberg, Oct. 1973.

Lieber, Ron. "Pictures of Themselves: The 2020 College Essays on Money." *The New York Times*, The New York Times, 28 Aug. 2020, www.nytimes.com/2020/08/28/your-money/pictures-of-themselves-the-2020-college-essays-on-money.html.

Mabillard, Amanda. "Contemporary References to King James I in Shakespeare's *Macbeth* (1605–06). *Shakespeare Online*. 20 Nov. 2011, http://www.shakespeare-online.com/plays/macbeth/jamescompliments.html.

———. "*Macbeth* Glossary [se'n nights nine times nine]." *Shakespeare Online*, 20 Aug. 2000, http://www.shakespeare-online.com/plays/macbeth/macbethglossary/macbeth1_1/macbethglos_seven.html.

———. "Shakespeare's Sources for *Macbeth*." *Shakespeare Online*, 20 Aug. 2000, http://www.shakespeare-online.com/sources/macbethsources.html.

"Macbeth." Differentiated learning activity for *Macbeth, Royal Shakespeare Company*, www.rsc.org.uk/shakespeare-learning-zone/macbeth.

"Macbeth." *Globe Player, Shakespeare's Globe*, 2013, globeplayer.tv/videos/macbeth-english.

Macbeth: The Graphic Novel. Classical Comics, script adaptation by John McDonald, pencils and inks by Jon Haward, 5 Nov. 2008, www.classicalcomics.com/product/macbeth-graphic-novel-hardback-us/?attribute_pa_text-version=original-text.

Matclock, Wesley. "Build Your Stack: Eight Metaphor-Rich Poetry Recommendations." *Literacy & NCTE*, 1 Oct. 2019, ncte.org/blog/2019/10/eight-metaphor-rich-poetry-recommendations/.

McGinnis, Mindy. *The Female of the Species*. Katherine Tegen Books, HarperCollins, 2016.

McIntosh, Peggy. "White Privilege: Unpacking the Invisible Knapsack." *Peace and Freedom*, July/August 1989, https://psychology.umbc.edu/files/2016/10/White-Privilege_McIntosh-1989.pdf.

Messenger, Tadeo. College application essay in "Pictures of Themselves: The 2020 College Essays on Money." *The New York Times*, 28 Aug. 2020, https://www.nytimes.com/2020/08/28/your-money/pictures-of-themselves-the-2020-college-essays-on-money.html.

Miller, Donalyn, with Susan Kelly. *Reading in the Wild: The Book Whisperer's Keys to Cultivating Lifelong Reading Habits*. Jossey-Bass, 2014.

Miranda, Lin-Manuel. *Hamilton*. Original Broadway cast recording, composed and written by Lin-Manuel Miranda, Atlantic Recording Corporation, 2015.

Nunn, Trevor, director. *Macbeth* [Video of live performance]. *YouTube*, 17 Oct. 2019, www.youtube.com/watch?v=7skhaOegpLA.

O'Connor, Flannery. "Revelation." *Sewanee Review*, Spring 1964.

Price, Eoin. "*Macbeth* in Original Pronunciation (Shakespeare's Globe) @ Sam Wanamaker Playhouse, 2014." *Reviewing Shakespeare*, 22 July 2014, bloggingshakespeare.com/reviewing-shakespeare/macbeth-original-pronunciation-shakespeares-globe-sam-wanamaker-playhouse-2014/.

Reynolds, Jason. *Long Way Down*. Atheneum, 2017.

"Riddle Poems." *ReadWriteThink.org*, 2003, readwritethink.org/sites/default/files/resources/lesson_images/lesson169/RiddlePoems.pdf.

Roberts, Julia L., and Tracy F. Inman. *Assessing Differentiated Student Products: A Protocol for Development and Evaluation*. Prufrock Press, 2015.

Rodríguez, Luis J. "Watts Bleeds." *Poetry Foundation*, 1991, www.poetryfoundation.org/poems/147105/watts-bleeds.

Sawyer, Ethan. "College Essay Guy: Get Inspired." *College Essay Guy*, www.collegeessayguy.com/.

———. "Why This College Essay Guide + Examples." *College Essay Guy*, www.collegeessayguy.com/blog/why-this-college-essay.

"Seeing White." *Scene on Radio*, season 2, https://www.sceneonradio.org/seeing-white/.

Shakespeare, William. *The Tragedy of Macbeth*. [1623, Entire play online] MIT, *The Tech*, shakespeare.mit.edu/macbeth/full.html.

Shin, Sun Yung. "(Riot Police)." *Poetry Foundation*, 2012, www.poetryfoundation.org/poems/142187/riot-police.

Smith, Clint. "Why Confederate Lies Live On." *The Atlantic*, June 2021, https://www.theatlantic.com/magazine/archive/2021/06/confederate-lost-cause-myth/618711/.

Smith, Danez. "Tonight, in Oakland." *Poetry Foundation*, www.poetryfoundation.org/poems/58027/tonight-in-oakland.

Stone, Nic. *Dear Martin*. Crown Books, 2017.

Tamaki, Mariko. *Laura Dean Keeps Breaking Up with Me*. First Second, 2019.

Teaching Tolerance. "Let's Talk! Discussing Race, Racism and Other Difficult Topics with Students." *Teaching Tolerance*, http://www.tolerance.org/sites/default/files/general/TT%20Difficult%20Conversations%20web.pdf.

Tillyard, E. M. W. *The Elizabethan World Picture*. Vintage Books, 1988.

Tomlinson, Carol Ann. *How to Differentiate Instruction in Mixed-Ability Classrooms*. 2nd ed., ASCD, 2001.

Tomlinson, Carol Ann, and Jay McTighe. *Integrating Differentiated Instruction and Understanding by Design: Connecting Content and Kids*. ASCD, 2006.

"Tomorrow, and Tomorrow—Ian McKellen Analyzes Macbeth speech (1979). *YouTube*, 25 May 2012, https://www.youtube.com/watch?v=zGbZCgHQ9m8.

Trailer for *Macbeth*. [Kurzel, 2015] Movieclips Trailers, *YouTube*, 2015, https://www.youtube.com/watch?v=YqHhKuCQmoY.

Trailer for *The Tragedy of Macbeth*. [Polanski, 1971] *YouTube*, 2015, https://www.youtube.com/watch?v=Ysd5gwHfG1w.

"Trump Says His Misleading Coronavirus Comments Were Meant to Show 'Strength.'" NPR, 10 Sept. 2020, https://www.npr.org/2020/09/10/911608521/trump-says-his-misleading-coronavirus-comments-were-meant-to-show-strength.

Wilde, Oscar. *The Picture of Dorian Gray*. Ward, Lock, 1891.

"Young Black Poets: Ten Teenage Writers Show the Future of Poetry." Introduction by Maya Phillips, *The New York Times*, 9 Oct. 2020, www.nytimes.com/interactive/2020/10/09/arts/young-black-poets.html.

Yousafzai, Malala. *Malala's Magic Pencil*. Little Brown, 2017.

Zuckert, Michael P. "'Something Wicked This Way Comes': Machiavelli, *Macbeth*, and the Conquest of Fortuna." *The Review of Politics*, vol. 78, no. 4, 2016, pp. 589–607, doi:10.1017/s0034670516000607.

Index

The letter *h* following a page locater denotes a handout. Activities and Scene Lessons are capitalized.

Author

Lyn Fairchild Hawks holds a BA in English and an MA in education from Stanford University. She has taught English, creative writing, theater, and other humanities courses for more than fifteen years in public and independent schools and was recognized as a Distinguished Teacher with the Presidential Scholars program, among other awards. She also served for fifteen years as instructor, curriculum developer, teacher trainer, and director of curriculum and instruction for online learning in the Duke University Talent Identification program. Hawks is coauthor of *The Compassionate Classroom: Lessons That Nurture Wisdom and Empathy* and *Teaching* Romeo and Juliet: *A Differentiated Approach* and author of *Teaching* Julius Caesar*: A Differentiated Approach*.

An MFA candidate in creative writing for children and young adults at the Vermont College of Fine Arts, Hawks also runs Success Story Essay Consulting, helping students use storytelling strategies to write a standout college admissions essay, and works with College Essay Guy training educators and coaching students. She is author of the YA novel *How Wendy Redbird Dancing Survived the Dark Ages of Nought* and the middle grade novella *Minerda*, and is represented by Tara Gelsomino of One Track Literary. Hawks lives in North Carolina with her husband, singer-songwriter Greg Hawks, and what the Bard would call a "brindled cat," her master and familiar, Sonny. Her stepson, Henry, does sound design for film and TV in Hollywood. Connect with her at www.lynhawks.com, at her Teachers Pay Teachers store Success Story www.teacherspayteachers.com/Store/Success-Story, @lynfairchildhawks on Instagram, www.facebook.com/FairchildHawks on Facebook, and @FairchildHawks on Twitter. Go to lynhawks.com/extramacbeth and log in for exclusive content with the password wyrdsisters.

This book was typeset in Palatino and Helvetica by Barbara Frazier.
Typefaces used on the cover include Copperplate Gothic, Aquinas, and Berkeley.
The book was printed on 50-lb. White Offset paper by Gasch Printing.